The European Union in a Changing World Order

Antonina Bakardjieva Engelbrekt
Niklas Bremberg • Anna Michalski
Lars Oxelheim
Editors

The European Union in a Changing World Order

Interdisciplinary European Studies

palgrave
macmillan

Editors
Antonina Bakardjieva Engelbrekt
Department of Law
Stockholm University
Stockholm, Sweden

Niklas Bremberg
Department of Political Science
Stockholm University
Stockholm, Sweden

Anna Michalski
Department of Government
Uppsala University
Uppsala, Sweden

Lars Oxelheim
School of Business and Law
University of Agder (UiA)
Kristiansand, Norway

Research Institute of Industrial
Economics (IFN)
Stockholm, Sweden

ISBN 978-3-030-18000-3 ISBN 978-3-030-18001-0 (eBook)
https://doi.org/10.1007/978-3-030-18001-0

Cover illustration: Robsonphoto / Shutterstock

This Palgrave Macmillan imprint is published by the registered company Springer Nature Switzerland AG
The registered company address is: Gewerbestrasse 11, 6330 Cham, Switzerland

Contents

Notes on Contributors

Claes G. Alvstam is Professor (Emeritus) of Economic Geography at the Department of Business Administration, School of Business, Economics and Law at the University of Gothenburg. His research interests include international trade and investment, and regional economic integration, with a special focus on Central/Eastern Europe and Asia.

Antonina Bakardjieva Engelbrekt is Professor of European Law and Torsten och Ragnar Söderberg Professor of Legal Science (2015–2018) at the Faculty of Law, Stockholm University. She is Chair of the Swedish Network for European Legal Studies (SNELS). Her research interests include Europeanization and globalization and their influence on national law and institutions.

Sofie Blombäck is Lecturer in Political Science at the Department of Social Sciences, Mid Sweden University. Her research interests include political parties, populism, and multilevel elections, especially involving the European Parliament.

Pontus Braunerhjelm is Research Director at the Swedish Entrepreneurship Forum and Professor in Economics at the Department of Industrial Economics and Management, Royal Institute of Technology. His research interests include entrepreneurship, innovation and market dynamism.

Niklas Bremberg is an associate professor at the Department of Political Science at Stockholm University and a senior research fellow at the Swedish Institute of International Affairs. His research interests include EU foreign and security policy, European diplomatic practices, and climate-related security risks.

Douglas Brommesson is Associate Professor in Political Science at the Department of Political Science, Lund University. His research interests include Foreign Policy Analysis, religion and politics, party politics.

Per Cramér is Professor of International Law and Dean at the School of Business, Economics and Law at the University of Gothenburg. He holds the Jean Monnet Chair in European Integration Law at the University of Gothenburg. His research interests include the external identity of the EU, especially the relationship between the Common Foreign and Security Policy and the Common Commercial Policy.

Ann-Marie Ekengren is Professor of Political Science and Deputy Head of the Department of Political Science, University of Gothenburg. Her research interests include foreign policy decision-making, with a particular focus on Sweden and comparative case studies.

Johan E. Eklund is CEO of the Swedish Entrepreneurship Forum and Professor of Industrial Economics at the Department of Industrial Economics, Blekinge Institute of Technology. His research interests include entrepreneurship, industrial economics and regulations.

Björn Fägersten is Senior Research Fellow and Director of the Europe Programme at the Swedish Institute of International Affairs. He holds a Ph.D. in Political Science from Lund University. His research interests include European security, intelligence cooperation and political risk.

Sverker C. Jagers is Professor of Political Science and Director of the Centre for Collective Action Research (CeCAR) at the Department of Political Science, University of Gothenburg. His research interests include environmental politics, especially public attitudes, democracy and sustainable development.

Lena Lindberg is Deputy Director at the Department for Asia and the Pacific, Swedish Ministry for Foreign Affairs. She holds a Ph.D. in Economics from the University of Gothenburg. Her research interests include international trade and regulations, with a special focus on EU trade relations with Asian countries.

Anna Michalski is Associate Professor of Political Science at the Department of Government, Uppsala University. She is Chair for the

Swedish Network for European Studies in Political Science (SNES). Her research focuses on European foreign policy, EU-China relations, and socialization in international organizations.

Frida Nilsson is Research Assistant at the Department of Business Administration, School of Business, Economics and Law at the University of Gothenburg. She holds a Master's Degree in Political Science from the University of Gothenburg. Her research interests include environmental politics, public trust and collective action.

Lars Oxelheim is Professor of International Business and Finance at the University of Agder. He is the founder of the Swedish Network for European Studies in Economics and Business (SNEE). His research interests include economic and financial integration, corporate governance, and risk management.

Thomas Sterner is Professor of Environmental Economics at the Department of Economics, School of Business, Economics and Law at the University of Gothenburg. His research interests include discounting and instrument design for climate and environmental policy.

Erik O. Wennerström is Director General for the Swedish National Council for Crime Prevention, Stockholm, Sweden. He holds a Ph.D. in Law from Uppsala University. His research interests include rule of law and human rights, particularly in relation to the development of EU law.

Karolina Zurek is Senior Advisor at the National Board of Trade in Sweden. She holds a Ph.D. in Law from the European University Institute. Her research interests include international trade and regulations, especially with a focus on sustainability and development.

List of Figures

List of Tables

CHAPTER 1

The European Union in a Changing World Order: What Is at Stake?

Antonina Bakardjieva Engelbrekt, Niklas Bremberg, Anna Michalski, and Lars Oxelheim

Introduction

The international system is in a state of upheaval. In the last decade, much of public debate has been dedicated to global power shifts away from the United States and Europe and towards countries with strong economic growth or development potential, such as China, India, Brazil, and South

A. Bakardjieva Engelbrekt
Department of Law, Stockholm University, Stockholm, Sweden
e-mail: antonina.bakardjieva@juridicum.su.se

N. Bremberg (✉)
Department of Political Science, Stockholm University, Stockholm, Sweden
e-mail: niklas.bremberg@statsvet.su.se

A. Michalski
Department of Government, Uppsala University, Uppsala, Sweden
e-mail: anna.michalski@statsvet.uu.se

L. Oxelheim
School of Business and Law, University of Agder (UiA), Kristiansand, Norway

Research Institute of Industrial Economics (IFN), Stockholm, Sweden
e-mail: lars.oxelheim@telia.com

A. Bakardjieva Engelbrekt et al. (eds.), *The European Union in a Changing World Order*,
https://doi.org/10.1007/978-3-030-18001-0_1

Africa. This trend grew stronger in the wake of the financial and economic crisis in 2008–2010, the Eurozone crisis in 2010, and the relatively weak economic recovery in numerous parts of the western world, which further underlined the vulnerability of the liberal market model (see e.g. Bernitz et al. 2018). New security threats in the form of terrorism and acts of violence by non-state actors are shaking Europe and its neighbours, while war, instability, poor governance, and climate change have forced over 65 million people from home (see e.g. Bakardijeva Engelbrekt et al. 2018a, b). Meanwhile, major technological shifts in the form of digitization, robotization, and artificial intelligence have already begun to upset traditional patterns of economic and social interaction (see e.g. Teigland et al. 2018).

These developments have the effect of seriously unsettling the liberal international order as we know it. This order was shaped in the decades following World War II and it lead to the exponential spread of democratic norms and values after the end of the Cold War. However, this liberal order is now facing severe challenges, threatening ultimately to lead to its demise. In terms of external challenges the growing influence of rising great powers is particularly notable. Many of these great powers do not share western values, and are openly defying established principles of international cooperation by advocating alternative world orders. In terms of internal challenges, equally vociferous contestation towards the liberal world order have been coming from inside the West, where populism and nationalism are posing a threat to the very foundations of liberal democracy. As we are approaching the end of the 2010s, most European countries are wrestling with anti-democratic forces that are challenging prevailing values and forms of government whereas the United States is being torn apart by a growing partisanship divide while President Trump is openly defying long-cherished rules and government practice.

In 2018 the EU celebrated the 60th anniversary of the entry into force of the Treaty of Rome. In the course of its history, the Union has suffered serious setbacks and navigated through a number of crises. Yet, the above described foundering of the liberal world order arguably constitutes the Union's most complex challenge to date. Much of the complexity resides in the fact that the EU is at once the product of this world order and a guarantor of the same. The mutual dependency between the EU and the liberal world order raises fundamental questions: How should the EU work to maintain international free trade in a context marked by an escalating trade war, and how is the new protectionist US trade policy affecting the EU and the Euro? Can the strong waves of neo-mercantilism triggered by a number of great powers be stopped, and what effects will economic nationalism have on the advancement of global financial regulation? Can the European-style welfare state survive in a changing world order that is marked by uncertainty and divisiveness? How is the weakening of multilateralism and global regulation influencing EU's capacity to act in the rest of the world? What impact will Brexit have on European cohesion and the future shape of the EU? What influence will right-wing populist parties have on EU member states capacity to act in common and pursue European policies? Can international law and the rule of law survive in an increasingly illiberal world order, and how can the consistency of the EU legal order be ensured against nationalist forces? How will the media image of the EU and EU communications policy be affected not only by social media but also by disinformation and propaganda?

This is the second book in Palgrave's Interdisciplinary European Studies book series. The book is published at a time when the EU is facing the most complex challenge of its existence: that is, how to stay true to the principles of its own inception in an increasingly less liberal world order. Considering the profound changes arising from global power shifts and contestation towards liberal values and forms of government, the book's interdisciplinary, holistic approach is particularly apt. Order at the international level, however, is a complicated concept. In various ways, therefore, the authors of this book address how a changing world order is affecting the EU and how the EU, in turn is trying to shape the emerging new order by recalibrating its policies and actions in various domains, ranging from the Union's relations with the rest of the world, the relations among the member states and EU institutions as well as the impact of the Union's current and future policies. In order to pave the way for the following chapters in the book, this chapter, by way of introduction, aims to shed light on how tightly the EU and the liberal international order are entwined and discuss the likely impact on the EU of a changing and, most likely, less liberal world order.

The EU and the Emergence of the Liberal World Order

The founding of the European Economic Community (EEC) with the entry into force of the Treaty of Rome in 1958 marked a key step in the creation of what is now the EU. At the time, a customs union was created through the EEC among the six original member states: West Germany, France, Italy, the Netherlands, Belgium, and Luxembourg. Following the creation of the customs union, the EEC also crafted a common external trade policy. The customs union and the trade policy can both be regarded as important components of the US post–World War II goal of promoting economic exchange between the countries in the "free" (western) world. US efforts to strengthen the liberal order, primarily through the Bretton Woods Institutions, were further advanced by several significant free trade talks in the 1940s, '50s, and '60s within the framework of GATT (General Agreement on Tariffs and Trade), in which the EEC was able to negotiate as a unified party. Another important dimension of the European external trade policy was the possibilities it offered countries like France, Belgium, and the Netherlands to maintain economic influence over the former colonies in Africa and Asia as well as to uphold the responsibility for ensuring efficient trade with these countries through the establishment of trade and cooperation agreements with the same, from Yaoundé (1963–1975) to Lomé (1975–2000).[1]

As economic integration within the European Community (EC) deepened in the following decades, more western European countries joined the organization, starting with the United Kingdom, Ireland, and Denmark in 1973. This was soon followed by the accession to the EC by the southern European countries, first Greece in 1981 and soon thereafter Portugal and Spain in 1986. For these three new member states, the decision to seek and obtain membership of the EC was aimed at securing democratic consolidation and bolstering the difficult path to socioeconomic modernization (Michalski and Wallace 1993). Then, in the beginning of the 1990s, the deepening of market integration and the momentous geopolitical shift in guise of the end to the Cold War both contributed to the creation of the European Union (EU) through the Maastricht Treaty in 1993. The end of the Cold War also allowed for the accession in 1995 of Sweden, Finland, and Austria, whose neutrality had hitherto prevented such a step. The swift "EFTA enlargement" that brought in the three members of the European Free Trade Association into the EU was succeeded by a long period of adjustment to conditions of membership for the ten formerly communist countries in Eastern and Central Europe, along with Cyprus, and Malta, which acceded to the EU in 2004 and

[1] On the development of EU trade policy and its role in the global economy, see e.g. Tsoukalis (1997), Meunier (2005), Baldwin (2006).

2007. In a way, the role of the EU as a stabilizing force in Europe came to fruition with this major eastern enlargement. That the EU had, in a sense, found its geopolitical calling in a united continent was apparent in the increasingly explicit conditions imposed on countries that applied for membership, which were compelled to demonstrate a functioning market economy, democratic government, and the effective rule of law (Schimmelfennig and Sedelmeier 2005). The European integration process and the role of the EU in the emerging liberal order were thus entwined from the outset, and in that sense the process of market integration in Europe and the regulation of international trade can be regarded, from a European perspective, as two sides of the same coin.

But European integration has obviously not only served a strictly economic purpose. The safeguarding of liberal democracy in Europe has been equally important, partly in the attempt to prevent the return of fascism to countries like Germany and Italy and partly as a way to counteract Soviet influence in Europe. The refusal to allow the authoritarian regimes in Spain, Portugal, and Greece to join the EEC before the 1980s is thought to have helped garner support for democratization among national elites, and EU membership has thus become strongly associated with liberal democracy and the rule of law (Linz and Stepan 1996). US support, primarily in the form of economic aid to rebuild Western Europe after World War II and later as a guarantor of national security during the Cold War, also strengthened the impression that European integration and liberal democracy work hand in glove (Dinan 1994). This was further strengthened by the EU enlargements in 2004 and 2007, which were made possible by several years of democratic and free market reforms in Central and Eastern European countries supported by the EU's pre-accession policy (Michalski 2014). In this process, the EU worked with other regional organizations dedicated to democracy, market economy, the rule of law, and human rights, such as the Council of Europe, the European Bank for Reconstruction and Development (EBRD) and the Organization for Security and Co-Operation in Europe (OSCE) (see e.g. Checkel 2007; Sadurski 2012). The sustained focus on democracy, rule of law and human rights in the course of this last EU enlargement contributed not least to the stronger constitutionalisation of these values and principles within the Union itself (De Burca 2003; Sadurski 2004).

However, the US and the EU have not always seen eye-to-eye on foreign and security policy, and they have tended to put economic and political considerations above their inclination to defend human rights around the world. Although the US and the EU have diverging views on matters including power, global governance, and national obligations in the global community, they have nonetheless been driving forces in the spread of liberal democracy and free trade that the world has witnessed since the end of the Cold War (Anderson et al. 2008). The EU and the US are thus both essential components of the liberal world order. The question of whether this world order is still viable is therefore crucial, as is the question of what the EU can do to safeguard important advances on the international level.

Geopolitics and Multilateral Institutions in a Changing World Order

Order has multiple meanings.[2] In the everyday sense, "order" usually refers to something that occurs regularly and is relatively formalized. Regular cooperation that arises spontaneously when individuals have similar interests or shared problems constitutes a kind of order, even if it naturally does not uphold the same measure of formality as the legal order through which the rights and obligations of citizens are regulated in modern states governed by the rule of law. The term "world order" can also be said to encompass both these aspects. First, there is the notion that a world order is apparent in the regularity with which states and other important actors interact with each other, which can be regarded in terms of social practice and is manifested in, for example, the diplomatic code of conduct (Bicchi and Bremberg 2016). Secondly, the term refers to the structure of the international system, which in its liberal version is informed by generally accepted norms and organizations, such as UN bodies and the World Trade Organization (WTO). According to the realist perspective on international politics, it is problematic to imagine an international order being anything more than a balance of power among the global great powers that dominate geopolitics in any given epoch (see e.g. Waltz 2010 [1979]; Gilpin 1983). Accordingly, prospects for achieving a permanent and peaceful international order are dim, and when such order does arise, as in the nineteenth-century Congress System in Europe, it is subordinate to great power politics. Historically speaking, international order has ultimately been upheld by a hegemonic power, such as Spain in the sixteenth century, Great Britain in the late nineteenth century, and the US since 1945.

[2] On the concept of order in international politics, see e.g. Bull (2012), Guzzini (2013).

In contrast to the realist understanding of international order, the liberal perspective on international politics suggests that order is created when states and other actors, especially economic actors, believe there are advantages to common rules and institutions (see e.g. Moravcsik 1997; Slaughter 2009). US hegemony was indeed essential for the emergence of the liberal world order as it emerged after World War II but what made it distinct from previous orders was that the interests, values, and vulnerabilities (particularly the common threat from the Soviet Union) of the US and leading western European states coincided to a large extent. After the end of the Cold War, the liberal world order expanded through free market and democratic reforms in many areas of the world. In connection with this transition, Francis Fukuyama (2012 [1992]) famously expressed the idea in *The End of History and the Last Man* that liberal democracy and market economy had settled all ideological battles about which model of society can best meet the needs of humanity. Geopolitical developments have, however, shown that liberal norms and values are not easily transferable to countries beyond the West, and may even be perceived as a threat to the status of national elites in many countries. In addition, political developments in Western countries since the 2010s have laid bare the vulnerability of pluralist political systems to domestic criticism and populism, where citizens' anxiety about the future must clearly be addressed.

In contrast to realist-inspired analyses of ongoing power shifts from the West to Asia that emphasized the increased risk for armed contestation (e.g. Mearsheimer 2010), John Ikenberry (2011) has argued that these risks might be overstated and the odds that the liberal international order will survive are actually better than they might seem at first sight. While Ikenberry does not deny the force of this power shift, he contends that the liberal order should be able to persist even if the US loses its hegemonic position. His argument is based on the assumption that rising great powers like China and India will ultimately benefit by preserving the order because it provides for a range of public goods in the form of common rules for world trade and institutions for collective action to manage shared challenges such as security threats and climate change.

According to Ikenberry, it would be much easier (and more advantageous) for the rising powers to embrace the liberal international order than to overturn it. A prerequisite for Ikenberry's scenario, however, is that the US and the EU are capable of integrating the new great powers into liberal institutions and concede that they are going to affect the structure of these institutions, for instance, through an adjustment of the current rules. Even though the EU and its member states have demonstrated a relatively high degree of flexibility on this issue, such as by supporting China's membership in the WTO and its right to vote in the International Monetary Fund (IMF), the US has shown reluctance to give rising powers, China in particular, a place at the table. Consequent upon Donald Trump becoming US President, the American attitude has hardened with regard to the country's role as a world leader. Paradoxically enough, the Trump administration's repudiation of the liberal world order and aversion to honouring previous agreements has considerably weakened the international stature of the US and eroded trust among its allies in the western world.

But the actions of the US President are not the only reason that faith in the political success of the liberal world order has recently been displaced by uncertainty and increasingly pessimistic visions of the future. The Russian annexation of Crimea in 2014 is a violation of international law and a breach of the security order in Europe, which relies on the norm of the inviolability of national borders. But in Russian rhetoric, its actions are merely a response to the threat it perceives in post–Cold War EU and NATO enlargements. In addition, the governments of several EU member states, such as Hungary and Poland, have been actively working for some time to undermine liberal principles and, above all, the rule of law, in their own countries while painting the EU as a threat to their national sovereignty. Populist politicians like Marine Le Pen in France, Geert Wilders in the Netherlands and Matteo Salvini in Italy also depict the EU as a threat to the sovereignty of the French, Dutch and Italian peoples. What unites these actors is their explicit opposition to the values and principles that are the pillars of the liberal world order.

The Role of the EU in a Changing World Order

For most of the EU's (and its predecessors) existence, the question of its role in the liberal world order was never made explicit. From a geopolitical perspective, its obvious place was to implicitly facilitate peace and stability in Europe and spread democracy and market economics as fundamental components in the process of post-World War II modernization and development. With the Maastricht Treaty, the Union's foreign and security policy role was strengthened. In the major geopolitical shift in the early 1990s caused by the fall of the Soviet Union, the EU's role became more explicitly to promote security and stability in Europe, but this time in relation to the countries of Central and Eastern Europe. The inherent symbolism that the EU (with the accession of these countries) would unite basically the whole of the European continent led to greater self-awareness of the role of the EU in the global system.

What role was the EU meant to assume? In academic debates, the EU has often been called a normative power, to use a term coined by Ian Manners (2002). Manners argues that the power of the EU is derived from the values and norms upon which the Union was created and that are written into its treaties. But in many ways "normative power" is more a description of the EU's self-image as a foreign policy actor than an accurate description of its actions. Nonetheless, the EU is something of an anomaly in the international system: an actor that is not a state and yet displays clearly state-like features and whose actions can in many ways be equated with those of a state. It would therefore be more accurate to describe the EU in terms of a post-sovereign actor called upon to uphold aspects of the liberal system that further its interests and reflect its specific composition and nature. The EU is therefore expected to assume special responsibility for disseminating values such as human rights, democracy, rule of law, and international law, as well as principles of global governance, such as multilateralism and a rules-based international system (Van Vooren 2013). These values and principles are the framework of the EU's approach to international cooperation and bilateral agreements with countries and international organizations. The EU's climate change policy, development assistance, and neighbourhood policies are notable expressions of this approach. In addition, the EU has demonstrated a predilection for multilateral negotiations and close cooperation with international organizations, like the Organization for Economic Cooperation and Development (OECD), the World Bank, and UN bodies that approach global issues in a similar way.

Nevertheless, the EU's rules-based, functionalist-oriented approach has come under increasing pressure since 2003, when power politics and ideologically motivated interests once again dominated the international system, partly as a result of the US invasion of Iraq. Power politics is also the clearest driver of Russian foreign policy and coincides well with how international politics is understood in China and many other emerging powers. In addition, a number of non-state actors that are propelled by ideology with religious overtones are having profound influence on security in Europe and surrounding regions. But power politics and self-interested orientations have also advanced their positions in areas other than security and stability and have changed the conditions of global governance. World trade is now dominated by regional or bilateral trade agreements, international development assistance is increasingly regarded as a foreign policy tool, and rich countries like China are enticing poorer countries in Africa, Asia and eastern and southeast Europe with investments, loans, and direct financial aid, thus influencing the global political economy. Finally—and not least importantly—the liberal system is being challenged by several countries with populist governments in the western sphere that are touting economic egoism, isolationism, and nationalism as answers to widening domestic income gaps.

This development is challenging the EU on several fronts. It has even been couched in terms of existential survival by the Union's representative for foreign and security policy, Federica Mogherini, in the EU Global Strategy of 2016 (EU 2016). In this context, the EU has been forced to navigate between a multilateral, rules-based international system and increasingly bold power politics. Thus far, the Union's approach has been informed by two principles. The first can be regarded in terms of a balancing against the prevailing power perspective in which the EU has chosen a middle way, where this power perspective is acknowledged but multilateralism is simultaneously presented as—to quote former President of the European Commission, José Manuel Barroso—"the right mechanism to build order and governance in a multipolar world" (2010). This can be seen in the EU's success at making association and partnership agreements with South Korea, Canada, Japan, and, not least importantly, Ukraine, and at initiating talks with New Zealand and Australia, as well as in EU support for the Paris Climate Change Convention, even though its logic was not the one primarily championed by the Union.

The second principle can be expressed in terms of the EU seeking to solidify its position in the international system by reinforcing its identity and agency, and by strengthening its capacity to act through the more effective use of common resources. The foreign policy identity of the EU is being articulated with increasing clarity in terms of opposition to the policies of the Trump administration, solidarity in the face of Brexit, and in more forceful action against Polish and Hungarian reforms of the judicial system and media that are questionable from a rule of law perspective. Its agency has been reinforced by building bilateral agreements with key states in "strategic partnerships" and by taking a more realistic position in the fight against terrorism, organized crime, and illegal immigration.

Moreover, the EU has taken new initiatives aimed at strengthening the Union's external border controls.

How Does a Changing World Order Affect the EU and What Can the EU Do About It?

The following nine chapters of this book address in various ways the question of how the unfolding crisis of the liberal world order is influencing the EU and how the EU can influence the emerging new world order. As the US under Trump is changing the course of its foreign policy to the point of undermining multilateral international cooperation and international free trade regimes, how is this affecting the conditions for autonomous action by the EU in foreign and security policy? What can the EU do to continue promoting global free trade based on fair and effective rules? Should the EU recast its overall strategy for promoting external trade and focus even more narrowly on bilateral and regional trade agreements? How should the EU protect the value of sustainable development in light of ongoing shifts of power? Can we expect the EU to remain a leading force in international climate change policy in the future? What must the EU and its member states do to ensure the survival of the welfare state in an era of mass migration? How is EU foreign and security policy affected by the spread of mediatization and new forms of digital communication in international politics? How can the EU best respond to the challenges to the rule of law and liberal democracy presented by the rising wave of populism in Europe, and what means provided under EU law and the EU treaties can be used to safeguard the fundamental values upon which the European project is based? These are some of the questions addressed in the book.

In the book's second chapter Björn Fägersten analyses how the EU as a foreign and security policy actor is being affected by a changing world order. Fägersten argues that the EU is in many ways a product of the liberal order that has shaped international relations since 1945. But the liberal order is now being shaken to its foundations, as manifest in various ways in Europe. Fägersten argues that the turbulence is leading to a fragmented world order in which cooperation among state and non-state actors is patchy and occurring in changing constellations. Furthermore, two overarching logics of interaction co-exist side by side—cooperation-oriented globalism and geopolitical competition, although they are affecting various policy areas in different ways.

To determine how this fragmented world order is affecting the EU as a foreign and security policy actor, Fägersten develops a framework of analysis that stipulates that a collective actor needs coherence (consensus), capacity (resources for pursuing policy), and context (a permissive setting). He argues that the EU is in some areas being strengthened by the prevailing turbulence. For example, both Brexit and Trump have enhanced coherence in parts of the EU and created potential for further capacity building in foreign and security policy. But at the same time, Brexit is impairing coherence and capacity in the EU because when the UK leaves, it will take military and diplomatic capacity with it out of the EU, while widening differences in values in the EU are exacerbating the risk of schisms among the member states. Fägersten recommends that the EU should make better use of the intelligence gathering that the Union is capable of so that it can act with greater congruence in its strategic sphere. The EU should also engage in structured and constructive cooperation with the UK in the area of security policy to mitigate the negative consequences of Brexit. The EU should also prepare alternative strategies to promote the Union's values and interests if Trump's lack of goodwill towards the liberal world order proves to be a symptom in the US of increasing and persistent disdain for the same.

The third chapter by Per Cramér seeks to identify structural changes in the regulation of international trade consequent upon Trump and Brexit. The point of departure is that both of these political changes were driven by similar populist-tinged lines of argument in which matters related to the design of foreign trade policy are central. The chapter begins with a retrospective look at the main elements of the development of international trade regulation. Cramér argues that a field of tension has arisen since 1945 between a multilateral ideal, on the one hand, and the development of regional and bilateral preferential trade agreements, on the other, in the form of free trade areas or customs unions. Against this backdrop, the chapter recounts the changes in US foreign trade policy during the current administration and the likely effects of the British withdrawal from the EU. The primary result of Brexit will be that the country's foreign trade policy relationships will be regulated largely through bilateral agreements. Brexit also entails a change of the internal dynamics in the EU, which will inevitably affect the shape of the Union's external trade policy in the future, with potentially serious consequences.

Cramér describes four trends in international trade that will inevitably be strengthened by Brexit and the Trump administration's international trade policy agenda. In short, these trends involve higher prioritization of bilateral trade agreements combined with weaker multilateral regulation within the framework of the WTO and accelerated use of trade policy protection measures, which risk leading to a general increase in protectionism. Moreover, the ongoing shifts in the geopolitical balance are being hastened, resulting in a weakening of US and European influence, in relative terms, over the design of regulation of international trade conditions. In light of historical experience, Cramér concludes his chapter by underscoring how important it is that the EU manages to buck these trends and actively works to bring about modernized multilateralism that more fully responds to the challenges facing global society, not least by promoting non-economic considerations such as basic working conditions, environmental protection and actions to prevent climate change within the framework of multilateral cooperation.

Claes G. Alvstam and Lena Lindberg discuss in the fourth chapter of the book the EU's common external trade policy in light of economic and political changes in the world. The authors establish that EU external trade policy is currently facing some of its greatest challenges ever. This is not only a consequence of Brexit, considering the equally great demands for continuous adjustment to worldwide structural changes in international trade. In the past, an oft-used rule of thumb was that the growth rate in external trade of a state was about twice as high as its GDP growth, but this seems no longer to be the case. Despite the fact that trade in goods and services has stagnated in recent years, global GDP has nevertheless increased during the same period. The question that Alvstam and Lindberg address in this chapter is how EU trade policy vis-à-vis the rest of the world should be modified and renewed in pace with external changes.

The chapter analyses the changing world order in the form of a new US trade policy, the British withdrawal from the EU, and China's increasingly prominent place in the international arena. In light of this, the authors consider various possible alternatives for the EU's external trade policy. Is the most appropriate strategy to try to assume the role of global leader in defending the multilateral trade order in the vacuum left in the wake of Trump, or would it be more realistic to instead intensify efforts to achieve far-reaching bilateral and regional agreements with key partners in various parts of the world? The role that the relationship with the post-Brexit UK will play in formulating an effective trade policy for the EU is a central question here. In conclusion, the authors present what they consider an important recommendation: the EU should first and foremost take vigorous action to defend the multilateral trading system. In other words, the EU should work to "Make the WTO Great Again," in harmony with continued initiatives towards ambitious bilateral and regional agreements.

The fifth chapter of the book by Karolina Zurek examines the efforts of the EU to promote sustainability within the framework of the Union's free trade agreements. From the vantage point of the changing nature of global trade, the chapter first describes how sustainability issues have been managed within EU external trade policy. Although there are strong tendencies towards greater protectionism all over the world, international trade has come to be regarded as a central tool for achieving the Sustainable Development Goals under the UN 2030 Agenda. At the same time, global civil society is pressing ever-higher demands for a socially and environmentally aware trade policy. The chapter recounts how the EU is striving to meet these challenges by focusing on the implementation of and compliance with the sustainability provisions of the EU's free trade agreements with international partners. Since 2008, the EU has systematically included horizontal Trade and Sustainable Development (TSD) chapters in its free trade agreements. Zurek investigates both substantive and procedural aspects of the TSD chapters and discusses the proposed reform on stronger implementation recently presented by the European Commission.

Against the backdrop of an ongoing and growing discussion of the scope of the EU's authority and competence in external trade policy, Zurek considers two aspects of the European Court of Justice's opinion on the Singapore agreement. First, the court confirms that the TSD chapter falls under the EU's exclusive competence. Second, the Court confirms that a breach of the commitments concerning sustainable development in the free trade agreement should be regarded as a breach of the Vienna Convention and thus be sanctioned, regardless of whether the agreement itself provides opportunities for sanctions for breaches of the sustainability provisions. In light of the Singapore opinion and based on the European Commission's proposed reform, Zurek concludes by presenting a number of recommendations aimed at strengthening implementation of and compliance with sustainability provisions in present and future EU free trade agreements.

As EU member states are about to implement the Paris Agreement, EU climate change policy is pursued in a new international context, according to the sixth chapter of the book by Sverker C. Jagers, Frida

Nilsson and Thomas Sterner. New economic powers have emerged on the scene in recent years and, along with declining economic power and diminishing emissions reductions in the EU, the Union no longer retains the prominent position in international climate change negotiations it had historically. With an increasing number of economic players in the game, it has become more difficult to achieve binding climate agreements that all parties perceive as fair. With the Paris Agreement, the international community has reached a compromise, but at the expense of clear burden sharing of emissions reductions. The authors argue that the EU presented a strong, united front in the process leading up to the Paris Agreement, but there are clear differences in terms of both ambition and approach in the actual climate change policies of EU member states, is due to variation in political culture, values, and political institutions in European countries.

With this in mind, the chapter considers the EU's role as an actor in climate change policy with regard to its historical role, current position, and future status. The authors begin by presenting Europe's early industrialization, which led to prominence in terms of both economic power and the level of emissions of greenhouse gases. Relying on statistics covering GDP, population, and greenhouse gas emissions in recent decades, the authors determine that Europe's position looks very different today, and they emphasize that even though the EU maintains a united front in climate negotiations, climate policy differs widely among EU member states. Jagers, Nilsson, and Sterner stress that it does not seem too likely that the EU will be able to implement a common, and effective, EU-wide climate policy. The authors conclude by recommending that decision-makers must be responsive to the various national contexts within the EU and show openness to applying different control mechanisms in different countries. Regarding the EU's future as a climate policy actor, they suggest that the EU is likely to become less important, but could in a positive scenario still play a significant role as a forerunner in an increasingly fragmented world order.

The seventh chapter of the book by Johan E. Eklund and Pontus Braunerhjelm asks how migration might affect the economies of European welfare states. The welfare state is put in the perspective of the refugee crisis that Europe has experienced since 2015 and the massive reception of asylum-seekers, particularly in Sweden and Germany. The chapter seeks to shed light on the economic costs and benefits that migration can generate against the background of comprehensive welfare ambitions and economic redistribution in many European countries. Conditions in Europe are compared with the US, and the authors refer to research showing that immigrants are often a very heterogeneous group with regard to level of education and language skills and that this has profound impact on opportunities for economic integration in recipient countries. Large-scale asylum-based immigration often entails economic costs for the recipient country, at least initially, but the authors also show that immigrants often contribute to economic development through innovation and new networks. Demographic developments and aging populations are also putting pressure on European welfare states that could be alleviated by higher levels of immigration.

Eklund and Braunerhjelm underscore that an effective integration policy is critical to national economic performance, as well as the future scope and design of welfare policies. One of the main issues brought up in the chapter is whether the most expansive welfare states in Europe will be able to maintain their universal nature or whether welfare entitlements must somehow be differentiated. Consequently, there is substantial policy scope to shape the ultimate outcome of higher immigration. The authors argue that a successful integration policy in EU member states must employ several different instruments with regard to aspects including wage formation, social transfers, and investments in education. At the end of the chapter, the authors recommend that the EU should strengthen the common asylum and migration policy and establish mechanisms to make it easier for EU member states to learn from each other in order to strengthen economic and social integration in European societies.

Douglas Brommesson and Ann-Marie Ekengren engage, in the eight chapter of the book, in a critical discussion of the mediatization of policy in general and of EU foreign and security policy in particular. According to a large body of research on mediatization, alignment with media norms and practices in society is increasing due to factors including the impact of social media and other social changes, mainly of a technical and economic nature. The burgeoning interest in digital diplomacy and "fake news" in the wake of Donald Trump's twitter storms are clear signs of the times. A common argument in public debate and in research is that the media logic, with its focus on polarization, intensification, and personification is increasingly affecting how policy is formulated. Brommesson and Ekengren are critical of this, as they see it, oversimplified perspective, and they also analyse EU foreign and security policy from the opposite point of view in this chapter. Foreign policy is usually described as a conservative policy area, in the sense that it is informed by caution and a long-term perspective, and foreign policy is not the subject of public debate to the same extent as other policy areas. Based on this reverse perspective, the authors ask whether policy actors are actually taking advantage of the opportunities provided by mediatization to strengthen long-term policy objectives.

The chapter sheds light on the relationship between policy and mediatization through a comparative analysis of two important strategy documents within the framework of EU foreign and security policy: the European security strategy of 2003 and the EU global strategy of 2016. The authors discuss the overarching question of whether the formulation of EU foreign and security policy is dominated by media logic, in other words, whether this policy has been mediatized. The authors determine that although aspects of media logic have increased since the turn of the millennium, its effects on the formulation of EU foreign and security policy are limited. Based on their analysis of elements of media logic in EU global strategies, Brommesson and Ekengren outline two general recommendations. First, the EU and its representatives should continue to focus on political institutions and policy content and, second, should carefully use the opportunities that media logic nevertheless offers. It is worth pointing out that policy-makers at the European and national levels in the area of foreign and security policy still have tremendous power to choose whether to use the media or not.

Populism as a challenge to the EU and democracy in Europe is analysed in the ninth chapter of the book by Sofie Blombäck. Even though populism as a phenomenon has received a great deal of attention lately, there is no consensus, in political debate or in social science research, as to how it should be defined. Blombäck argues that what primarily defines populism is the anti-pluralist notion that a homogeneous people stands in moral opposition to a more or less corrupt elite. Populists often present themselves as the true champions of the people against the elite. And because populist messages can be combined with other ideological positions, there are populist parties on both the left and right sides of the political spectrum. The chapter also addresses the important role that crises play in populist rhetoric, and Blombäck argues that populist parties can influence the content of the EU project through their presence in governing bodies at the EU level, but success at the national level is required to fundamentally change the European project. It is also at the national level that the complicated relationship between populism and representative democracy can most clearly be appreciated.

The chapter presents an analysis of election outcomes for populist parties in various European countries during the period 2010–2017, which shows wide variation among EU member states. Some countries have no populist parties in their parliamentary assemblies, while others have several. The notion that the European Parliament election of 2014 was a particularly successful one for populists is true, insofar as that the percentage of votes for populist parties increased compared to the preceding national elections. On average, the increase has continued in national elections held since 2014, but this actually obscures the fact that there were both major increases and major decreases in individual member states. Still, there is no generally available answer to the question of how the challenge to representative democracy and liberal values from populist parties should be handled. Blombäck recommends that it is, first, important to understand how populism works and how it differs from other political challengers. Not all populist parties are necessarily anti-democratic. Second, a rise in populism should be seen primarily as a warning signal, rather than an immediate threat, and should therefore be dealt with through political means. The message is that when the political system is able to resolve crises and deal with economic and social problems, this undermines the appeal of populist parties. It is important that the EU and its member states consider this carefully in an era when established parties and institutions are often depicted as part of the problem, rather than the solution.

The tenth and final chapter by Erik O. Wennerström analyses the EU's endeavours to define common, fundamental values and defend those values against member states that are challenging these values either deliberately or owing to lack of capacity. The chapter provides an overview of how the EU's fundamental values emerged and how they are used, as well as the various protective mechanisms created to monitor compliance with these values. The preparations leading up to the EU enlargements in the latter half of the 1990s and early 2000s were at the heart of this process. The successive reforms of EU treaties, with the Treaty of Lisbon being the latest stage in the process, have also been fundamental. However, many of the legally binding mechanisms that the EU has developed since the 1990s have never been used, even though, as Wennerström notes, there have been several situations in various EU member states where they could have been applied. A key argument in the chapter is therefore that the EU's various protective mechanisms seem not to be particularly user-friendly and it is possible that they were never meant to be that.

But values protected by unusable mechanisms are at risk of being undermined, Wennerström argues. He goes on to discuss a development that can be said to strengthen the fundamental values of the EU from the inside. Some of the EU's values that are defined in the treaties have not gained sufficient political support, and it has therefore been impossible to build legally binding protective mechanisms in their defence. It can be argued that the European Commission has confirmed this, as it has stopped referring to all the fundamental values of the EU. Instead, the Commission focuses on the values regarded as vital, which coincide with the values that the Council of Europe promotes. Herein rests a normative power that should not be underestimated: when there is consensus between the EU and the Council of Europe concerning fundamental values, the legitimacy of the values is reinforced, as are the opportunities to protect them. Finally, Wennerström argues that the member states that are intent on safeguarding the EU's values should, first, confirm the prioritization of and convergence surrounding the values of democracy, the rule of law, and human rights and, second, support the European Commission in its earnest efforts to influence the member states that are challenging the values, since attempts to influence them politically via the EU Council of Ministers, where national interests tend to outweigh matters of principle, are unlikely to succeed.

Conclusion: The EU Needs to Actively Defend Liberal Democracy in a Changing World Order

The nine chapters of this book touch upon important aspects of the position of the EU in a changing world order. The EU can approach this development by either accepting it (and adapting to new conditions) or by actively attempting to influence the emerging order. In other words, the EU can either choose to be a passive, relatively insignificant actor, or assume a more active role by seeking to exert impact on the actual conditions, as well as principles and beliefs about how the international order should be shaped going forward. Naturally, it remains to be seen to what extent the EU will in the future be able to pursue a more goal-oriented foreign policy, whether political consensus can be reached, and whether strategic autonomy can be realized. Lacking these components, the EU is at risk of assuming a vague and, in the worst case, marginal role in the emerging world order.

The authors show that the Union is facing a number of internal and external challenges. An overall message to the EU is that sustained cohesion is important, along with stronger capacity and autonomy to act on the internal and external stages in order to implement policy that the Union has decided to uphold. Climate change and international trade crystallize as the policy areas where the EU is capable of pursuing common policies and where the Union can safeguard interests that go beyond the solutions and agreements that are the usual focus of global negotiations. Also, the EU's *raison d'être* as a global actor is tightly linked with perceptions of its legitimacy. Its ability to communicate with both external and internal publics is therefore important, especially because many people see Brexit as a weakening of the EU. Wisdom and moderation are required here, as is clarity concerning the norms and values that the EU represents as a whole. But the EU also has a duty to defend the interests of the Union, whether these involve security, economic and social development, democratic values and practices, or equipping EU citizens for taking on the major societal changes brought by digitization and robotization. Such interests are defended not only by upholding a rules-based international trade system and an effective global climate policy, but also by helping the member states protect their welfare systems against internal and external shocks. Paradoxically, at least if one recalls past discussions of the EU as a threat to democracy, the Union now has a duty to act forcefully, we believe, both against member states and outside forces that seek to dismantle or weaken liberal democracy in Europe.

References

Anderson, J. J., Ikenberry, G. J., & Risse, T. (Eds.). (2008). *The End of the West?: Crisis and Change in the Atlantic Order*. Ithaca, NY: Cornell University Press.

Bakardijeva Engelbrekt, A., Michalski, A., Nilsson, N., & Oxelheim, L. (Eds.). (2018a). *The European Union: Facing the Challenge of Multiple Security Threats*. Cheltenham: Edward Elgar Publishing.

Bakardijeva Engelbrekt, A., Bremberg, N., Michalski, A., & Oxelheim, L. (Eds.). (2018b). *Trust in the European Union in Challenging Times*. Basingstoke: Palgrave Macmillan.

Baldwin, M. (2006). EU Trade Politics: Heaven or Hell? *Journal of European Public Policy, 16*(6), 926–942.

Barroso, J. M. (2010). The European Union and Multilateral Global Governance. Speech at the European University Institute. Retrieved October 16, 2018, from http://europa.eu/rapid/press-release_SPEECH-10-322_en.htm.

Bernitz, U., Mårtensson, M., Oxelheim, L., & Persson, T. (Eds.). (2018). *Bridging the Prosperity Gap in the EU*. Cheltenham: Edgar Elgar Publishing.

Bicchi, F., & Bremberg, N. (2016). European Diplomatic Practices: Contemporary Challenges and Innovative Approaches. *European Security, 25*(4), 391–406.

Bull, H. (2012 [1977]). *The Anarchical Society: A Study of Order in World Politics* (4th ed.). London: Macmillan International Higher Education.

Checkel, J. T. (Ed.). (2007). *International Institutions and Socialization in Europe*. Cambridge: Cambridge University Press.

De Burca, G. (2003). Beyond the Charter: How Enlargement Has Enlarged the Human Rights Policy of the European Union. *Fordham International Law Journal, 27*(2), 679–714.

Dinan, D. (1994). *Ever Closer Union: An Introduction to European Integration*. Basingstoke: Palgrave Macmillan.

European Union. (2016). Shared Vision, Common Action: A Stronger Europe. A Global Strategy for the European Union's Foreign and Security Policy. Retrieved October 16, 2018, from http://eeas.europa.eu/archives/docs/top_stories/pdf/eugs_review_web.pdf.

Fukuyama, F. (2012 [1992]). *The End of History and the Last Man*. London: Penguin Books.

Gilpin, R. (1983). *War and Change in World Politics*. Cambridge: Cambridge University Press.

Guzzini, S. (2013). The Ends of International Relations Theory: Stages of Reflexivity and Modes of Theorizing. *European Journal of International Relations, 19*(3), 521–541.

Ikenberry, G. J. (2011). The Future of the Liberal World Order: Internationalism After America. *Foreign Affairs, 90*, 56–68. (May/June Issue).

Linz, J. J., & Stepan, A. (1996). *Problems of Democratic Transition and Consolidation: Southern Europe, South America, and Post-Communist Europe*. Baltimore, MD: Johns Hopkins University Press.

Manners, I. (2002). Normative Power Europe: A Contradiction in Terms? *JCMS: Journal of Common Market Studies, 40*(2), 235–258.

Mearsheimer, J. J. (2010). The Gathering Storm: China's Challenge to US Power in Asia. *The Chinese Journal of International Politics, 3*(4), 381–396.

Meunier, S. (2005). *Trading Voices: The European Union in International Commercial Negotiations*. Princeton, NJ: Princeton University Press.

Michalski, A. (2014). The Enlarging European Union. In D. Dinan (Ed.), *Origins and Evolution of the European Union* (2nd ed.). Oxford: Oxford University Press.

Michalski, A., & Wallace, H. (1993). *The European Community: The Challenge of Enlargement*. London: Royal Institute of International Affairs.

Moravcsik, A. (1997). Taking Preferences Seriously: A Liberal Theory of International Politics. *International Organization, 51*(4), 513–553.

Sadurski, W. (2004). Accession's Democracy Dividend: The Impact of the EU Enlargement upon Democracy in the New Member States of Central and Eastern Europe. *European Law Journal, 10*(4), 371–401.

Sadurski, W. (2012). *Constitutionalism and the Enlargement of Europe*. Oxford: Oxford University Press.

Schimmelfennig, F., & Sedelmeier, U. (Eds.). (2005). *The Europeanization of Central and Eastern Europe*. Ithaca, NY: Cornell University Press.

Slaughter, A. M. (2009). *A New World Order*. Princeton, NJ: Princeton University Press.

Teigland, R., Holmberg, H., & Felländer, A. (2018). The Importance of Trust in a Digital Europe: Reflections on the Sharing Economy and Blockchains. In A. Bakardijeva Engelbrekt, N. Bremberg, A. Michalski, & L. Oxelheim (Eds.), *Trust in the European Union in Challenging Times*. Basingstoke: Palgrave Macmillan.

Tsoukalis, L. (1997). *The New European Economy Revisited*. Oxford: Oxford University Press.

Van Vooren, B., Blockmans, S., & Wouters, J. (Eds.). (2013). *The EU's Role in Global Governance: The Legal Dimension*. Oxford: Oxford University Press.

Waltz, K. N. (2010 [1979]). *Theory of International Politics*. Long Grove, IL: Waveland Press.

CHAPTER 2

European Autonomy in a Changing World Order

Björn Fägersten

Introduction

Europe and European integration are undeniably going through a phase of geopolitical turbulence. A few years ago, the term "crisis upon decline" was coined to refer to the parallel processes of home grown European crises and the relative power shift away from Western states more generally. Today, some of the European Union's (EU) most acute crises, such as on Eurozone cohesion and the shortcomings of a common approach to migration, have been managed in the short term, but turbulence has arisen elsewhere. The United Kingdom's decision to leave the EU (so-called Brexit) on the basis of a referendum and the election of Donald J. Trump as President of the United States have shaken the pillars that support the international and European order. While this turmoil in the world order challenges the EU as an actor in security policy, it has also led to a renaissance of thought on European autonomy and the idea that Europe itself must be able to *promote* its strategic interests (see e.g. Bartels et al. 2017). Throughout Trump's two first presidential years, there have been regular statements about the end of the liberal world order, mainly because Trump

B. Fägersten (✉)
Swedish Institute of International Affairs, Stockholm, Sweden
e-mail: bjorn.fagersten@ui.se

A. Bakardjieva Engelbrekt et al. (eds.), *The European Union in a Changing World Order*,
https://doi.org/10.1007/978-3-030-18001-0_2

does not seem to see any benefit in maintaining this order and in some cases has actively undermined its functioning. The liberal world order has been put under pressure in the past, but mainly from countries outside the "Western hemisphere". The fact that Trump's rhetoric and actions arouse so much concern for the liberal world order indicates how closely bound up this arrangement is with "the West" as a political entity in the world. To understand how Europe, as a fundamental part of the political West, is influenced by shifts in the world order, it is essential to appreciate what the previous system consisted of, who was included in it and what made it liberal.

This chapter provides an analysis of how the liberal system manifests itself in Europe and shapes the EU as an international actor, while also analyzing the effects of current changes to the world order on the EU as an actor in foreign and security policy. The chapter examines three overall questions: (a) how Europe and the EU have affected and were in turn affected by the world order that is now undergoing change; (b) how the outside world, together with Europe's internal problems, have *impacted* the opportunities for the EU to be a player in international affairs; and (c) how the EU's actorness affects its autonomy, that is, the EU's ability to act independently in relation to both its member states and vis-a-vis outside powers? To answer these questions, a theoretical framework is used that focuses on coherence, capacity and context. Coherence refers here to the ability of EU member states and institutions to agree on a goal and work unitedly for that goal. Capacity is the material and institutional resources that can be used to support the EU's collective action. Finally, context refers to the strategic environment, which affects the scope and impact of what the EU can achieve as an actor. The chapter concludes with a number of recommendations for the EU, most notably on the importance of finding a better balance between means and goals within the EU's foreign and security policy in order to promote the EU's interests and protect liberal values in international politics.

A World Order in Disorder

The liberal world order is a term for the collection of norms, rules, institutions and hierarchies that have surrounded and shaped international politics since the end of World War II (Bull 1977). The victorious Western forces, with the US as the driving force, established this order in which states' external relations were based on the same principles that governed the internal life of the liberal states: sovereignty, political freedom, a market economy and strong institutions. The US, however, had a special position as guarantor of the system. This hierarchy was partially legitimized by the fact that during the Cold War, there was an opposing political order—Soviet communism—which also had a strong inherent hierarchy. During the Cold War, the liberal world order brought relatively clear advantages to the actors involved. The US benefited from this order since it strengthened the power resources that could be put up against the Soviet Union in the bipolar system of the time. Other states benefited from US security guarantees vis-à-vis the Soviet Union and partly from global goods, such as open seas and satellite navigation, that the US provided the world. The liberal aspect of this order consisted primarily of economic liberalism, a common vision that later developed into the so-called "Washington consensus", but also political liberalism, which distinguished it from the Soviet Union's authoritarian regime.

After the end of the Cold War, all the supporting elements of the liberal world order (the liberal element, the system's geographical scope and its internal order) changed. The economic and political liberalism of the Cold War order were joined by a belief system within international politics that was close to that of *academic liberalism*, that is, assumptions about the effects of international organizations as expressed in the liberal school of International Relations. In trade, the General Agreement on Tariffs and Trade (GATT) developed into the institutionally more muscular World Trade Organization (WTO), the European Security Conference (ESC) gained a wider mandate and organizational resources and was renamed the Organization for Security and Cooperation in Europe (OSCE), the International Criminal Court was established and the EU took a big step towards closer and more institutionalized cooperation through the 1992 Maastricht Treaty. As far as the scope of the liberal order is concerned, a rapid spread of its values and principles took place at this time. Globalization accelerated, former-communist states were liberalized both economically and politically, and China and Russia were admitted into the WTO. The liberal system, or at least several of its sub-areas such as the market economy, the environment and, in part, security, now became a genuine *world order*.

Finally, the nature of the order changed. The US which had previously been a hegemon in the liberal order now became a hegemon in a unipolar system devoid of any competing actors. This had an effect on the legitimacy of the world order. In the early 2000s, US unilateralism and its possible negative effects were discussed both in the US and among its traditional allies (Anderson et al. 2008). Another change in the nature of the order was the relative displacement of the principle of the inviolability of states. Westphalian sovereignty, which had been incorporated into the postwar liberal order, was now challenged by political liberalism—for example, a certain view on human rights and the principle of the Responsibility to protect (R2P)—as well as stronger, even, supranational, international institutions. Around the Millennium, various liberal principles of the expanded liberal world order thus came into conflict with the state's traditional role in the same order. Not only would the sovereign powers of the state be questioned, but the state itself would also face competition as a reference point in the new order. Regional organizations, with the EU at the forefront, took an increasingly active role in world politics, while cities in many cases ran their own international policies, companies stepped into areas formerly dominated by the state, such as defense and the maintenance of currency systems, and a small number of individuals acquired material resources and influence that far exceeded that of many states in the international system. States were hardly out-competed, but they no longer played the dominant role in all policy areas which had been the case since the foundation of the Westphalian system.

The EU's Role in the Liberal World Order

It is worth pointing out that the EU was not only affected by, but also a driving force in the developments described above. In documents such as the 2003 European Security Strategy, its "effective multilateralism" set as a goal the integration of different formats and actors into world politics. The EU also took the initiative to regulate new areas such as space and encouraged regional integration in other parts of the world. The EU thus affected this phase in the development of the liberal order as an actor, while also providing an example of how international policies could be conducted in new ways.

However, this "updated" liberal order would have only a short period in the sun after the end of the Cold War. During the first term of US President George W. Bush, the norms of multilateralism and the importance of international institutions were questioned. Critiques of globalization were already widespread but after the US reaction to the attacks on its territory of September 11, 2001 and the conduct of the 2003 Gulf War, primarily became criticisms of the role of the USA as hegemon. The political science literature of the early 2000s questioned whether "the West", and by extension the liberal world order, could survive the transatlantic rupture that occurred following the Iraq war. Thomas Risse, Jeffrey Anderson and John Ikenberry (Anderson et al. 2008) have demonstrated that the discussions were about not just the world system itself, but also the agreements that underpin cooperation in the Euro-Atlantic area. In parallel with the expansion of the transatlantic divide during the Bush administration, which was somewhat narrowed during Barack Obama's presidency, the liberal world order was being challenged by the rise of non-Western countries. Brazil, Russia, India and China (later joined by South Africa, the so-called BRICS) presented proposals that could be seen as alternative arrangements in certain fields. Although in the West there was talk of revisionist ambitions, this accusation could be regarded as hypocritical given the way in which the Western countries had themselves revised the liberal order after the Cold War. However, the questions of whether the BRICS wanted to revise or replace the current world order, and of how the US and its allies should react, have dominated the political and academic debate on international order for the past decade. Part of this discussion has concerned the very nature of the system itself: are the countries on the rise so strong that that we are on the verge of entering a multipolar rather than a unipolar system? How would such a development affect the allies of the US in Europe? Are the rising powers sufficiently interlinked to form their own pole in a multipolar system?

Today, the liberal world order is also under pressure in its traditional "heartland", which represents perhaps its biggest challenge so far. The various aspects of this fragmentation of the world order are the focus of the analysis in this chapter. In the US, President Trump clearly challenges the norms and principles of the liberal order, expressing doubts about it and whether it is in the country's own interests to maintain leadership. Dissatisfaction can be seen in relation to all of its structural elements: economic liberalism, where Trump leans toward protectionism and mercantilism; and political liberalism, where both at home and abroad Trump places little value on the attributes and principles of liberal democracy. Rather than a rules-based and coordinated arrangement in which open societies interact in an environment of strong institutions, Trump has voiced his belief in an order in which strong states (their domestic governance and degree of transparency seem to be of minor importance) compete through traditional means of power projection without the supporting elements in the form of international law and international institutions.

This line was perhaps most clearly expressed by Trump's former National Security Advisor, H.R. McMaster, and former Chief Economic Advisor, Gary Cohn, in an article in the Wall Street Journal in May 2017:

> The president embarked on his first foreign trip with a clear-eyed outlook that the world is not a "global community" but an arena where nations, nongovernmental actors and businesses engage and compete for advantage. We bring to this forum unmatched military, political, economic, cultural and moral strength. Rather than deny this elemental nature of international affairs, we embrace it.

A rules-based multilateral system is no longer the aim. Instead, it is stated that world politics is an arena of competition between actors using classical power instruments, and the US welcomes this geopolitical paradigm. This message, about conflict rather than order and unhinged sovereignty rather than interdependency, resurfaced in the 2017 US security strategy as well as in President Trump's United Nations General Assembly speech of 2018. This shift in the official US worldview of how world politics should look and how it should be conducted is significant and speaks to the ambition of the Trump administration.

Even in Europe the liberal system is reeling. The UK has decided to leave the EU, which manifests many of the principles behind the liberal world order and actively pursued the development of this order after the end of the Cold War. The mantra of "taking back control", which reached a crescendo during the referendum campaign, indicates a certain amount of nostalgia for the nation state's control capabilities in a fast-paced and globalized world. Interestingly, the UK carried out a comprehensive and ambitious review of the balance between national powers and the value of collective action in the EU before the referendum (United Kingdom 2012). This review showed that the balance between member state and EU competences was reasonable, given the policy issues involved. Reverting more competences to the EU member states might therefore be said to risk the control capabilities of several of today's cross-border issues. The UK's decision to disengage from cooperation is a significant setback to the European integration project. At the same time, however, the country had long been seen as a difficult partner with only a lukewarm interest in the more political aspects of integration. A bigger problem in the long term for the European project is the revolt against liberal democratic principles taking place within the EU. Countries such as Poland and Hungary have made clear departures from the internal rule of law while also challenging supporting principles such as compliance with EU law (see Wennerström in this volume). In the background, there are the conflicting interests with other states and the EU institutions regarding solidarity on the migration issue, but the ideological element should not be underestimated. Hungary's Prime Minister, Viktor Orbán, has explicitly argued for an end to the imposition of the values of Western Europe and is looking to establish an illiberal state. This development raises questions about the consolidation of the European integration and the status of the common values that are said to provide stability to the EU (see e.g. Petersson 2018; Nergelius 2018).

A Two-Faced World Order

It thus appears that the liberal world order is now resting on shaky ground. John Ikenberry (2014) argues that a stable world order requires three things: support from a strong enough powerbase represented by one or more states; that the rules and institutions of the order must enjoy a certain degree of legitimacy; and that the order must resolve collective problems and/or offer benefits to actors in the order. As discussed above, support for the liberal system has been eroded from both within and outside the Euro-Atlantic area. The institutions of the liberal world order are often perceived to lack legitimacy and the guarantor of that order, the US, is now ruled by a president who openly questions its benefits. One assumption is that when existing arrangements are perceived in this way, and technological and political trends mean that these arrangements no longer reflect real power resources, a new order will be established by the powerful but displaced actors in the current order. This is a typical realist perspective, which appears in Robert Gilpin's (1983) classic work on international order. In today's world, however, no alternative actor seems capable of establishing an order that meets Ikenberry's three criteria. The different geopolitical starting points of the BRICS, the difficulties in establishing legitimate forms of governance and the fact that these countries benefit greatly from current liberal arrangements, such as free trade, all counteract the development of competing orders. David Lake, for example, demonstrates how non-liberal states have difficulty maintaining legitimate international regimes and hierarchies, as their internal political systems lack barriers to abuse of power and arbitrariness (Lake 2009). A more likely scenario than a competing order is a continuation of the trend we see today: that we are moving towards a system of fragmented order in which groups of states in various configurations work together in specific fields in a looser regime than that which has existed since the end of the Cold War.

Two partially contradictory paradigms can thereby be said to coexist in the context of this turbulent contemporary world order. One is the liberal globalization paradigm that permeated the development of the liberal order and dominated it between the end of the cold war and the turn of the millennium. Somewhat simplified, it consists of assumptions about the ability of globalization to make countries interdependent, the positive effects of democratization on the behavior of states and the benefits of international trade. A central assumption is that more frequent and faster patterns of international interaction and information flows have changed the meaning of time and space. Even today, much political and economic development is governed by the logic of this globalization paradigm, such as the effects of digitization and global value chains that tie together economic operators across time and space (see Alvstam and Lindberg in this volume).

The opposing paradigm that has been increasingly emphasized in recent years is geopolitical, and rooted more closely to the realist school of international relations. Geopolitics assumes that interests—and hence conflicts of interest—are territorially bound. Since territory is something that accrues to states, these become the central political actors. Geopolitics is thus characterized by states regaining their interest in territory, the struggle for natural resources and zero-sum games. From this perspective, the economy is also an obvious arena of power; hence, the return of "geo-economics" in which states seek short-term relative gains, where the ideals of free trade and development are weak and the market is increasingly used as a weapon. It is in this perspective that Russia's President Putin would feel threatened by EU economic cooperation within the Eastern Partnership, which includes countries such as Ukraine and Georgia, and US presidential candidate Hillary Clinton hoped that the defunct Transatlantic Free Trade Agreement (TTIP) would become an "economic NATO". In this view, economics is power and should be treated as such. The essence of geopolitics and geo-economics appears perhaps most clearly if you put them in relief against their counterparts: the belief in the power of globalization to dissolve the importance of territories, human agency as an explanatory factor in international relations and the importance of structural factors other than geography such as class, race, norms or ideology. In conclusion, a state-based perspective that elevates the importance of territory and a materialistic understanding of power can now be said to coexist with the globalization paradigm, and the logic of both perspectives can be said to have a bearing on politics, albeit within different domains, in today's turbulent world.

Order, Actorness and Autonomy in Europe

The remainder of this chapter is devoted to analyzing how today's challenges affect the EU's actorness and, in the long run, its autonomy based on a relatively straight-forward theoretical framework. The basic elements of this framework—coherence, capacity and context—are presented below. First, however, the link between the concepts of order and actorness must be clarified. First and foremost, an order constitutes what type of political entity that forms the basis for a political system, something that can be called the macro-order. The liberal world order of 1945 rests on the Westphalian system, with sovereign states as the central players in the scheme, although developments since the end of the Cold War have demonstrated greater openness to other forms of actors. Second, each type of order has some form of leadership and/or hierarchy that shapes the strategic behavior and scope of other actors. In the liberal world order, the US has played a leadership role, making it possible for US-European partnerships in international politics, while also limiting the room for maneuver. Viewed from a European horizon, the EU as an actor has thus been surrounded by two formative dimensions in the liberal order: the European nation state and US hegemony.

To start with the nation state, it is possible to say that the EU's actorness is based on the fact that its members have the political will to act jointly and in this sense are prepared to delegate power to a central institution to enable collective action. The study of European integration has largely been the study of the development of this capacity for collective action and how it is influenced by the outside world, domestic interests and existing forms of cooperation. The central questions here are how and why member states delegate power to central bodies and what this means for the influence and sovereignty of member states. These questions clearly illustrate the tensions that exist within the liberal order between the norms of cooperation, multilateralism and the role of international institutions, on the one hand, and the rights and obligations of sovereign states to define and protect their own interests, on the other.

Also its relation to the hegemon of the world order has defined the EU's actorness. Within the liberal world order, it is possible to see a "Euro-Atlantic suborder", based on a number of geopolitical agreements. Ikenberry (2014) describes three such agreements: US security guarantees to Europe within the framework of NATO; US support for European reconstruction and integration after the end of World War II, manifest in the Marshall Plan; and European support for US leadership of the liberal system at different levels and within different policy areas. While this was of course in Europe's interests, it was also in the interests of the US as it prevented conflict between European countries, strengthened transatlantic trade exchanges and increased Europe's resilience in relation to the ideological and military threat of the Soviet Union.

It is also important to highlight what was not part of this Euro-Atlantic pact. For example, it did not prevent the US from pursuing its own policies toward other regions, such as South America and the Middle East, which were not necessarily calibrated in tandem with its European allies. Nor did support for primarily economic integration in Europe mean automatic support for collective European actorness in a broader political sense. The US and some of its closest allies in the EU, such as the UK and in recent years the countries of Eastern Europe, have had difficulty accepting that the EU should formulate an independent security policy and risk weakening NATO and challenging the Euro-Atlantic regime. In 1998, US Secretary of State Madeleine Albright warned of "discrimination, disconnection, duplication" if the EU conducted its own security policy. With regard to discrimination, she wanted to lay down a marker that non-EU member states would not be discriminated against in future cooperation. She expressed concern that European and North American security might not be seen as common, and that material and capabilities should not be developed in parallel with NATO resources, resulting in waste and duplication.

US reluctance or at best ambivalence with regard to Europe designing its own security policy has made it controversial for the past two decades to suggest that the world is about to get several new centers of power and that the US is losing its status as the sole superpower. In other words, the EU as an early security policy actor was challenging for the US on two levels. In principle, it paved the way for a multipolar system, which was seen as a challenge to the US role as hegemon. On a more political level, the partnership entailed potential conflicts of interest and competition with the USA in relation to the Middle East and other regions. In conclusion, the EU's actorness is based on hegemonic support in terms of military guarantees and acceptance of integration, but also limited as in the long run it challenges some of the fundamental agreements that underpin the Euro-Atlantic alliance.

The EU's foreign and security policy has thus been shaped by the sovereignty of its member states and by US hegemony. At the same time, there is an inverse relationship in the sense that EU member states, to the extent that they are able to act together, can affect the development of this order. The international order and European actorness are to some extent mutually constitutive. Joint action by EU member states has helped to update the liberal order since the end of the Cold War, in regard partly to the areas to regulate but also to which actors are given a place in the order. While a certain degree of common European actorness is in line with the Euro-Atlantic bargain (it can be seen as a cost-effective way for EU member states to maintain their part of agreements), its role as a more developed actor, and specifically the idea of autonomy, are undoubtedly a cause of tension in the relationship. The concept of autonomy, or strategic autonomy, has a long history, but in simple terms it means that EU member states can act together in the security policy field, independently of the US, and the realization that this effectively requires close cooperation between those states. It was this idea of autonomy that Albright opposed. Since then, however, the criticism has been toned down as, in practice, strategic autonomy goes hand in hand with European capacity-building, which is also of value to NATO. Interestingly, the greatest resistance to EU autonomy today can be seen as coming from those EU member states that see the transatlantic alliance as vital to their national security. In practice, developments are also hampered by European countries finding it difficult to agree on how such autonomy should be built—it would, for instance, require specialization and integration on a completely different level than exists today—and how it should be used. Countries still have quite different starting points regarding threats, interests and the use of force as an instrument of policy.

However, within these constraints, instruments, strategies and capabilities that increase European autonomy and actorness are being developed. The question however remains: how far can it go within the current order? Given the crucial links between international and Euro-Atlantic arrangements, and the way European actorness is dependent on these arrangements, it is worth asking how the EU is affected by the turbulence in the world order. A framework for analyzing collective action should determine the internal prerequisites for decisions as well as the strategic environment in which an actor operates. In this way, analyzing the EU's prospects of becoming an actor—its actorness—has a long tradition. Scholars such as Gunnar Sjöstedt (1977) were already analyzing the EU's opportunities for actorness back in the 1970s.

In this chapter, the EU's actorness is analyzed in terms of coherence, capacity and context. *Coherence* refers to the ability of member states and institutions to agree on a goal and to work coherently to achieve it. Coherence benefits from shared values, threat perceptions and overall interests. In addition, arrangements and processes that make it easier to reach a decision, such as majority voting, can be said to increase coherence, which has long been studied within the institutional school of international politics. *Capacity* is the material and institutional resources that can be used to support collective action. In the first case, this may include crisis management equipment, defense equipment, financial assets, intelligence and diplomatic resources. In the latter case, these may be networks and processes that allow for the effective implementation of a course of action. Finally, an actor's *context* influence scope and the impact that it is possible to achieve. Context refers to the surroundings, and the obstacles and opportunities these raise for a specific actor. Is there acceptance of a collective actor? Are there any political or geographical conditions in which a particular actor can be assumed to be more efficient than another? In the existing literature, there is disagreement about whether contextual factors should form part of actorness or be seen as a different dimension altogether. In an analysis of the EU, however, is it reasonable to see contextual factors as part of the actorness itself, since EU foreign and security policy has so clearly been formed by its surrounding environment.

Coherence: EU Cohesion During Disorder

Coherence refers to the degree of cohesion between EU member states. As a collective actor for which foreign and security policy decision-making is of an intergovernmental nature, coherence is vital to potential actorness. How is this coherence affected by the current changes inside and outside Europe? President Trump's challenge to the order that the US created and has led since 1945 has taken various forms, most notably doubting the value of NATO, contempt for EU integration and its institutional manifestations, a general mistrust of multilateralism and an almost mercantilist view of trade. This line has undoubtedly increased coherence among EU member states, or at least among the 27 countries that intend to remain within the union. The UK has faced difficulties reconciling Trump's policy pronouncements as they make exiting the EU more difficult and leave the UK even more dependent on US support. Other EU member states have balanced Trump's actions by supporting an active policy on climate change while also supporting NATO, as well as new EU initiatives on free trade agreements with countries such as Australia, New Zealand and Mexico (see Jagers et al. and Zurek in this volume). One area in which cohesion has been reduced, however, is values, where some member states appear to have been inspired by Trump's success in their campaigns against the EU's liberal values.

With regard to Brexit, the effect has been to unite the remaining member states, at least in relation to the UK and the negotiations. The European Commission has been given a clear mandate and the split over the negotiations that some had feared has not materialized. In other policy areas, too, Brexit can be said to have increased coherence, either because the UK can no longer prevent progress or because the remaining member states have felt it necessary to demonstrate unity and progress. For example, defense cooperation has taken great strides since the British vote, with a decision on a new limited headquarters, the establishment of a Defense Fund and a stronger commitment to achieve enhanced cooperation in smaller groups within the framework of Permanent Structured Cooperation (PESCO) as stipulated in the Treaty of the European Union. There are several reasons for this—such as internal institutional developments based on an ambitious new global strategy and the election of a US president who, in various ways, has signaled that Europeans must be better able to take responsibility for their own security—but coherence certainly increased once the UK took a much more permissive attitude within this domain. This effect was multiplied by the fact that other formerly more cautious countries such as Sweden understood the political cost of keeping their foot on the brake now the UK had ended its resistance, leading to a more cooperative stance (Fägersten 2017). Another similar multiplication effect is the probability that the remaining countries will move towards more majority voting in the security policy field due to the lack of British resistance. The possibility of majority voting is itself a tool for creating greater coherence for a collective actor such as the EU. Finally, Brexit has made the remaining member states more willing to invest in enhanced cooperation in order to demonstrate the EU's dynamism and avoid the contagion effects of the British decision to leave. For this reason, security policy emerged as a mature area with broad public support for greater cooperation and with clear gaps to fill.

Another change in the internal order with a bearing on coherence within the EU is the fact that some governments are now openly questioning the core principles of liberal democracy. The lack of internal coherence in terms of liberal democratic values obviously has implications for the EUs internal composition and the ability to enforce EU principles externally. It also exposes the vulnerability of the EU as a foreign policy actor, and increases the possibility that an external power might split the union. Mitchell A. Orenstein and Daniel Kelemen (2017) have stated that the EU has a problem with "Trojan horses", meaning that individual member states might be able to obstruct or thwart decisions that affect certain external parties, as most recently illustrated when Greece prevented the EU from taking a united line on China's human rights violations. Alternatively, the EU might agree to take a certain foreign policy approach, such as sanctions against Russia, but some member states could pursue a directly opposing policy on a national basis, such as making their own energy agreements or selling defense equipment to the country in question. The stronger the EU becomes as a foreign policy actor, the more external parties have to gain from trying to limit the EU's power with the help of sympathizers inside the EU. This vulnerability could be increased if the anti-liberal norms manifest by, for example, Russia and China are increasingly seen as desirable in some EU member states.

Capacity: Conditions for Implementing EU Policies

Capacity is the combination of resources a collective actor can draw on to achieve its foreign and security policy aims. Coherence without capacity produces a virtual or symbolic political actor with negligible effects. In the same way as President Trump's unwillingness to invest in the liberal world order has increased the coherence of EU member states, it can to some extent also be said to have increased their capacity. More resources have been promised by several countries in areas where the US is cutting back, such as certain forms of targeted aid and support for mitigating the effects of climate change. Even in the field of security policy, leading countries, such as Germany, have clearly indicated that they intend to increase investment, but in a way that cannot be seen as a response to Trump's insistence that Europeans "pay their debts to NATO and the United States". Outside of the EU, France has spearheaded a new European Intervention Initiative to facilitate European responses to crises in the neighborhood. In practice, this means that capacity are created that could be utilized within an EU-framework and thereby resulting in a certain capacity increase for the EU as an actor. On the other hand, a clear confrontation with the Trump administration could jeopardize strategic resources such as intelligence material, strategic air lift capacities and ammunition that the US has under certain conditions made available to European countries. EU capacity would then be reduced as an effect.

The UK's planned exit from the EU also has the potential to reduce capacity in the foreign and security policy field. The UK has significant diplomatic and military resources that, to some extent, it makes available to the EU. The capacity that it has provided for analysis and decision-making within the European Council structures and the European External Action Service has been crucial to the development of the EU's actorness. One example is the intelligence arena, where the UK has played a crucial role both in public and behind the scenes (Fägersten 2015). The British contribution to EU civilian and military operations has been more limited in recent years, but the potential capacity is still a decisive factor in the common European capability. Against this potential loss of capacity, however, must be set the momentum within the EU's security cooperation that Brexit has helped to create. The increased coherence between the remaining 27 member states has largely aimed to increase foreign and security policy capacity through investment in management and planning capabilities, defense cooperation on neglected areas, and efficiency gains and synergies through better coordination of national defense investments. What the net effect on capacity might be of all these changes is difficult to say, but one factor that speaks to a positive net effect is that the UK appears to be seeking continued close cooperation with the EU in the field of security policy. Its security policy position papers in the Brexit negotiations, published in September 2017, as well as ongoing negotiations during 2018, suggest active participation in planning missions, participation in and funding of these missions, as well as a number of areas for continuing cooperation—including projects under the European Defense Agency and PESCO. If Brexit can lead to a new dynamism between the EU 27 without totally excluding British capacity support in the future, the net effect on overall European capacity would be clearly positive. This might, to some extent, be hampered by the potential loss of economic growth, especially in the UK, given the impact of its impending exit from the EU.

The internal gaps between EU member states can also have effects on capacity. The willingness to provide resources is a measure of solidarity within the EU as member states do not necessarily perceive the same threats or share the same interests. Traditionally, a balance has been sought between actions and expenses, linked to the South and to the East. With the UK on its way out, it is possible that the EU's focus might turn southwards, which could wreck the current balance and, in the long run, the willingness of member states to promote capacity. This would particularly be the case if the conflicts develop into a clear split between the so-called Visegrad countries (Poland, Slovakia, the Czech Republic and Hungary) and the rest of the EU.

Taken together, significant capacity building is under way within the EU with clear links to the turbulence in the transatlantic and European orders. On the other hand, this capacity increase does not appear to challenge the overarching European security arrangement. Instead, it might be said that the EU's role as a security policy actor is being refined by these developments. The current increase in capacity reinforces the EU's role as a broad security policy actor focused on small-scale crisis management, diplomacy and aid. If the UK is looking for close cooperation with its European partners, NATO will probably be the main platform for its commitment to European security. This, in combination with Russia's apparent violation of Europe's post-war order, makes it clear that NATO must return to its basic function of European territorial defense, and readiness for more demanding crisis management operations in Europe's neighborhood. The effect will be to consolidate and reinforce the division of labor between the EU and NATO, at least from a short- to medium-term perspective.

Context: The Surrounding Environment and External Expectations

The context is the demand for and acceptance of European actorness in the regions and policy areas where the EU aims to act. To some extent, this has been considered above by focusing on the direct effects of turbulence in the order. However, the changes in the order and in the parallel paradigms of geopolitics and globalization, as discussed above, also have an indirect effect through their impact on the context wherein the EU is likely to work. If the US view of the liberal world order is not just a product of President Trump, but rather the effect of a structural change in how the US views the outside world, this raises the issue of European actorness in a more fundamental way. Will the EU be prepared to increase investment in order to maintain elements of the current order? This could be done, for example, in collaboration with Canada, Mexico, Japan, Australia and New Zealand, with which the EU is currently conducting trade negotiations. Another question is whether the more distant US role in Europe's neighborhood, which began well before Trump was elected, will increase the demand for European commitment. Previous studies of the euro crisis and its importance for European actorness have shown that despite the challenging crisis years, the model of cooperation that Europe represents and the toolbox it uses were still in demand in, for example, North Africa and sub-Saharan Africa (Fägersten 2014). As countries in these regions have a lot to gain from wider security solutions and interregional cooperation, it might be assumed that they will continue to accept and demand European commitment even in times of global turmoil and a diminished US role.

It can also be assumed that the shift from a globalization paradigm to a greater role for geopolitical logic will have an asymmetric effect on Europe and, in the long run, its actorness. A comparison between the EU's leading member states, Germany and France, provides a good illustration. For Germany, developments in Russia and the United States are a threat since relations with both are central to the German economy and its security. A harsher power policy presents challenges for Germany, which is heavily invested in regulated and institutionalized international relations. For France, on the other hand, the turmoil in the world order presents both problems and opportunities. France's relationship with Russia is less significant than Germany's, and France is better equipped mentally, strategically and in resource terms for a world order that leaves more room for geopolitical logic. With the UK on its way out, France is the only remaining EU member state with nuclear weapons, a permanent seat on the UN Security Council and a tradition of clearly articulating national interests. In this way, a system based more on geopolitics would allow France a more central role in the EU and an opportunity to balance Germany in a relationship that has become increasingly unbalanced in recent years. Political logic both globally and in the EU's neighborhoods thus affects the position of the member states and ultimately their role in European collective action.

Another example is the role of the European Commission in much of the EU's policy towards its neighborhoods. The Commission is responsible for EU enlargement policy and programs targeted at neighboring countries. This division of labor has led to criticism that even neighboring states lacking an enlargement perceptive have been treated according to the same logic, that is, in a relatively technocratic relationship where EU member states have a smaller role. As more and more countries in the immediate area have become politically unstable and Russia pursues an active destabilization policy in parts of the region, the EU's approach has emerged as naïve. Should the current trend for a greater degree of geopolitical logic be accentuated, the Commission might be forced to stand back in favor of member states that want to pursue a more active and traditional foreign policy towards the countries in the immediate neighborhood. In this way, EU actorness will change in response to contextual changes.

In conclusion, it is too early to assess the long-term effects of the turbulent order and how it will affect the context in which the EU operates. The fact that the logics of globalization and geopolitics coexist in the region, however, has made the EU as a whole an actor that is more accepted and welcomed in some areas than in others. As noted above, such a logic can also shift the balance between EU member states and EU institutions, as they have different conditions for taking action according to a globalized or a geopolitical game plan. This strengthens the image initially painted of a fragmented world order with pockets and fields of cooperation.

A Better Balance Between Goals and Resources Can Strengthen EU Actorness and Europe's Autonomy

This chapter has analyzed the turbulence in the liberal world order and how it has affected the EU's actorness. Three dimensions of fragmented and strained order—the US ambivalence to the global liberal order, British withdrawal from a collaboration that demonstrates the basic values of this order and the opposition of a small number of European countries to these liberal values—have been analyzed to assess their bearing on EU coherence, capacity and context. With regard to coherence, both Trump's actions and the UK's decision to leave the EU have increased cohesion among the EU's remaining members. However, it should be noted that the effect of losing an actor that often worked to prevent further integration will also reveal differences—for example, between Germany and

France—that have not previously been to the fore. At the same time, the internal fragmentation in the view of liberal democratic core values constitutes a clear barrier to consensus in the foreign policy arena and increases the risk of "Trojan Horses". Even the EU's capacity for action, in terms of both material and institutional resources, could be affected, albeit in a more indirect way. A collapse of the international order, for example, in the form of a wrecked global trade system, would be hard for Europe to cope with. Furthermore, the loss of the UK's capacity in the field of foreign policy will be hugely relevant to the EU's potential actorness. The net effect of the increased coherence within the EU after the Brexit vote, which manifests itself primarily through a series of capacity-building commitments, and the capacity losses that Brexit itself would mean is difficult to predict.

However, it is reasonable to assume that if the UK establishes a close relationship with the EU on defense and security policy, as stipulated in its position paper, the net effect of Brexit would be a capacity increase. The EU 27 would increase its collective capacity while the UK moved from skeptical member to constructive partner. Finally, the turbulence in the liberal order may in the long run affect the context in which the EU operates and in some sense alter the EU's actorness. A reduced US presence in Europe's neighborhood would be likely to lead to increased demands for EU commitments. In the same way, US lack of interest in a continuation of multilateral trade liberalization would increase demand for bilateral trade agreements with the EU. However, the contextual changes caused by a fragmented order would not all be to the EU's advantage. A more geopolitical logic to neighborhood and international relations would weaken the EU, at least based on the tools, mechanisms and values that currently govern its foreign policy.

Overall, the EU could be said to have the potential to become a leaner and sharper actor in an increasingly difficult strategic landscape. Without the UK, but with increased capacity and greater consistency between its institutions and the remaining member states, the EU can become more efficient, albeit in relation to a more limited number of tasks. Small-scale conflict management, mediation, cyber and hybrid issues, as well as other areas that benefit from the EU's broad toolbox would be the focus, with more demanding military efforts still in the future. This has a number of implications for Europe's security and autonomy. For example, the relationship between Europe's security institutions becomes clearer. The strengthened EU actor capacity, as discussed above, increases the EU's ability to live up to the ambitions already stated in the Common Foreign and Security Policy. In this way, the division of labor that in practice already exists between the EU and NATO means that NATO will continue to be responsible for the continent's territorial defense. This procedure is further cemented by the fact that the UK, as part of its ambition to maintain responsibility for European security, will probably strengthen its commitments in NATO.

Moreover, this development will have a somewhat ambiguous effect on ambitions for European strategic autonomy. On the one hand, the EU's ability to plan and carry out smaller efforts with its own resources will increase. On the other, it is hard to see how the EU could be the platform for more demanding military efforts after the UK's exit, as British capacity as well as its strategic culture will be absent from the EU in the future. With President Trump in the White House, however, European autonomy will probably not be demonstrated through a European pillar of NATO, an old idea that is revived periodically. Given Trump's dubious and changing views on NATO, the European NATO countries have every reason to fully integrate their interaction with US troops, not isolate their contribution to NATO in the form of an autonomous European arm.

In conclusion, inasmuch as European countries are able to act autonomously in more demanding military situations, this will in the medium term be realized in the shape of a voluntary coalition of sufficiently strong states. The EU is not irrelevant in such scenarios, but its role would be that of an enabling and capacity-enhancing actor for some of the coalition members, not a decision-making forum. In sum, different dimensions of fragmentation of the liberal system in Europe and globally will have significant effects on the EU's actorness. However, these effects go in different directions and affect the different aspects of actorness (coherence, capacity and context) to varying degrees. The movement toward a stronger but to some extent more limited actorness, and the effects of the internal and external unpredictability generated by the fragmented world order, mean that certain actions are called for at the EU level.

First, the EU should strengthen its ability to be a *strategic* actor, not just an actor. As Engelbrekt (2008) (see also Chappell et al. 2016) has emphasized, it is precisely the interaction between the constituent parts of actorness that give rise to strategic actorness. Coherence should constitute not just consensus, but agreement on overall and long-term goals. Capacity should be seen in relation to these goals, and both objectives and resources should be balanced against the context in which they are to be implemented. Strategic actorness requires, in other words, internal prioritization of goals and resources, constant analysis and information retrieval about the context in which it seeks to work and an ongoing learning process whereby the outcomes of previous actions and activities influence future action. In other words, a collective actor such as the EU requires a high level of information sharing between member states in order to achieve adequate knowledge of the outside world and each other's preferences. A number of steps that could be taken are described in previous research on information management and actorness (Fägersten 2015, 2016). For example, the EU could better utilize and develop the analytical capabilities of its external representations to increase strategic awareness in Brussels and national capitals. Similarly, the EU could jointly train intelligence analysts in order to build the trust needed for multilateral information exchange.

Second, the EU should try to minimize both the uncertainty and the loss of capacity resulting from the UK's departure. There are good reasons to connect the UK as closely as possible in a number of areas, such as intelligence cooperation, crisis management, defense issues and counterterrorism. However, there is a risk that the EU's security policy relationship with the UK would then develop into a series of agreements and practical arrangements in demarcated areas without any overall strategic orientation or political ownership. Therefore, the ambition should be to supplement these agreements with a comprehensive political declaration of intent. A security and solidarity pact between the EU and the UK would increase the predictability and the strategic value of the future relationship. This is of particular importance for the non-NATO members of the EU.

Third, the EU should prepare to take greater responsibility for the liberal order, both inside and outside of Europe. As this chapter has shown, Europe and the EU are hugely affected by illiberal trends, both globally and locally. Much of the concern that many Europeans have felt with regard to President Trump's policy—the hesitancy over Article 5 of the North Atlantic Treaty, the lack of interest in European integration and its institutions, and resistance to international organizations and free trade—is a side-effect of his views on the liberal world order and how this system is unfavorable to the US. If Trump is not the sole reason for the US turnaround in relation to the liberal world order, but rather a symptom of a more deep-seated change within the American society, the EU must prepare to take greater responsibility for maintaining parts of this order. This could involve more support for multilateral institutions or rules-based cooperation, as well as leadership in areas such as environmental, cyber and space issues. However, taking the lead role in the liberal order globally would require acceptance of and insight into the importance of these values locally. It is essential that the EU, and not least its member states, persevere with regard to a values-based community under the treaties.

Finally, the EU will need to develop actorness beyond the boundaries of current and future orders in order to maintain international political relevance. This chapter has described a world order that is becoming "less global" and more fragmented. This development poses more of a problem for the EU than for many other actors. The current order covers only a few regulatory areas and, more importantly, the state actors that make up the system are restrained by it to different degrees.[1] In the case of the US, for example, while the country has functioned as the backstop of the liberal world order it understood early on that this order would not cater for and cover all US interests. Hence, the US made certain by enjoying hegemonic military status and building a network of alliances to maximize its power in the security realm. The liberal world order therefore did not cover the full realm of US security policy and the country maintained tools and capacities that offered it actorness beyond the order. Countries that came late to the order and with much less buy-in, such as Russia and China, also maintained the will and capacity to act outside of the system. This is in stark contrast to the EU, which has developed its entire foreign and security policy repertoire within the liberal order. As this order shrinks, it will eventually be imperative for the EU to develop agency beyond the agreed order. In practice, the EU will need to equip itself to be able to act autonomously in areas other than traditional diplomacy, in order to avoid becoming irrelevant. In this sense, some level of strategic autonomy will be needed if the EU wants to retain even a minimal degree of actorness in a future where the world order will most likely be less comprehensive than the one that has served us up until now.

[1] For a discussion on the scope and limits of order from a US perspective, see Friedman Lissner and Rapp-Hooper (2018).

References

Anderson, J., Ikenberry, G. J., & Risse, T. (Eds.). (2008). *The End of the West? Crisis and Change in the Atlantic Order*. Ithaca: Cornell University Press.

Bartels, H.-D., Kellner, A. M., & Optenhögel, U. (Eds.). (2017). *Strategic Autonomy and the Defence of Europe: On the Road to a European Army?* Bonn: Dietz.

Bull, H. (1977). *The Anarchical Society: A Study of Order in World Politics*. London: Palgrave Macmillan.

Chappell, L., Mawdsley, J., & Petrov, P. (2016). *The EU, Strategy and Security Policy: Regional and Strategic Challenges*. New York: Routledge.

Engelbrekt, K. (2008). Conclusion: A Strategic Actor Under Permanent Construction? In Kjell Engelbrekt och Jan Hallenberg (Ed.), *The European Union and Strategy: An Emerging Actor*. Adbingdon, Oxon: Routledge.

Fägersten, B. (2014). The Implications of the Euro Crisis for European Foreign Policy: Lessons from Crisis Management and International Trade. *European Foreign Affairs Review, 19*(4), 483–502.

Fägersten, B. (2015). *Intelligence and Decision-Making Within the Common Foreign and Security Policy*. Stockholm: Sieps 2015:22epa.

Fägersten, B. (2016). *For EU Eyes Only? Intelligence and European Security*. Report published by the European Union Institute of Strategic Studies, Paris.

Fägersten, B. (2017). *Transatlantic Turbulence and European Security: Effects of President Trump's Foreign Policy Agenda and Brexit*. Stockholm: The Swedish Institute of International Affairs.

Friedman Lissner, R., & Rapp-Hooper, M. (2018). The Day After Trump: American Strategy for a New International Order. *The Washington Quarterly, 41*(1), 7–25.

Gilpin, R. (1983). *War and Change in World Politics*. Cambridge: Cambridge University Press.

Ikenberry, G. J. (Ed.). (2014). *Power, Order and Change in World Politics*. Cambridge: Cambridge University Press.

Lake, D. A. (2009). *Hierarchy in International Relations*. Ithaca: Cornell University Press.

Nergelius, J. (2018). What Explains the Lack of Trust in the EU Among Its Member States? A Constitutional Analysis of the EU's "Value Crisis". In A. Bakardijeva Engelbrekt, N. Bremberg, A. Michalski, & L. Oxelheim (Eds.), *Trust in the European Union in Challenging Times*. Cham: Palgrave.

Orenstein, M. A., & Kelemen, D. (2017). Trojan Horses in EU Foreign Policy. *Journal of Common Market Studies Volume, 55*(1), 87–102.

Petersson, B. (2018). Perspective on the Eastern Enlargement: Triumph of the EU or Seed of Its Destruction? In A. Bakardijeva Engelbrekt, N. Bremberg, A. Michalski, & L. Oxelheim (Eds.), *Trust in the European Union in Challenging Times*. Cham: Palgrave.

Sjöstedt, G. (1977). *The External Role of the European Community*. Farnborough: Saxon House.

United Kingdom. (2012). Review of the Balance of Competences. Retrieved October 5, 2018, from https://www.gov.uk/guidance/review-of-the-balance-of-competences.

CHAPTER 3

Brexit, Trumpism and the Structure of International Trade Regulation

Per Cramér

Introduction

The political processes that led to the outcome of the British referendum on continued membership in the European Union (EU) and the installation of Donald Trump as president of the USA demonstrate clear similarities. In gaining support of the electorate, the successful Trump and Brexit campaigns were both dominated by populist messages, expressed in a strong nationalist rhetoric, externalizing responsibility for an undesired development within the nation and explicitly criticizing existing international trade agreements as well as the acceptance of the jurisdiction of supranational structures for dispute resolution. This said, it is important to note the differences between these two political decisions. The British decision to withdraw from membership in the EU is an extraordinary decision in a specific concrete question with large repercussions regarding foreign trade regulation. The election of Donald Trump as president and the installation of a new U.S. administration is a choice within the ordinary political process with principal effects on the U.S. foreign trade policy.

P. Cramér (✉)
University of Gothenburg, Gothenburg, Sweden
e-mail: per.cramer@handels.gu.se

A. Bakardjieva Engelbrekt et al. (eds.), *The European Union in a Changing World Order*,
https://doi.org/10.1007/978-3-030-18001-0_3

The objective of this chapter is to contribute to a deeper understanding of how the recent political development in the UK and the U.S. will affect the structures for regulating the conditions for international trade. The chapter starts with a brief account of the historical development of the structures of international trade regulation. A specific focus is thereafter put on the increased priority of the development of bilateral trade agreements that has been demonstrated by the U.S. and the EU during the last decade. Against this backdrop, follows an analysis of the factual and potential changes in the structures of international trade regulation that are a consequence of the political developments in the UK and the U.S. The analysis constitutes a basis for defining a number of trends in this development and places these trends into a larger context, relating them to relevant historical experiences. The chapter finishes with a short reflection on how the EU could, and ought to, act in order to develop and strengthen the multilateral institutions for regulating international trade.

The Development of Regulatory Structures for International Trade

The established system for regulating the conditions for international trade through reciprocal agreements between states on bilateral, regional and multilateral levels is the result of a relatively recent development. Starting in the early nineteenth century the dominance of mercantilism was gradually substituted by an understanding of the welfare gains that follow from opening up for the comparative advantages of states through international trade. The international economic system during *la belle epoque*, from the 1860s up until the advent of the Great War 1914, was characterized by high economic growth furthered by a rapid scientific and technological development in combination with a high degree of asymmetric internationalization. This period was also an era of relative peace between the European Great Powers within the balance of power system that had been established through the outcome of the Vienna Conference 1815. The competition between these nations was primarily taking place outside Europe in the establishment of colonial empires. To an increasing extent, the trade relations between industrialized states became based on the principle of reciprocity and a densely spun network of bilateral trade agreements between these states developed successively

(Lazer 1999).[1] In addition to mutual obligations on liberalizing the conditions for trade these agreements included a prohibition on discrimination between trading partners; that the parties to the agreement should be given the same treatment as the most favoured trading partner—the principle of Most Favoured Nation (MFN). The conditions for trade and capital flows between these states were moreover stabilized by fixing the value of the national currencies to a gold standard.[2]

Outside the northern hemisphere military instruments were utilized to establish colonial empires within which highly asymmetric relationships of economic integration between colonial power and colonies were developed, relationships that in many instances led to the de-industrialization of the colonial dependencies (Bairoch 1993: 88–98). Armed force was also used to open up previously restricted markets, such as China and Japan.[3] These actions were confirmed through unequal bilateral trade agreements between the dominant industrialized states and the states that were forced to submission.[4] The core of these agreements was non-reciprocal obligations for the latter to guarantee market access and not to discriminate between trading partners in accordance with the MFN-principle. The primary motive for including this asymmetric version of the MFN-principle in these agreements was to avoid conflict between the great powers.

The development of multilateral structures for regulating the conditions for international trade was very limited during this period and the first initiatives in this direction took place towards the end of the nineteenth century, when the tensions between the European Great Powers were increasing and the fragile system of bilateral agreements for trade

[1] This development commenced 1860 through the conclusion of the Cobden-Chevalier Treaty between France and Great Britain.

[2] The gold standard was established in Great Britain during the 1820s. The majority of European states followed suite during the following decades. By the end of the 1880s the gold standard had been established by a majority of the world's nations.

[3] The Chinese market was opened up for European trade primarily as a consequence of the Chinese submission after the defeat in the first Opium War with Great Britain 1842. Japan was forced to open its market to international trade under threat of an American armed intervention 1853.

[4] See, for example, Treaty between China and Great Britain, signed at Nanking, 29 August 1842, (93 CTS 465), Treaty of Peace, Amity, and Commerce, between the United States of America and the Chinese Empire, Signed at Wang Hiya, 3 July 1844, (97 CTS 105) and Treaty of Peace and Amity between Japan and the United States, signed at Kanagwa, 31 March 1854, (111 CTS 377).

liberalization was rapidly eroding.[5] These multilateral initiatives were focusing on regulating trade in times of war, most importantly through a number of the conventions that were signed at the Peace Conferences in Haag 1899 and 1907.[6] These peace conferences constituted an attempt to stabilize the complicated balance of power structure that had developed since the Vienna conference, This attempt notoriously failed, and the escalation of competition between the European Great Powers, fired up by strong nationalist rhetoric and a cultural glorification of armed conflict as a heroic activity[7], led to a war of hitherto unimagined proportions and destructive effects.

The first decade after the end of the Great War breathed of hope and optimism for the future expressed in cultural modernism, the breakthrough of democracy in most European states, scientific and technologic development, economic growth, increasing international trade and a strong belief in international organization. Through the Statute of the League of Nations, the right to use armed force as an instrument in the relations between states was limited for the first time in history. Moreover, a number of multilateral organizations of functional character were established, most importantly the International Labour Organization (ILO). The explicit motive behind the formation of this organization was a conviction that social justice constituted a prerequisite for a stabile international peace order.[8]

[5] The erosion of the system of bilateral trading agreements between the European states started with the German introduction of new tariffs 1879. The Cobden Chevalier Treaty was terminated through the French introduction of the Méline tariff 1892.

[6] In particular II Convention respecting the Limitation of the Employment of Force for Recovery of Contract Debts (Treaty Series 537), XI Convention relative to Certain Restrictions with regard to the Exercise of the Right of Capture in Naval War (Treaty Series 544), and XIII Convention concerning the Rights and Duties of Neutral Powers in Naval War (Treaty Series 545).

[7] For a contemporary illustrative example of cultural expressions glorifying the state of war, see Brooke (1915).

[8] ILO constitution signed at Versailles 28 June 1919 (Treaty Series 874) states, in its Preamble "Whereas universal and lasting peace can be established only if it is based upon social justice; ...Whereas also the failure of any nation to adopt humane conditions of labour is an obstacle in the way of other nations which desire to improve the conditions in their own countries; The High Contracting Parties, moved by sentiments of justice and humanity as well as by the desire to secure the permanent peace of the world, and with a view to attaining the objectives set forth in this Preamble, agree to the following Constitution of the International Labour Organization".

In parallel with this multilateral development, attempts were made to recreate the system for regulating the conditions for international trade that had existed during the latter half of the nineteenth century. A large number of reciprocal bilateral trade agreements were concluded in the early 1920s including provisions for liberalization of trade conditions and non-discrimination through the application of the MFN-principle. In addition, the gold standard was reintroduced in most industrialized stated.

The general optimism for the future that dominated the early 1920s was however soon substituted with despair and eroding societal structures. The economic depression that hit the world after the stock market collapse on Wall Street 1929 soon led to shrinking economic activity, social instability and the demise of the political systems in a large number of states. In a majority of European states this led to an erosion of democracy and the rise of populist, nationalist authoritarian regimes of different political shades. Nationalism was partly expressed in increasing protectionism through increased tariffs, quantitative restrictions and devaluations of the national currencies. The gold standard, that was considered to have exaggerated the economic downturn, was abandoned by most states in the early 1930s (Bernanke and James 1991). The combination of economic depression and increased protectionism led to international trade becoming virtually non-existent for many states.

In a similar manner, the hopes that had been knitted to the development of multilateral organization, and an international peace order, within the framework of the League of Nations were crushed by the early 1930s when the world witnessed the collapse of the organization's collective security system and a number of states left the League. In this environment, an increasing number of authoritarian states developed increased military aggressiveness and the weakened institutions for international cooperation could not prevent the outbreak of a second world war.

The Structural Development of the Regulation for International Trade Conditions After 1945

At the San Francisco conference in 1945, the victorious powers agreed upon the establishment of a centralized global collective security system that was realized through the Charter of the United Nations. The wartime alliance, that was a prerequisite for the functioning of this system, did however deteriorate rapidly after the common enemy was defeated and was substituted by a Cold War between two nuclear armed great power blocs. Within the framework of this bi-polar balance of power, two competing economic systems developed. As internal trade in both of these blocs expanded rapidly in accordance with radically different theoretical frameworks, trade between the blocs became heavily restricted, largely as a result of security policy considerations, and therefore stayed at very limited levels.

Within the Western bloc, the basic structures for the economic order and international economic co-operation were set up through the Bretton Woods agreement in 1944.[9] As a part of this order, the General Agreement on Tariffs and Trade (GATT) was established in 1947 as the first reciprocal multilateral structure for regulating the conditions for international trade. The fundamental principle of the GATT was, and is, the general prohibition on discrimination between trading partners that is expressed in the MFN-principle; that each signatory party shall treat all other signatory parties no less favourable than it treats its most favoured trading partner (GATT, article I). In its multilateral reciprocal expression, the MFN-principle thus became a foundation for creating a levelled playing field for international trade. However, the agreement also included a fundamental derogation from this principle in that it allows for the creation of regional preferential areas, in the formats of Free Trade Areas and Customs Unions, under conditions specified in the agreement (GATT, article XXIV). Thereby a field of tension between multilateralism, regionalism and bilateralism was created within the structure of the GATT.

During the following decades the GATT-system was developed through a number of negotiating rounds between the signatory parties leading to normative clarifications and successive reductions in customs tariffs for trade in industrial goods. Moreover, largely as a consequence of the dismantling of the European colonial empires, the number of signatory parties increased successively from the original 23 states to 99 in 1990. However, simultaneously the signatory parties also invoked the derogation from the MFN-principle by establishing regional preferential areas in an increasing number of cases. Thus, the multilateral order developed in parallel with an increased number of regional and bilateral preferential

[9] Formally named the United Nations Monetary and Financial Conference. Representatives from all 44 states that were allied in the war participated in the negotiations and signed the Final Act, including the Soviet Union. The Final Act was ratified by all states participating except the Soviet Union.

agreements. The extent to which these two lines of development should be perceived as complementary or competing did soon become a fiercely debated issue both in politics and in legal and economic doctrine.[10]

In this context, the establishment of the European Economic Community (EEC) in 1957 constitutes a ground-breaking example of far reaching regional economic integration. Based on the customs union, the objective of EEC was to establish a common market with internally free movement of products—goods and services, and the factors for production—capital and labour. As a logical consequence of the customs union, a supranational common commercial policy was established including the exclusive competence to enter international trade agreements.

The development of GATT together with the establishment of the EEC constitute examples of functional international co-operation influenced by the theories developed by the sociologist and political scientist David Mitrany during the early 1940s (Mitrany 1941). This theory was developed against the backdrop of the experiences drawn from the destructive powers unleashed during the two world wars and the instability and fragility of the imperfect international order established during the interwar period. The fundamental idea in Mitrany's theory is that, through the successive establishment of multilateral structures for international co-operation in functional areas of mainly technical-legal character, mutual dependence between states will gradually increase. The objective is that this over time will lead to increased mutual trust between the states involved and increase the costs for initiating international conflicts, thereby contributing to the establishment of a stabile international peace order. In this connection, it shall be observed that Mitrany explicitly pointed out the tension between multilateralism and regionalism and hoisted a flag of warning that regional structures may find a need to define real or imagined external enemies in order to strengthen internal cohesion and loyalty. Structures for regional co-operation, if they are not effectively included in a multilateral framework might, according to Mitrany, therefore contribute to the increase of international tensions (Mitrany 1941).

After the fall of the Berlin Wall and the disintegration of the Soviet empire in the early 1990s the western economic system rapidly developed into a global multilateral structure. Based on the GATT, the World Trade Organization (WTO) was established in 1995 as an institutional framework

[10] The pioneering analysis of this tension in the regulatory system for international trade is found in Bhagwati (1991).

for an expanded global code of conduct for international trade. In addition to trade in goods, regulated in a revised GATT, the WTO-system covers trade in services, and a baseline for the protection of trade related intellectual property rights, regulated in separate agreements under the WTO umbrella.[11] In addition, an independent system for dispute resolution regarding the interpretation and application of the WTO-agreements was established through the Dispute Settlement Understanding (DSU). Through the establishment of this dispute settlement system, the normativity of the agreements was strengthened and an extensive case-law on the interpretation of the WTO-rules successively developed.

The membership of the WTO was soon expanded and in 2018 it includes 164 states which stand for approximately 95 per cent of world trade. Important steps in this development were the accession of China 2001 and Russia 2012 to the WTO-treaties. The establishment of WTO and the following expansion of the organization took place in an environment of high hopes for the future world order in the wake of the end of the Cold War, based on the values that had been developed in the West since 1945; an environment which might be illustrated by the claim by the political scientist Francis Fukuyama that the world, after the collapse of the Soviet Union and the triumph of liberal democracy and market economy, had arrived to the end of history (Fukuyama 1989).

Multilateral negotiations for a further development of the WTO-system were initiated in 2001 within the framework of the Doha Development Agenda (DDA). The Doha Round did however soon end up in a stalemate as a result of conflicting interests primarily between developing states and established industrialized states. The negotiations, that were planned to be concluded in 2005, are still continuing, albeit with very meagre results. Partly as substitute for the absence of development at the multilateral level, the proliferation of bilateral regional preferential trade agreements has been increasing at a rapid pace during the last decades.[12]

This quantitative increase has been combined with a qualitative development of more ambitious agreements that in addition to liberalization of direct hindrances to trade include provisions on harmonization and

[11] General Agreement on Trade in Services (GATS) and General Agreement on Trade Related Intellectual Property Rights (TRIPS).

[12] Between 1995 and 2018 the number of regional trade agreements in force increased from 54 to 459. An updated account of the cumulative development of regional preferential trade agreements is found at the WTO Regional Trade Agreements Information System, available at: http://rtais.wto.org/UI/PublicMaintainRTAHome.aspx.

co-ordination of product related regulation, technical standards, market access for services, public procurement and in some cases investment protection. A result of this development is that the multilateral ideal that is expressed in the MFN-principle has become partially eroded and spurred an intensified discussion on the relationship between multilateralism and bilateralism/regionalism.[13] This development has taken place in parallel with an increased propensity to adopt protective safeguard measures.[14] It shall in this connection also be noted that the growth in international trade in goods stagnated during the same period while the character of such trade has been undergoing a change through the development of global value chains and closely knit transnational production networks, underlining the interdependence between exports and imports (see Alvstam & Lindberg in this volume).

Finally, it shall be observed that while the negotiations within the Doha Round have been non-conclusive, the multilateral development has demonstrated an increasingly greater awareness of the necessity to handle existential challenges of global character. This is reflected in a number of international treaties and agreements, most importantly the UN Framework Convention on Climate Change (UNFCCC) 1994 with the agreements for its implementation; the Kyoto Protocol 1997 and the Paris Agreement 2015 (see Jagers, Sterner & Nilsson in this volume). Moreover, the increased awareness of the necessity to change the behaviour of humanity in order to secure sustainable conditions for its long term survival is reflected in the 17 Sustainable Development Goals which constitute the core of the Agenda 2030 adopted by the UN General Assembly 2015. This development has, in spite of the obvious functional relationship, only to a very limited extent been reflected in the multilateral regulations for international trade.[15]

[13] As examples of the contemporary discussion on this theme, see Lamy (2002), Lindberg and Alvstam (2012), and Melo Araujo (2014).

[14] Since the financial crisis in 2008 and the following recession, until 2016, more than 1500 anti-dumping and countervailing duties were introduced by states in the G-20 group (WTO 2016).

[15] Regarding the question of a establishing a functional relationship between the UNFCCC and the WTO, see Cramér (2012).

Development of Bilateral and Regional Trade Agreements by the EU and the U.S. After the End of the Cold War Up Until 2016

Both the EU and the U.S. were strong supporters of the strengthening of the development of the multilateral regulatory system leading to the establishment of the WTO and its following geographical expansion. However, since the beginning of the twenty first century, in the shadow of the stalemate of the Doha Round both these actors have increasingly focused on the development of ambitious bilateral and regional arrangements.

The Scope of European Union Treaty Making Competence for the Common Commercial Policy

Since its establishment, the Common Commercial Policy (CCP) of the EEC demonstrated a clear focus on the development of the multilateral WTO-system in combination with bilateral and regional preferential agreements with the near abroad and a preferential relationship with states that have former colonial relationships with the Member States. The changes in the geopolitical situation after the end of the Cold War called for an adaptation of the European integration process to a new reality. Through a comprehensive substantive deepening of the co-operation and a successive enlargement the EEC came to be transformed into the EU. As a consequence of this transformation, the scope of the CCP of the EU was successively expanded through the treaty amendments negotiated in Maastricht, Amsterdam, Nice and Lisbon. Thereby, exclusive EU treaty making competence in the domain of the CCP, through the entry into force of the Lisbon Treaty 2009, became largely congruent with the functional area covered by WTO regulation. The following tension between the Union and its Member States concerning the limits of exclusive treaty making power did however not get clarified until 2017 through the opinion 2/15 by the Court of Justice of the European Union (CJEU) concerning the treaty conformity of the proposed free trade agreement between EU and Singapore. In general terms, the CJEU concluded that the EU has exclusive competence to enter international agreements covering all aspects of the CCP including transportation, trade related intellectual property issues, public procurement and sustainable development issues related to trade (see Zurek in this volume). Moreover the CJEU concluded that agreements relating to the protection of international non-direct investments and provisions on Investor-State Dispute Settlement (ISDS) fall within the area of competence that is shared between the EU and its Member States.[16]

In practice, the tension between the EU and its Member States concerning the limitations of EU treaty making competence has since long been solved in a pragmatic way by concluding all comprehensive trade agreements as so called mixed agreements that are ratified by decisions in the Council and European Parliament according to the Treaty on the Functioning of the European Union (TFEU) as well as by all Member States in accordance with national constitutional provisions. Thereby competing claims concerning sovereignty are neutralized and each Member State is given a power of veto concerning the conclusion of the Agreement. This procedure has furthered the legitimacy of trade agreements entered into. Simultaneously, the power of veto has become a token that enables individual Member States to influence specific aspects of proposed agreements and in several cases the entering into force of agreements has been delayed due to failing national ratification in individual Member States. Recent examples of this are the Wallonian parliament's decision not to adopt the proposition on ratification of the Comprehensive Economic and Trade Agreement with Canada (CETA) 2016 and the negative result in the Dutch facultative referendum on ratification of the Association Agreement with Ukraine 2016. In both these cases, final decisions on national ratification were adopted with a considerable delay and an eroded democratic legitimacy.

The Development of the EU Portfolio of International Trade Agreements

The trade agreements with third states that have been concluded by the EU may be divided into four categories with different motivations. The first category concerns relations with a number of smaller, economically strong, European states with close economic connections to the internal market but have chosen to stay outside the process of deeper political integration and therefore not applied for EU membership. The central agreement for this category is the EEA-agreement that, with the exception of Switzerland, integrates the members of EFTA into the internal

[16] For an insightful analysis of Opinion 2/15, see Cremona (2018).

market, an agreement that can be described as a substitute for membership. The second category consists of the Association Agreements that the Union has concluded with states in the near abroad within the frameworks of the Eastern Partnership and Southern Neighborhood. These bilateral agreements are primarily motivated by the Union's interest to promote, and influence, economic development and political stability in the near abroad. A number of these agreements have a transitory ambition as waiting rooms for possible future membership. The trade- and cooperation agreements with the so called ACP-states, primarily developing states with a former colonial relationship to Union Member States, constitute a third category. These agreements are primarily motivated by development objectives.

The fourth, and for this chapter most relevant, category consist of the ambitious bi-lateral trade agreements that the Union has concluded, or is negotiating, with industrialized states outside Europe. The growth of this category of agreements constitutes a relative recent development and shall be seen as a consequence of a strategic shift in the CCP which took place in 2006. This shift, which was concurring in time with the suspension of the Doha Round negotiations, meant downplaying the priority of actions strengthening the multilateral WTO and opening up for the conclusion of comprehensive bi-lateral trade agreements with industrialized states (European Commission 2006, see also Melo Araujo 2014). At the basis, these ambitious bi-lateral agreements establish free trade areas. When tariffs and quantitative restrictions for trade in industrial goods largely have been done away with within the framework of the WTO, the focus of these agreements is put on the removal of technical barriers to trade through convergence of product related regulation and standard setting, market access for services and public procurement and investment protection, including dispute resolution through ISDS. The development of these agreements is primarily motivated by an economic rationale; to strengthen European competitiveness on the global arena.

In accordance with the present EU trade policy strategy of the Commission, *Trade for all—Towards a more responsible trade and investment policy*, adopted in 2015, the Union has a clear ambition to conclude comprehensive bilateral trade agreements with economically developed states outside its geographical proximity.[17] EU bilateral agreements shall,

[17] On the different kinds of trade and association agreements that the EU has developed with third countries, see Alvstam and Lindberg in this volume.

according to the strategy, have a high level of ambition and include reciprocal market access. In the autumn of 2018 the EU had concluded agreements of this type with Chile and South Korea. Agreements with Canada and Singapore have been signed and are presently in the process of ratification. Negotiations with Japan have been finalized and negotiations with Mexico, Malaysia, Thailand, India, Indonesia and the four Latin American States within MERCOSUR are underway, albeit at different speeds. Moreover the European Commission has announced its interest to initiate negotiations on agreements with New Zealand and Australia.

The conclusion of the negotiations between EU and Japan to enter a comprehensive free trade agreement has been designated by the Commission as the most important step for the Union on the bilateral trail so far. It has been described as a model for a new generation of comprehensive bilateral free trade agreements between developed economies, in particular when it includes mutual obligations relating to international agreements on safeguarding non-economic interests such as the ILO Core Labour Standards, UNFCCC, and the Paris Agreement. The Commission has also attached a geopolitical importance to the design of the agreement and stated that it will strengthen the European influence in the development of international trade regulation in accordance with the Union's core values (European Commission 2017a). In this respect, the agreement with Japan has become a substitute for the more grandiose, but postponed, project of developing the Transatlantic Trade and Investment Partnership (TTIP) with the U.S.

Finally, it shall be noted that in the agreements with Japan and Singapore, the issues relating to investment protection have been separated from the body of the free trade agreements and expressed in separate agreements on investment protection, including ISDS. Thereby, the comprehensive trade agreements fall within the scope of exclusive Union treaty making competence and the conclusion of the agreements do not need ratification by the Member States in accordance with national constitutional provisions (see also Zurek in this volume). However, the foreseen adjacent separate bilateral agreements on investment protection standards and investment protection dispute resolution have to be entered into as mixed agreements (European Commission 2018a). Thus, the Commission seems to have been guided by the definition of the scope of exclusive Union treaty making competence established by the CJEU in opinion 2/15 in combination with the experiences gained from the delayed processes for ratification of the CETA and the Ukraine Association Agreement.

The U.S. Portfolio of International Trade Agreements

In comparison with the EU, the U.S. development of bilateral and regional trade agreements is more recent and less ambitious. A first bi-lateral free trade agreement with Israel entered into force in 1985. Thereafter the regional North America Free Trade Agreement between the U.S., Canada and Mexico was established in 1994, largely in parallel to the establishment of the WTO. As in the EU, this development accelerated in parallel to the stalemate and suspension of the Doha Round Negotiations. During the twenty first century, the U.S. has concluded a regional free trade agreement with a group of Central American states (CAFTA-DR) and a number of bi-lateral agreements of which the most economically important are those with Australia, Chile, Singapore and the Republic of Korea. This development was further accelerated during the Obama administration, most importantly through the negotiations to establish a regional free trade area around the Pacific Basin (with the exception of China, and North and South Korea), i.e. the Trans-Pacific Partnership (TPP) and the above mentioned bi-lateral TTIP between the U.S. and the EU. Both the TTIP and the TPP were motivated by a combination of economic and political considerations. In the case of TPP, it was a clear U.S. ambition that the agreement would be an instrument for establishing fundamental principles for trade and economic collaboration in the Pacific basin under U.S. foremanship before the increasing Chinese influence in the region made such a development increasingly difficult.

Increased Challenges to the Legitimacy of the International Regulation of International Trade

Since the mid-1990s, the legitimacy of the increased economic internationalization that has been furthered by the development of multilateral, regional and bi-lateral trade agreements has increasingly been challenged, both in national political processes and by extra parliamentary opinion building. This critique of the regulatory structures for international trade has increased in the aftermath of the economic crisis of 2008 and during the following recession. Concerning the WTO, the inability of the Member States to reach concrete results within the framework of the Doha Development Round has inevitably led to a decreased trust in development of the multilateral order. In addition, the WTO-structure has been criticized for not taking due account of safeguarding non-economic interests. The most ardent criticism in this connection concerns the weak or non-existent co-ordination between the WTO regulatory structure and multilateral agreements on core labour rights, environmental interests and combatting climate change. The passivity of WTO has however led to this type of critique increasingly focusing on regional and bilateral trade agreements.

Moreover, on a more general level, the perception that economic internationalization constitutes a threat to the upholding of national rules safeguarding non-economic interests, negatively affects national employment, increases inequality in distribution of incomes and wealth and threatens what are considered as specific national values, has gained an increasingly stronger foothold in many industrialized states. Thus, in national political debates proposed regional and bilateral trade agreements have become an often used target for criticism, a target that many times seems to be given an almost symbolic character.

In a similar way, the internal economic and political integration within the EU has been criticized as constituting a threat against national interests. This strain of criticism has been accentuated as a result of the increased cultural and economic divergences within the Union resulting from the enlargement process in combination with a parallel deepening of the integration process. Clear examples are found in the shaky processes for ratification of treaties revising the Treaty on European Union and the explicit denial on the part of individual Member States and national courts to accept the claim of EU Law to be an autonomous order of law superior to the national laws of the Member States as a consequence of its inherent character. The challenge to EU legitimacy is aggravated by the seemingly permanent low public interest in the elections to the European Parliament. The British decision to withdraw from membership in the European Union and the election of Donald Trump as president of the U.S. can partly be seen as populistic outflows of this increased criticism of the structures for regulating international trade and economic collaboration.

Brexit and Its Plausible Consequences

Without getting deeper into the political background, it is a well-known fact that the UK on 23 June 2016 held a referendum on the country's continued membership in the EU. Among the advocates for a withdrawal, general arguments on the desire to regain national legislative and judicial sovereignty were mixed with specific arguments relating to the control over persons passing the national territorial border. Following the result of the referendum, the process of withdrawal was formally initiated, in accordance with Article 50 of the TEU, by the notice that was submitted by Prime Minister Theresa May to the European Council 29 March 2017. According to the TEU the negotiations on an agreement defining the conditions for withdrawal shall be concluded within two years from the notice, if not the European Council, in agreement with the UK, decides to prolong this time period. If no agreement is reached during the set time period the application of the European Treaties will *ipso facto* cease with regard to the UK.[18]

The future consequences of Brexit must be seen in two different interrelated basic dimensions. The first concerns the future relationships of the UK to the EU as well as to third states with which the EU has concluded trade agreements. The second dimension concerns the changes in the internal dynamics of the EU that will follow from the divorce.

The UK Dimension

During the negotiations it has been firmly maintained by the Union that no negotiations on the conditions for the future relationship between the Union and the UK can be held until an agreement on the conditions for divorce has been concluded.[19] From a trade regulation perspective, the essence of a withdrawal is that the UK regains its national sovereignty within the area of foreign commercial policy. Thus, as a fully sovereign member of the WTO, the UK will have to enter into national tariff commitments according to GATT and commitments regarding market access to services according to GATS. These commitments constitute a foundation for the UK entering into bilateral or regional preferential agreements with the Union and third states. In order to simplify this process the UK could mirror the present WTO commitments of the

[18] For detailed analyses of the article 50 procedure and its application in the negotiations between the EU and the UK see Dougan (2018) and Hillion (2018).

[19] This firm stance of the EU could arguably be seen as non-congruent with the wording of TEU Article 50, which explicitly states that negotiation on the conditions for withdrawal shall take the future relations between the withdrawing state and the EU into account.

EU. Nevertheless, this process has to find acceptance among all 164 WTO-members.

Concerning the future relationship between the UK and the Union, the main positions held by the UK seem to be relatively steady since the initial notice sent to the European Council 29 March 2017. The positions have since been elaborated in a number of policy documents and positions on specific issues. From these it appears clear that the UK has well understood the principle that the free movement of goods, services, capital and persons constitute an indivisible whole. As a consequence of the country's clear determination to regain full national sovereignty when it comes to control over persons moving across the territorial border a future participation in the free internal market is not possible. Thereby a British accession to the EEA Agreement is ruled out. Moreover, the UK government takes a clear stand to regain sovereignty over the external commercial policy, which bars the establishment of a customs union between the UK and the EU. Nevertheless, in its position paper of July 2018, the British government proposes a comprehensive free trade agreement that would allow for the continued free, *frictionless*, movement of goods but not persons, thereby disaggregating the components of the free internal market (United Kingdom 2018). To no surprise, this element of the UK proposal has been heavily criticized by the EU negotiators (Barnier 2018).

Taken together, this leaves two general options for structuring the future trade relations between the UK and the Union. A minimalistic, but highly unlikely, scenario is that the bilateral relations would only be regulated through the WTO-structure. The second scenario, and in my eyes the most plausible, is that the UK enters into an ambitious free trade agreement with the EU. Such a reciprocal agreement should, as a minimum, include provisions for free trade for goods, extensive market access for services, freedom for capital movements, market access for public procurement and obligations relating to mutual recognition/standardization of product related rules with the objective to avoid technical barriers to trade. From a British perspective there is furthermore a strong interest to include special provisions regarding financial services including passporting rights. Such an agreement would further the movement of goods services and capital between the UK and the EU at considerably lower level of integration compared with today. During the negotiations inspiration could be found in the bilateral agreement between the EU and Canada (CETA).[20]

It shall in this connection be underlined that the upcoming negotiations on a trade agreement between the UK and the EU will have a unique and previously rarely experienced character. This is due to the fact that the negotiations will take place between parties which at present are joined together within a free internal market based on a customs union. Accordingly, the objective is not to reduce existing hindrances to trade but in a controlled manner limit future increased hindrances. Under a future bilateral free trade agreement there will undoubtedly be a number of non-tariff barriers through the application of rules of origin and the reinstitution of border controls. A relationship regulated by a free trade agreement will, with high probability, incur the successive increase of technical barriers to trade as a consequence of the challenges to uphold the principle of mutual recognition of product related regulation in a longer time perspective. Thus, the general predictability regarding the conditions for trade between the UK and the Union will decrease. It should be noted that, given the logic of a free trade agreement, this structure would open up for the use of safeguard measures, such as anti-dumping and countervailing duties in the bilateral relationship.

With regard to third countries, the British withdrawal means that the UK ceases to be a part to the 39 preferential agreements that the Union has concluded with 65 Non-member States. A large part of these agreements are conceived as mixed agreements that have been concluded through decisions in the Council and the European Parliament as well as through ratification in all Member States, including the United Kingdom. To the extent that substantial provisions of these agreements fall outside Union competence, the UK will continue as contracting party based on the national ratification. This constitutes a special legal/technical complexity that should be solved during the negotiations on conditions for withdrawal in close dialogue with concerned Non-member States.

A pragmatic solution would be that the majority of the trade agreements that the Union has concluded with Non-member States are duplicated by similar bilateral agreements between the UK and the concerned states. On condition that mutual political will exists, this will probably be

[20] In its position paper the UK Government, with reference to CETA, explicitly states that the "UK's arrangements with the EU should not be constrained by EU FTA precedents" (United Kingdom 2018).

a way forward regarding all free trade agreements that do not have an objective to prepare for an institutional association with the Union. For the large group of partnership agreements between the EU and states in its geographic proximity a reasonable solution would be to duplicate the substantial parts of these agreements that relate to conditions for trade into bilateral free trade agreements with the UK.

Of a greater potential importance are the declared UK ambitions to enter into free trade agreements with states that do not currently have such a contractual relationship with the Union. This group includes the U.S., Australia and New Zealand (United Kingdom 2018: 48). This development can however not commence before the UK has seceded from the Union Treaties, regained its sovereignty in external commercial policy, and made new tariff commitments under GATT. Thus, there is a risk that a time gap will emerge between the date on which the existing Treaties will cease to be applicable for the UK and the time when new bilateral treaties would be concluded. Accordingly, in order not to fall into an unregulated lacuna the agreement on the conditions for withdrawal must include a transitional period under which the UK can conclude bilateral agreements both with the Union and with Non-member States with which the Union has established relations based on bilateral agreements that the UK has an interest to uphold.

In March 2018 a draft agreement on the conditions for the UK withdrawal had been agreed upon in principle by the negotiators for the EU and UK (European Commission 2018b). This draft for a Withdrawal Agreement is presently under legal scrutiny before it is planned to be presented for ratification in October 2018.[21] Simultaneously the European Council adopted guidelines for the Union negotiators regarding the opening of negotiations on a framework for the future relationship between the Union and the UK. The Draft Agreement on Withdrawal includes provisions on a transitional period of 21 months, from the UK's withdrawal from the Union, 29 March 2019 to the end of 2020. During this period the UK would retain access to the EU internal market and Customs Union on its current terms. UK participation in Union institutions, including

[21] It should be noted that a number of open issues of specific character could stall the ratification of the Withdrawal Agreement. The presently most contentious such issues relate to the arrangements at the territorial border between the Republic of Ireland and Northern Ireland and the Spanish objections to the inclusion of Gibraltar in the scope of the arrangement.

voting rights would however cease when the divorce takes place on 29 March 2019.[22] Regarding Union agreements with Third States, the UK will not have a right to benefit from these agreements during the transition period, unless the third country agrees, however the UK will be bound to give effect to these agreements even if there is no reciprocity.

The limited transition period will put considerable pressure on the UK and the EU to finalize an agreement on the long-term future conditions for their bilateral relationship. It also incurs an immediate challenge for the UK to engage in negotiations with the Third States with which the Union has concluded bilateral or regional trade agreements with the aim to retain reciprocity during the transition period and to agree upon long-term conditions for bilateral trade conditions after the expiry of the transition period. It is an evident risk that this will not be possible. The process forward is accordingly still highly uncertain. It shall in this connection be noted that the Draft Agreement on Withdrawal does not include any provision concerning prolongation of the transition period in the case no agreement on the long-term conditions for the relationship between the Union and the UK has been reached by 31 December 2020.

Possible Effects of Brexit for the EU Common Commercial Policy

The UK has since 1945, with a great deal of consistency, upheld a policy position supporting liberal conditions for world trade. Since the country entered the EEC 1972, the UK, as one of the larger Member States in alliance with a number of highly trade reliant smaller Member States, has influenced the formulation of the CCP in a liberal direction and promoted the strengthening of the multilateral regulatory level. As has been shown empirically through analysis of alliance building within the Council, the UK has since the mid 1990s, primarily found a communality of interests with smaller northern Member States such as the Netherlands and Sweden (Huhe et al. 2017). The secession of the UK from Union membership will thus alter the internal dynamics within the Union in a way that probably will lead to that the CCP will be given a somewhat less liberal, or more protectionist, character. With the same logic it could also be argued that the political conditions for a more effective integration of non-economic

[22] The UK has secured limited rights of consultations on proposed new Union legislation during the transition period.

interests into the CCP might improve as a consequence of a British withdrawal.

Based on the EU Trade Policy Strategy of 2015 and the Commission's "Reflection Paper on Harnessing Globalisation" of May 2017, it stands clear that the Commission has the ambition to prioritize an expansion of the Union's bilateral free trade agreements with industrialized states outside its geographic proximity (European Commission 2015, 2017b). At the same time there is also a strong expression of loyalty to the multilateral regulatory order and that the development of bilateral agreements shall take place in concordance with this order. According to the Commission "[t]he EU needs to pursue bilateral and regional arrangements in a manner that supports the returning of the WTO to the centre of global trade negotiating activity" (European Commission 2015: 29). Moreover, a rule based ethos is emphasized as well as the importance of effective safeguard measures when motivated and a functioning dispute settlement system. The Commission does also attempt to formulate a constructive answer to the social anxiety that increased economic internationalization in general, and international trade agreements in particular, has incurred. This is mirrored in an emphasis on the importance of developing an effective multilateralism and that the regulation of international trade is coordinated with international agreements on environmental protection, minimum rules on labour conditions, obligations relating to combatting climate change and the sustainable development goals defined in Agenda 2030 (see Zurek in this volume).

Moreover, the Commission underlines the importance of national measures to further social inclusion in a situation of radical structural changes following from increased international competition and rapid technological development. To which extent the Union, and its Member States, will be able to mobilize the political leadership that is necessary to fulfil this ambitious agenda is uncertain. This uncertainty is emphasized by the change in internal dynamics that will follow from the UK withdrawal from the Union, a change that may both erode the bargaining power of the Union and tilt the substance of the CCP in a more protectionist direction. It shall in this connection be noted that a number of protectionist initiatives, primarily directed against China have been signalled within the Union during the last year. In addition, the position of the Union, and its ability further its trade policy agenda has become increasingly challenged by the trade policy agenda of the U.S. under the presidency of Donald Trump.

The Consequences of Trumpism on the Regulatory Structures for International Trade

After a presidential election campaign under which a rosary of political forecasts was proven incorrect, Donald Trump was installed as president of the United States 10 January 2017. The fundamental theme of the Trump campaign was a promise to make "America great again", primarily through giving a stronger priority to the furthering of the national interest in international relations. Accordingly, the trade policies of earlier administrations were heavily criticized. During his campaign presidential candidate Trump often returned to that the U.S. ought to leave the WTO if the organization cannot uphold what he defined as fair conditions for trade. Moreover, it was underlined that the regional and bilateral free trade agreements that the U.S. had concluded, and was about to conclude, did not further U.S. interests. A concrete promise was made to abort the process of ratifying the agreement on the TPP that had been negotiated during the Obama administration. The North American Free Trade Agreement (NAFTA) was described as the worst trade agreement ever concluded and the U.S. therefore ought to leave this agreement. Using similar rhetoric, the Trump campaign argued that also the free trade agreement with the Republic of Korea (KORUS) should be terminated.

Since the new U.S. administration was installed in the White House, the bombastic trade policy rhetoric has become somewhat more nuanced. At the same time it is now evident that the trade policy actions taken by the present U.S. administration point in a very clear direction; prioritizing bilateral arrangements over multilateral and regional in combination with an increased propensity to use protectionist safeguard measures and consequent downplaying of the normative effects of the WTO. In The President's Trade Policy Agenda presented to Congress 2017 it was explicitly stated that "it is time for a new trade policy that defends American sovereignty, enforces U.S. trade laws, uses American leverage to open markets abroad, and negotiates new trade agreements that are fairer and more effective both for the United States and for the world trading system" (United States 2017a).

The process for U.S. ratification of the TPP was terminated in January 2017 which led to the agreement being put on shelf. This decision will most probably produce long-term geopolitical effects when it leaves the table free for other models for structuring economic co-operation in East- and Southeast Asia. In the vacuum that has developed, Chinese initiatives for regional economic integration have rapidly gained ground, most importantly the ambitious Belt and Road Initiative (BRI) which is centred around the establishment of transport corridors at land and sea from the Chinese east coast to Europe. The BRI includes massive investments in infrastructure in states along the road through credits from the Asian Infrastructure Development Bank, in which China is a dominant actor. In addition, the negotiations on establishing a free trade area between the ten members of ASEAN and China, Australia India, Japan, New Zealand and The Republic of Korea through a Regional Comprehensive Partnership (RCEP), have been launched as an alternative to the TPP.[23] The shelving of the TPP has also stimulated the development of bilateral agreements between the EU and states in Asia and the Pacific region. The most evident example is the recent agreement to conclude a free trade agreement between the Union and Japan. Nevertheless, the U.S. administration has declared its ambitions to conclude bilateral trade agreements with all the eleven states that were signatories to the draft TPP treaty.[24]

Regarding the EU, the U.S. administration has, at least temporarily, withdrawn from the negotiations on the agreement for the TTIP. Since the advent of the Trump administration, no constructive negotiations have taken place and it is not clear if, or when, they will be continued. In this connection it can be noted that the U.S. has offered the UK to conclude a bilateral transatlantic free trade agreement after the withdrawal process from the EU has been concluded (United States 2018a: 11–12).

Regarding the geographical close proximity, the U.S. has initiated a renegotiation of the NAFTA with Mexico and Canada. The stated objectives for these negotiations were to improve the U.S. terms of trade with these two states, primarily through the changes in the rules of origin and commitments on market access for U.S. products. The negotiations commenced in August 2017 and were scheduled to have been concluded in seven months. During the negotiations the U.S. Administration introduced, and threatened to introduce, protectionist measures with regard to imports from Mexico and Canada. Moreover, the U.S. Administration, on several occasions during the negotiations stated that it is not clear if the

[23] The negotiations on RCEP were formally launched in November 2012 and are expected to be concluded 2019.

[24] The U.S. has existing bilateral free trade agreements with six of the eleven TPP states; Canada, Australia, Mexico, Chile, Peru and Singapore. The U.S. administration has declared its intention to establish closer trade relationships with the remaining five; Japan, Vietnam, Malaysia, New Zealand and Brunei.

U.S. will accept the maintaining of a regional structure for the agreement or will propose a development of two separate bilateral agreements with Mexico and Canada respectively (Globe and Mail 2018). The negotiations were concluded in October 2018 with an agreement that largely fulfils the U.S. priorities; the U.S.-Mexico-Canada Agreement (USMCA) which is planned to enter into force 2020.[25] Of special interest is that the agreement stipulates that the signatory parties can withdraw from the agreement if one of them concludes a preferential trade agreement with a "non-market economy", a clause that is widely seen as an attempt to create an U.S. veto regarding Mexico or Canada entering a trade agreement with China (Draft USMCA clause 32:10). With regard to KORUS, the U.S. initiated discussions on modifications in autumn 2017.

Concerning the positioning with regard to the WTO structure, the U.S. has shown a very limited interest to participate in the development of the multilateral order for regulating international trade conditions. In the Presidents 2018 Trade Policy Agenda it is stated that "[t]he Trump Administration believes that the WTO has achieved positive results and has the potential to achieve even more in the future. However, for past two decades, the United States has been concerned that the WTO is not operating as the contracting parties envisioned. As a result, the WTO is undermining our country's ability to act in its national interest" (United States 2018a: 28). Moreover, in the Agenda the Trump administration explicitly declares that it will not negotiate off the basis of the DDA mandates or old DDA texts and considers the Doha Round to be a thing of the past (ibid: 29). Thus, the administration expresses a detached loyalty on condition that WTO regulation is not perceived as a hindrance to national interests. As a concrete outflow of this position the U.S. has questioned the legitimacy of the WTO Dispute Settlement System, especially the role of the Appellate Body (ibid: 22–28). The administration has underlined the fact that WTO decisions against the U.S. do not automatically lead to changes in U.S. law or practice and stated that it will aggressively defend the American sovereignty regarding trade policy (United States 2017a: 3). Moreover, the U.S. Trump administration has consistently been blocking the appointment of new members to the WTO Appellate Body, thereby

[25] The draft text of the U.S.-Mexico-Canada Agreement (USMCA) is accessible at https://ustr.gov/trade-agreements/free-trade-agreements/united-states-mexico-canada-agreement/united-states-mexico. (Latest accessed 22 October 2018).

causing the WTO dispute settlement to successively grind down to a halt (Payosova et al. 2018).

In addition the U.S. administration has successively intensified its rhetoric and actions regarding the introduction of protectionist safeguard measures.[26] This included initiating a number of anti-dumping and countervailing investigations which rendered criticism from the WTO. The Secretary of Trade, Wilbur Ross reacted to this criticism by stating that he considered this development to be positive and necessary for establishing balanced fair terms of trade and regretted that the actions taken were perceived as protectionism (Ross 2017).

This development has since accelerated. Through a presidential decree, in March 2017, U.S. agencies were urged to increase the rigor in application of the safeguard measures decided upon (United States 2017b). A special commission was established with the task of investigating the terms of trade with 16 states with which the U.S. runs a trade deficit. The objective being to define unfair trade conditions that could be counteracted through safeguard measures. In March 2018 the U.S. administration decided to introduce import tariffs on steel and aluminium, not justified as trade related safeguards but with reference to the protection of national security (United States 2018b). States affected, such as China, Canada and the EU protested and presented well founded arguments that the actions taken were incompatible with the U.S. obligations under the WTO. Nevertheless, several states let themselves into bilateral negotiations with the U.S. in order to strike deals for exemptions followed by the introduction of retaliatory measures and calls for consultations under the WTO Dispute Settlement System. Thus, the unilateral introduction of, and threats to introduce, clearly protectionist measures that are most likely to constitute an infringement of WTO rules is turned into a bargaining chip in a bilateral negotiation process. Later in spring 2018 a similar sequence of action and reaction developed as a result of President Trump declaring his intention to introduce import tariffs on passenger cars, formally justified by reference to the protection of national security. The same pattern can be observed in the summer of 2018 when the U.S. introduced additional tariffs on imports from China justified as a measure to protect domestic technology and intellectual property from alleged Chinese

[26] In the first year of President Trump's Administration it initiated 84 antidumping and countervailing duty investigations. This is an increase with 59 per cent in comparison with the last year of the Obama Administration.

discriminatory and burdensome trade practices. This action has been followed by Chinese retaliatory measures and bilateral negotiations under escalating tension.

Finally it shall be noted that the U.S., in June 2017 declared its intention to cease all participation in the 2015 Paris Agreement on the implementation of the UN Framework Convention on Climate Change (UNFCCC) (United States 2017c). Simultaneously, the State Department declared that the U.S. is open to re-enter into the agreement if it can be on conditions that are more favourable for the country than was initially agreed upon (United States 2017d). No such negotiations have been initiated yet.

Viewed together, these concrete actions taken by the U.S. administration constitute a clear shift in foreign trade policy. This shift includes an unequivocal stance for promoting unilateral national interest through the weakening of the multilateral regulatory order and giving priority to bilateral agreements where the substance is more in concordance with national interests as a result of the relative strength in bargaining power. From this follows that the U.S. increasingly steps back from the multilateral, and also regional, arenas. A related consequence is that the U.S. influence over the agenda setting when it comes to the future development of the multilateral order, and regional orders, for regulating international trade will most likely decrease, leaving the scene for other actors. Regarding the WTO, this clearly means that the prospects for a dynamic development will diminish in a medium term perspective.

Increased Bilateralism, Higher Degree of Protectionism, Weakened WTO and Hastened Geopolitical Power Shifts

The political development in the UK and the U.S. since 2016 will make an important imprint on the structure and substance of the regulation of the conditions for international trade. Partly, this means that already existing trends are amplified by Brexit and Trumpism. This development may be summarized in four interdependent points: i) The structure for regulating international trade will be given an increasingly bilateral character; ii) The terms of trade within certain areas will get less liberal and the use of trade safeguard measures will increase which might escalate into increasing protectionism in general; iii) The already evident weakening of the

WTO-system will continue, probably at an increasing speed; iv) The ongoing shift in the geopolitical balance will be faster when the European and American influence over the development of the regulation of the conditions for international trade is weakened in relative terms.

If we start with the structural shift towards increased bilateralism, we can see that the UK's withdrawal from membership in the EU will undoubtedly weaken European regionalism. Post-withdrawal, the UK is likely to conclude a large number of bilateral trade agreements with the objective of enhancing its international trade relations as a sovereign actor. Within the Union, it is likely that the British secession will lead to that the priority given to bilateral free trade agreements since 2006 will get stronger. The Union has a stated ambition to give these free trade agreements a more palpable social dimension through the integration of provisions relating to the fulfilment of obligations according to multilateral conventions on environmental protection, international agreements on minimum labour standards and the fulfilment of commitments relating to combatting climate change. Simultaneously, the bargaining power of the Union is likely to be weakened as a consequence of Brexit. Nevertheless, the Union's ability to conclude such agreements with Asian states has been furthered by the U.S. administration's decision not to ratify the TPP. Regarding U.S. trade policy, the present Trump administration has set a clear priority for bilateral relations over multilateral, and also regional, structures. The consequent critique of the WTO, the decision not to ratify TPP and the renegotiations of the NAFTA in combination with an expressed ambition to conclude new bilateral agreements are all concrete examples of this chosen direction. Structurally, bi-lateral relations are more or less asymmetrical and tend to favour the relatively stronger party both in the negotiations on the conditions for co-operation and in the application of these conditions.

Concerning the worsening of terms of trade, it is clear that the withdrawal of the UK from the EU will lead to increased hindrances to the movement of goods, services, labour and capital between the Union and the UK compared with the situation today. The withdrawal will also most probably lead to the opening up of the possibility for introducing trade safeguard measures in the future bilateral UK-EU relationship. Brexit will also induce a shift in the internal dynamics of the Union, which probably will lead to a somewhat higher propensity for introducing trade safeguard measures within the framework of the CCP. The U.S. administration has explicitly stated that it perceives an increased use of trade safeguard measures as a desirable instrument for furthering national economic and social interests. From recent experience we can also see that the use of safeguards, or the threat of introducing such measures, have become bargaining chips in bilateral negotiations between the U.S. and other states. The legality of an increased use of protectionist measures has at the bottom line to be handled by the dispute settlement mechanism of the WTO. In this system, the final consequence of a rule infringement is that the signatory party that has experienced damage as a result of the infringement is given a right to initiate retaliatory measures. This mechanism is meant to create a restraining effect on states that contemplate to introduce protectionist measures in violation of their obligations under the WTO treaties.

As the system of public international law in general, the WTO system is based on the principle of reciprocity between states. The reciprocity is the foundation for the system's normativity; that states choose to follow the obligations they have accepted by entering international agreements. In addition to costs in form of countermeasures, a violation also brings with it an erosion of the regulatory system at a structural level. Thus, it is only in the case that a state decides it is within the national interest to violate the treaty and that it *is prepared to pay the short and long term price* for this in the form of retaliatory measures and general erosion of the regulatory system, that the WTO-system will short-circuit and an uncontrolled protectionist escalation could occur. In a world characterized by high economic interdependence between states and cross-border economic activities in integrated production networks this risk must be appreciated as limited under the condition that political decision-makers act in a rational manner.

As mentioned above, there is reason to believe that the demise of the multilateral WTO system will continue. The U.S. interest to contribute to a reactivation of the negotiations on the DDA is non-existent and the U.S. administration is extremely clear in its priority of bilateral arrangements over regional or multilateral regulatory structures. The European Union, even if it confirms its loyalty to the multilateral WTO system, seems unable to muster the political leadership and the alliances necessary for strengthening this system. It shall in this connection be underlined that also the Union has an explicit ambition to give priority to the development of bilateral trade agreements with economically strong states outside Europe, an ambition that probably will be accentuated after the UK has left the member circuit.

Thus, ambiguity exists as to the motives behind the increased bilateralization described above. For the EU, bilateralism is primarily seen as a secondary substitute for a stalling, but desired, multilateralism. For the U.S., bilateralism is a natural consequence of downgrading the importance of multilateral structures for international co-operation and regulation. Disregarding the motives behind the development, the short term results are similar, leading to an erosion of the globalist MFN-principle. To which extent this development will lead to long-term erosion of the WTO-system, or could be a stepping stone for its future development is dependent on the ability of the community of states to articulate a common political will at the multilateral level. Finally, the WTO-system is at present increasingly challenged by the growing use of, and threats to make use of, trade safeguard measures. This development will increase the strain on the organization's system for monitoring and dispute resolution and thereby potentially also its legitimacy, a situation which is aggravated by the U.S. blockage of the appointment of new members to the WTO Appellate Body.

Lastly it seems clear that we can expect that the ongoing shift in the geopolitical balance will be accelerated by the fact that the American and European influence on the development of the regulation of the conditions for international trade has decreased. Since the installation of the Trump administration, the two projects that were initiated by the West during the first decade of the twenty first century with the objective to set a standard for the future regulation of international trade, TPP and TTIP, have both been shelved for a very uncertain future. After the U.S. decision not to ratify the TPP agreement, this project can probably be written off. This opens up a window of opportunity for other actors, primarily China, to take a stronger position in the formulation of a regulatory framework for economic cooperation and trade in the South East Asian region. The negotiations on TTIP are not formally terminated even if the U.S. interest to bring these forward seems to be very limited today. The future of the TTIP project will also be affected by the withdrawal of the UK from the European Union. As stated above this will affect the internal dynamics within the Union where the UK has, together with a group of smaller Member States such as Sweden, been among the strongest proponents of TTIP while other Member States have expressed a great deal of hesitance. Brexit will thus make it harder for the Union to reactivate the negotiations on the basis of the proposals that were presented in 2016. In addition, a Union without the UK will probably be a less attractive bilateral partner from the perspective of Washington. The hopes that were knitted to the TTIP agreement's potential of producing general normative effects are accordingly most probably dashed.

Look to the Past in Order to Move Forward

Even if the perceptions of reality that were expressed by the Yes-side in the British referendum on withdrawal and by the campaign that led to Donald Trump taking up the U.S. presidency, in many aspects cannot be verified by references to facts, the social unrest and lack of trust in established institutions that led to the decision on Brexit and the entry of the Trump administration must be taken seriously. Examples of similar political developments, furthering populist movements with an explicit nationalist taint, can today be observed in a number of other industrialized stated (cf. Müller 2016; Snyder 2017). This is a shift that probably will be accelerated in the near future as a consequence of new applications of digital technology and artificial intelligence, a development that will alter the conditions for established professions and the organization of society, changing patterns of life and rising demands for renegotiation of social contracts.

The concerns about our common future are furthermore aggravated by the understanding that established societal structures stand before anthropogenic challenges of existential character such as climate change, overconsumption of exhaustible resources, security policy instability and increasing international migration flows, all challenges that require multilateral cooperation in order to be handled or ameliorated. Confronting these problematic future scenarios, it is of value to reflect on the lessons to be learned from past experiences of mechanisms that have been dominating societal development in refractive periods of structural societal change.

In the early 1940s the economic historian Karl Polanyi, in his classical work *The Great Transformation*, described the evolution of the market economy and its emancipation from the social and political frameworks it had been embedded in (Polanyi 1944). In his path-breaking analysis, Polanyi described the development that had taken place during the nineteenth century up until the breakthrough of counter movements in the early 1920s; fascism, communism, social democracy and Christian democracy, movements that from very different ideological positions all had as an objective to re-embed the economic system in the political. At the core of Polanyi's analysis lies the hypothesis of a permanent tension between the uncontrolled expansion of the market forces and the political desire to regulate the market in order to avoid its tendencies towards social anarchy. This results in a pendular development that, in a situation where the legitimacy of the existing political structures is weak and the social conflicts escalating, may lead a majority of the citizens to turn their backs to the existing political system.

These observations ought, at a general level, to be a memento for the roles that the EU plays in a changing world order. In an economically highly globalized world, characterized by transnational production networks and highly integrated value chains transgressing national borders, the trust and legitimacy in multilateral regulative structures must be strengthened in order to avoid the destructive forces that may follow from increased protectionism in combination with a bi-lateralization of the regulation of the conditions for international trade. In order to strengthen the trust in, and legitimacy of, multilateral institutions, these must not be perceived as threats to specific societal interests but as instruments that can help to meet common contemporary societal challenges.

There are reasons to take the above mentioned warning flags hoisted by Mitrany concerning the effects of an eroding multilateralism seriously today. In the area of international trade this requires that the member states of the WTO are able to muster a common political will in order to strengthen the organization and to coordinate the development of multilateral regulation of international trade with the implementation of international agreements on core labour standards, environmental protection, measures to combat climate change and the 17 sustainable development goals defined by the UN General Assembly in Agenda 2030. Elements of the new generation of extended bilateral free trade agreements that the EU has concluded during the last decade, which include references to international agreements protecting non-economic interests, could thereby be given the role as forerunners to a desired multilateral development. Accordingly, the European Union, and its Member States, must clearly give priority to the development of a modernized multilateralism. Today the Union's ability to take up this responsibility, and political initiative, is however hampered, both by the lack of a clear common political will among the Member States and the present U.S. administration´s clear priority of bilateralism over multilateralism. Moreover, the ongoing successive geopolitical shift gives rise to a new, unmapped and less predictable context in which multilateral negotiations take place. In such a situation a regional structure, such as the EU, must not fall for temptation to strengthen its internal cohesion by enforcing the perception of external enemies.

References

Bairoch, P. (1993). *Economics and World History, Myths and Paradoxes*. London: Harvester Wheatsheaf.

Barnier, M. (2018). *An Ambitious Partnership with the UK After Brexit*. Brussels: European Commission. Retrieved from October 2, 2018, from https://ec.europa.eu/commission/news/ambitious-partnership-uk-after-brexit-2018-aug-02_en.

Bernanke, B., & James, H. (1991). The Gold Standard, Deflation, and Financial Crisis in the Great Depression: An International Comparison. In R. G. Hubbard (Ed.), *Financial Markets and Financial Crises*. Chicago: University of Chicago Press.

Bhagwati, J. (1991). *The World Trading System at Risk*. Princeton: Princeton University Press.

Brooke, R. (1915). *1914 & Other Poems*. London: Sidgwick and Jackson.

Cramér, P. (2012). The Doha Round and the Search for a Functional and Legitimate Co-ordination Between the UNFCCC and the WTO. *RSCAS Policy Papers* 2012/06, Florence; EUI.

Cremona, M. (2018). Shaping EU Trade Policy post-Lisbon: Opinion 2/15 of 16 May 2017: ECJ, 16 May 2017, Opinion 2/15 Free Trade Agreement with Singapore. *European Constitutional Law Review, 14*(1), 231–259.

Dougan, M. (2018). An Airbag for the Crash Test Dummies? EU-UK Negotiations for Post-Withdrawal "Status Quo" Transitional Regime under Article 50 TEU. *Common Market Law Review, 55*, 57–100.

European Commission. (2006). Global Europe: Competing in the World. A Contribution to the EU's Growth and Jobs Strategy. Retrieved October 2, 2018, from http://trade.ec.europa.eu/doclib/docs/2006/october/tradoc_130376.pdf.

European Commission. (2015). Trade for All – Towards a More Responsible Trade and Investment Policy. Retrieved October 2, 2018, from http://trade.ec.europa.eu/doclib/docs/2015/october/tradoc_153846.pdf.

European Commission. (2017a, December 8). EU and Japan Finalize Economic Partnership Agreement. Brussels. Retrieved October 2, 2018, from http://europa.eu/rapid/press-release_IP-17-5142_en.htm.

European Commission. (2017b). Reflection Paper on Globalisation. Retrieved October 2, 2018, from https://ec.europa.eu/commission/sites/beta-political/files/reflection-paper-globalisation_en.pdf.

European Commission. (2018a, April 18). European Commission Proposes Signature and Conclusion of Japan and Singapore Agreements.

Strasbourg. Retrieved October 2, 2018, from http://europa.eu/rapid/press-release_IP-18-3325_en.htm.

European Commission. (2018b, March 19). Draft Agreement on the Withdrawal of the United Kingdom of Great Britain and Northern Ireland from the European Union and the European Atomic Energy Community. Retrieved October 2, 2018, from https://ec.europa.eu/commission/sites/beta-political/files/draft_agreement_coloured.pdf.

Fukuyama, F. (1989). The End of History? *The National Interest.* Summer 1989: 1–18.

Globe and Mail. (2018, June 1). Trump Floats Replacing NAFTA with Bilateral Agreements with Canada, Mexico. *The Globe and Mail.* Retrieved from October 2, 2018, from https://www.theglobeandmail.com/world/article-trump-floats-replacing-nafta-with-bilateral-agreements-with-canada/.

Hillion, C. (2018). Withdrawal Under Article 50 TEU: An Integration-Friendly Process. *Common Market Law Review, 55*, 29–56.

Huhe, N., Naurin, D., & Thomson, R. (2017, August). With or Without You? Policy Impact in the Council of the EU After Brexit. *SIEPS European Policy Analysis.* Retrieved from http://www.sieps.se/en/publications/2017/with-or-without-you-policy-impact-and-networks-in-the-council-of-the-eu-after-brexit/.

Lamy, P. (2002). Stepping Stones or Stumbling Blocks? The EU's Approach Towards the Problem of Multilateralism vs Regionalism in Trade Policy. *The World Economy, 25*(10), 1399–1413.

Lazer, D. A. (1999). The Free Trade Epidemic of the 1860's and Other Outbreaks of Economic Discrimination. *World Politics, 51*(4), 447–483.

Lindberg, L., & Alvstam, C. (2012). The Ambiguous Role of the WTO in Times of Stalled Multilateral Negotiations and Proliferating FTA's in East Asia. *International Negotiation, 17*, 165–189.

Melo Araujo, B. (2014). The EU's Deep Trade Agenda: Stumbling Block or Stepping Stone Towards Multilateral Liberalisation? In C. Herrmann, M. Krajewski, & J. P. Terhechte (Eds.), *European Yearbook of International Economic Law 2014* (pp. 263–284). Berlin: Springer.

Mitrany, D. (1941). *The Functional Theory of Politics.* London: Martin Robertson & Company.

Müller, J. W. (2016). *What Is Populism?* Philadelphia: University of Pennsylvania Press.

Payosova, T., Hufbauer G. C., & Schott, J. J. (2018). The Dispute Settlement Crisis in the World Trade Organization: Causes and Cures. *Policy Brief* 2018: 5. Washington DC: Peterson Institute for International Economics.

Polanyi, K. (1944). *The Great Transformation: The Political and Economic Origins of Our Time.* New York: Farrar & Rinehart.

Ross, W. (2017, July 31). Free Trade Is a Two Way Street. *The Wall Street Journal*. Retrieved October 2, 2018, from https://www.wsj.com/articles/free-trade-is-a-two-way-street-1501542569.

Snyder, T. (2017). *On Tyranny: Twenty Lessons from the Twentieth Century*. London: Bodley Head.

United Kingdom. (2018, July). The Future Relationship Between the United Kingdom and the European Union, Presented to Parliament by the Prime Minister by Command of Her Majesty. Retrieved October 2, 2018 https://assets.publishing.service.gov.uk/government/uploads/system/uploads/attachment_data/file/725288/The_future_relationship_between_the_United_Kingdom_and_the_European_Union.pdf.

United States. (2017a). The President's 2017 Trade Policy Agenda. Retrieved October 2, 2018 https://ustr.gov/sites/default/files/files/reports/2017/AnnualReport/Chapter%20I%20-%20The%20President%27s%20Trade%20Policy%20Agenda.pdf.

United States. (2017b, March 31). Presidential Executive Order on Establishing Enhanced Collection and Enforcement of Antidumping and Countervailing Duties and Violations of Trade and Customs Laws. Retrieved October 2, 2018, fromhttps://www.whitehouse.gov/presidential-actions/presidential-executive-order-establishing-enhanced-collection-enforcement-antidumping-countervailing-duties-violations-trade-customs-laws/.

United States. (2017c, June 1). Statement by President Trump on the Paris Climate Accord. Retrieved October 2, 2018, from https://www.whitehouse.gov/briefings-statements/statement-president-trump-paris-climate-accord/.

United States. (2017d, August 4). Communication Regarding Intent to Withdraw from Paris Agreement. Office of the Spokesperson. Retrieved October 2, 2018, from https://www.state.gov/r/pa/prs/ps/2017/08/273050.htm.

United States. (2018a). Putting America First: The President's 2018 Trade Policy Agenda. Retrieved October 2, 2018, from https://ustr.gov/sites/default/files/files/Press/Reports/2018/AR/2018%20Annual%20Report%20I.pdf.

United States. (2018b, March 8). Presidential Proclamation on Adjusting Imports of Steel into the United States. Retrieved October 2, 2018, from https://www.whitehouse.gov/presidential-actions/presidential-proclamation-adjusting-imports-steel-united-states/.

WTO. (2016, June 21). *Report on G20 Trade Measures*. Retrieved October 2, 2018, from https://www.wto.org/english/news_e/news16_e/g20_wto_report_june16_e.pdf.

CHAPTER 4

The Challenges to EU Trade Policy in a Changing World Order

Claes G. Alvstam and Lena Lindberg

Introduction

The EU's common commercial policy is currently facing bigger challenges than it has ever encountered since the launch of the original customs union more than sixty years ago. These challenges include the United Kingdom's forthcoming leave and the impact of that exit for the remaining member states. At least equally important is the demand for continuous alignment of the common commercial policy with the structural changes that are continually occurring in foreign trade and the subsequent need for revisions of the trade policy map. To address these changes, the general direction of the trade policy strategy must be continuously revisited, re-assessed and revised.

The views expressed in this chapter are the views of the author, and do not necessarily reflect the official policy or position of the Swedish government.

C. G. Alvstam (✉)
University of Gothenburg, Gothenburg, Sweden
e-mail: claes.alvstam@handels.gu.se

L. Lindberg
Swedish Ministry for Foreign Affairs, Stockholm, Sweden
e-mail: lena.lindberg@gov.se

A. Bakardjieva Engelbrekt et al. (eds.), *The European Union in a Changing World Order*,
https://doi.org/10.1007/978-3-030-18001-0_4

One apparent indicator of the changing global economy is the fact that the growth rate for international trade in goods and services has stagnated remarkably in recent years. From 2012 to 2017, the average increase in volume was about 3.5 per cent per year, while it was about 6.6 per cent annually from 1999 to 2008. When measured in USD, the value of exported goods and services has actually declined from around USD 23,300 billion in 2013 and 2014 to about USD 22,700 billion in 2017. At the same time, the world's GDP has been increasing by about 3.5 per cent annually (IMF 2018a). Historically, the growth rate for foreign trade was about twice as high as the GDP growth rate, but this is no longer the case. This chapter examines how the EU's policy for trade should be revised in light of ongoing global changes. The chapter examines various options for the EU's external trade policy. Is the most appropriate strategy to take a more active global leadership role in defending the multilateral trade regime in the vacuum arising after the US's retreat? Is it more realistic to intensify attempts to achieve far-reaching bilateral and regional agreements with key partners in different parts of the world? A more radical option could be to lower the level of ambition for the EU's external trade policy and instead prioritize deeper integration within the internal market in accordance with a "Europe First" strategy. A central issue here is the role the EU's relationship with the UK will play as a powerful pan-European trade policy is formulated after the country's exit.

The chapter is structured as follows. First, we describe the history of the EU's common trade policy. Thereafter, we address some of the most important structural changes, including the effects of the international division of labour and specialization on trade policy content and geographical orientation. Significant changes in the form of a new US trade policy, the UK's exit from the EU and China's increasingly prominent role in the international arena are also discussed and analysed. Finally, we provide a brief overview of the EU's concluded, ongoing and future free trade negotiations with different constellations of countries, after which we offer several recommendations for the future direction of the EU's trade policy. An important policy recommendation based on the reasoning in the chapter is that the EU should vigorously defend the multilateral trading system. In other words, it should adopt the theme of "Make the WTO Great Again" while simultaneously continuing to conclude and implement ambitious bilateral and regional trade and economic partnership agreements with key partners.

The EU's Trade Policy in a Changing World Order

Global foreign trade growth has stagnated for several reasons. One important explanation is that Chinese exports, which long functioned as an engine of world trade, have experienced lower growth rates. In the rest of Asia, growth in foreign trade has also been weaker, while low growth figures were noted in Europe and North America even before the deep financial crisis in 2008 and 2009. The lower growth rates also reflect the fact that the gradual liberalization of foreign trade, which characterized the seven decades after World War II, has stalled. This is particularly true in terms of the creation and maintenance of a common trade policy framework for nearly all countries in the world within the World Trade Organization (WTO).

The WTO's first and, thus far, only general round of multilateral negotiations, the Doha Development Agenda (DDA), commenced in 2001. It should have been completed in 2005 but is yet to be concluded. At the same time, multilateralism as a basic idea has been challenged, while the conclusion of bilateral and regional trade agreements has become the most important strategy for pursuing the principles of free trade. However, even this road has been criticized (see, e.g., Bhagwati 2008). The two largest regional trade negotiations in the 2010s, the "Trans-Pacific Partnership" (TPP), which originally included 12 countries in the Americas and the Pacific, as well as the "Transatlantic Trade and Investment Partnership" (TTIP) between the EU and the US, collapsed and were laid on ice, respectively, in 2017 as a result of the new US president's view of foreign trade as a bilateral zero-sum game. In this view, the US economy is perceived as always having been the losing party and all previous free trade agreements are alleged to be disadvantageous for the US. Although the TPP negotiations later transformed into negotiations for a CPTPP ("Comprehensive and Progressive Agreement for Trans-Pacific Partnership"), these events show that the free trade ideal has increasingly come into question. At the same time, the critique of the globalization process from various ideological viewpoints has been strong and calls for a return to more protected national production and for the safeguarding of domestic employment and national self-sufficiency have become increasingly prominent. This applies not only in the US but also in several other countries.

It is in this wider context that the EU's external trade policy should be assessed. Foreign trade has undergone profound changes in content, geographical orientation and mode of operation in recent decades, including changes resulting from the emergence and proliferation of global and regional value chains. In addition, free trade agreements (FTAs) have become more ambitious and wider in scope, and now cover many new issues. At the same time, they have become more profound in terms of deeper commitments. These two shifts are reflected in new labels for these agreements, which are often referred to as "trade and investment partnerships", "deep and comprehensive trade agreements", "comprehensive economic and trade agreements" or "economic partnership agreements" rather than just "free trade agreements". However, the essential role of these agreements still relates to the management and regulation of economic transactions between states.

Foreign trade in goods and services is one of the few policy areas within the EU that is regulated by "exclusive competence" at the supranational level (Article 3 TFEU). A common commercial policy towards third countries (in the form of a customs union) was included in the 1957 Treaty of Rome, which established the European Economic Community (EEC). In a customs union, member states adapt their external tariffs to a common level and the trade barriers between member states are gradually eliminated.

At the time of the EEC's formation, the multilateral General Agreement on Tariffs and Trade (GATT) had been in force for a decade and had effectively contributed to a reduction of general tariff levels among its contracting parties. The GATT had also created an opportunity for two or more individual countries to speed up tariff elimination by reducing tariff rates among themselves as long as third countries were not put at a disadvantage. This condition was met by the six inaugural member states of the EEC. Over the span of a decade, free trade was created for a large part of internal foreign trade, while the common external barriers to trade continued to decrease as a result of the multilateral GATT Dillon Round (1959 to 1961) and the Kennedy Round (1963 to 1967).

Intra-regional foreign trade between "the original six" (West Germany, France, Italy, the Netherlands, Belgium and Luxembourg) amounted to about 25 per cent of their total foreign trade turnover in the mid-1950s. That figure rose to more than 50 per cent in the late 1960s. The ensuing GATT rounds (Tokyo, 1972–1979; Uruguay, 1986–1993) resulted in continued decreases in the common external tariff levels. At the same time, the European Community was enlarged from six member states in 1972 to 15 in 1995, all of which became part of the single internal market. Therefore, that market comprised the majority of the Western European countries. This combination of internal and external trade liberalization led to continued growth in intra-regional trade, but at a lower rate. The new members in western, northern and southern Europe were often already well integrated with the EU at the time of membership. The further enlargement to the east after the fall of the Berlin Wall in 1989 provided room for a further increase in the exchange of goods and services, but most of the thirteen member states added since 2005 are small economies that have only marginally contributed to an increase in intra-regional trade. The share of intra-regional trade to total external trade in goods has remained stable at around 65–70 per cent of total trade since the beginning of the 2000s. It amounted to about 64 per cent in 2017.

This apparent stagnation does not mean that the economic integration among member states has ceased. In fact, the launch of the European single market has entailed a gradual transition to deeper forms of integration. In particular, transactions involving services and direct investments between member states have expanded rapidly. Intra-regional supply chains have also continued to develop, linking producers and consumers closer to each other regardless of national borders. Therefore, the standardization of rules for manufacturing and service production has become an increasingly important component in new versions of free trade agreements. In addition, efficiency has been significantly improved through, for example, reduced requirements for documentation at border crossings, and the coordination of rules and regulations for trade procedures, all within the framework of the internal market's general principle of mutual recognition of each country's production. Moreover, at the WTO level, an important common agreement—the Trade Facilitation Agreement (TFA)—came into force in early 2017. The TFA is expected to simplify procedures and decrease transaction costs in international trade. Hence, it would be a mistake to view the last two decades as "lost" when it comes to trade liberalization. In fact, economic integration has taken new shapes and forms that may not be as evident or visible as tariff reductions.

One important reason why the EU's proportion of internal trade relative to total foreign trade has stagnated and declined in recent decades is that a large part of the growth in world trade has taken place outside of Europe, which implies that there has been an incentive for the EU to look beyond the union's borders (Ahnlid et al. 2011). In particular, foreign trade with Asia in general and China in particular has expanded. Therefore, over time, it has become increasingly important to not only prioritize the intra-regional trade relations but also actively work toward continued liberalization of foreign trade on the global level. The EU has been a driving force in the multilateral trade negotiations within the WTO, even though the outcomes have been modest. The basic principles and priorities of the EU's external trade policy were formulated in 2006 in the "Global Europe Strategy", which was followed up in 2010 by the Commission's Communication "Trade, Growth and World Affairs" (European Commission 2010), and in the 2015 "Trade for all—Towards a more responsible trade and investment policy" communication from the Commission (European Commission 2015). This latest strategy was followed by a reflection paper in May 2017 (European Commission 2017) and by President Juncker's State of the Union address in September 2017 and 2018.

As the negotiations within the WTO have largely been in a stalemate after 2005 (with the exception of the TFA) and as it has been difficult to achieve any major breakthroughs at the multilateral level, the EU has chosen to complement the basic multilateral strategy with a parallel focus on bilateral and regional trade initiatives. These ventures should not be seen as a contradiction to the principle of multilateralism, but rather as an opportunity to build a better platform for continued and deepened multilateralism through wide and deep free trade agreements that reflect the fact that foreign trade continuously takes on new forms. This approach, which is known as "multilateralizing regionalism", argues that ambitious and properly implemented bilateral and regional agreements can act as springboards in the attempt to push the multilateral process forward (Baldwin et al. 2009; Lindberg and Alvstam 2012a, b; Kommerskollegium 2018a). Recent studies show that about two-thirds of EU exports to partner countries make use of free trade agreements, while the corresponding figure for partner countries' exports to the EU is as high as 90 per cent (Kommerskollegium 2018b).

The Emergence of Global Value Chains: Continued Fragmentation of Global Trade?

Clearly, the challenges that today's trade policy negotiators face are far from minor. For years, the main issue has not been about reducing tariff levels. Nevertheless, high tariff rates still exist within individual countries and individual product groups, especially within the agricultural and food sector. Even though this sector only contributes with 5–7 per cent of world trade, it is often the most difficult industry to address in international trade negotiations, regardless of whether those negotiations are bilateral, regional or multilateral.

Today, there are different subtle technical barriers to trade that complicate transactions across national borders and make them more expensive. Such obstacles are often more difficult to describe, estimate and negotiate. The emergence of global value chains has made isolating the individual stages of manufacturing increasingly difficult. Production is no longer simply a matter of transforming raw materials into finished consumer goods within a domestic national production system. Specialization and fragmentation of production have long been prerequisites for improved efficiency and productivity. Firms may therefore outsource parts of production to external parties or transfer their own production to countries with lower manufacturing costs. This development has constituted the basic logic for the liberalization of foreign trade. In recent decades, it has been driven to ever higher levels as individual production units are moved further away from each other and goods cross national borders multiple times during the production process. A typical manufactured product (e.g., a car, lawnmower or mobile phone) consists of hundreds or thousands of individual pieces, semi-manufactured parts and components that are manufactured, refined and assembled, sometimes in 30–50 different countries. Total transport work for such global supply chains usually adds up to several turns around the globe.

These two processes (i.e., the specialization, fragmentation and division of labour on the one hand, and the liberalization of foreign trade on the other) have been mutually supportive. Requirements for continued specialization and division of labour within production have driven demands for further trade liberalization. The reduced trade barriers between countries have created additional opportunities for productivity improvements in manufacturing. The major remaining efficiency gains in continued trade liberalization lie in opportunities for further harmonization of standardization and certification rules among countries, since such regulations often contribute to "unnecessary" double work. Both parties must follow their countries' respective requirements and regulations, even though there are not always real differences in the level of ambition. Instead, the differences often reflect local traditions and modes of working.

The overwhelming majority of world trade thus consists of goods in different stages of processing (i.e., intermediate trade). In most countries, a substantial part of the export value of goods is made up of products that have previously been imported and have been further processed. Therefore, an export strategy requires an import strategy. In other words, we need to understand the entire supply chain, and how production and employment in one country depend on production and employment in other countries. In this regard, labels such as "Made in Japan" or "Manufactured in the US" have become obsolete and misleading. Given the decreasing barriers to trade, fragmentation and specialization have been driven so far that, in many industries, it is no longer possible to discern individual goods transported across national borders. This change has been called a transition "from trade in products to trade in tasks" and globalization's "second unbundling" (Baldwin 2014; Baldwin and Robert-Nicoud 2014).

Therefore, the question is whether there is an upper limit to specialization. One might argue that a final product's quality is adversely affected by a high degree of specialization, as the responsibility for the product is divided among numerous individual subcontractors in multiple stages. Furthermore, when a finished product generates such significant transport needs, one might question whether that product's geographically dispersed value chain is consistent with the ambition to create a more sustainable logistics system.

The trend towards fewer subcontractors delivering entire modules for final assembly may lower the number of border crossings and, thus, result in reduced gross-trade volumes as reported in foreign trade statistics. New technologies, such as the advent of 3D printing (i.e., additive manufacturing), may shift the logic of the global value chains toward a return to a higher proportion of "local" production (Laplume et al. 2016). The same forces that previously contributed to the liberalization of foreign trade may now move in the opposite direction, and contribute to global value chains becoming regional or even national. "Insourcing", "backshoring" and "reshoring" could become new trends in a period of reversed globalization and increased protectionist barriers between countries (Bremmer 2018; Cuervo-Cazurra et al. 2017; Kobrin 2017; Meyer 2017; The Economist 2017). However, evidence from Sweden suggests that the trend of "multinationals in retreat" is exaggerated (Vahlne et al. 2018).

Services: The "Invisible" Value Added in International Trade Transactions

Another fundamental change that has discreetly taken place in recent decades concerns the part of a product's total value added that comes from different kinds of services. In some cases, the product itself is a non-physical service. Services have traditionally been subject to multilateral regulations to a lesser extent than the manufacturing sector. This might be because the production and trade of services are, by nature, more "invisible" and "elusive", making them more complicated to measure, describe and regulate. The officially reported trade in services amounts to approximately 20–25 per cent of total world trade in goods and services. However, a significant part of service production is built into commodity production in the shape of research, product development, design, distribution and marketing. Many companies enjoy higher profit margins in their aftermarket activities than from the product itself. Accordingly, descriptions of their business models shift from, for example, "selling trucks" to "providing integrated mobility solutions". In most countries, employment now depends on the production of services. In advanced economies, the proportion of the economically active population involved in services is usually around 75–80 per cent. The decline in relative and absolute manufacturing employment and the subsequent rise of employment in the service sector is not a new phenomenon, but it has accelerated in advanced economies over the past fifty years. Thus, the main part of the final value of a physical product today often consists of different types of built-in services.

One problem in regulating trade in services is the high degree of geographical inequality in service production. The advanced service industries are usually located in the richest countries or in small isolated "islands" in the central business districts in developing countries' metropolitan areas. Many WTO member states are concerned that further in-depth multilateral regulation of foreign trade in services will deepen this inequality. As it has been difficult to proceed multilaterally on service trade issues, despite the common regulatory framework found in the "General Agreement on Trade in Services" (GATS), the EU together with a number of other advanced service economies launched negotiations for a "plurilateral" service agreement in 2013. While the negotiations for this "Trade in Services Agreement" (TiSA), have thus far failed to reach a conclusion and are currently at a standstill, aspirations for a re-start still exist. The TiSA negotiations have so far involved 23 WTO members, including the EU (50 economies in total), and a deal would encompass about 70 per cent of world trade in services.

Another factor making it difficult to agree on multilateral rules for trade in services is the fast pace of technological development in many industries, which means that the most advanced economies always have an advantage when it comes to generating high added value by being the first to apply a new technology. However, one example of success at the multilateral level was the 2015 renewal of the "Information Technology Agreement" (ITA) in which a holistic approach is taken to hardware and software in the IT area. In other words, the ITA combines trade in goods with trade in services.

One important matter, especially for the EU, is how to treat the growing field of e-commerce from a trade policy point of view (see, e.g., Teigland et al. 2018). The increased service content in advanced production also means that it has become more important in international trade policy to indicate *how*, rather than *where*, a product is manufactured, as most goods have multinational origins. In a marketing context, we increasingly see designations such as "Made *by* Sweden", "Designed in the USA", "assembled in China" or "Proudly made in France".

Foreign Direct Investment: The "Janus Face" of Trade in Goods and Services

The interactions and interdependencies between foreign trade and foreign direct investment (FDI) have also been neglected. While trade has generally been regulated on a multinational level, international investment agreements have usually been bilateral. Moreover, the long growth period after World War II resulted in a continuous internationalization process in virtually all business sectors and the gradual emergence of globally coordinated production. Big multinational companies manage production, suppliers and customers in a large number of countries at the same time. As such, they have an integrated approach to imports, exports and FDI. The process of moving manufacturing closer to sales markets and attempts to avoid barriers to trade have been natural parts of producers' internationalization. Market-driven investments in the shape of relocated manufacturing may result in a decline in export flows, but production expansion abroad can also serve as a springboard for additional exports in cases where subcontractors who previously delivered components to a domestic plant can start supplying the new foreign plant. At the same time, the differences between "domestic" and "foreign" production have become blurred. If about 90 per cent of a finished product's value-added is generated in the host country and contributes to employment in that country, it is difficult to assert that it is a foreign product, even if the manufacturing company is wholly or partly foreign-owned. It follows that a significant proportion of total world trade consists of intra-corporate trade in which companies in the same group act as sellers and buyers in transactions across national borders.

The logic behind this kind of foreign trade is different from cases in which the transaction takes place "at arm's length" between stand-alone buyers and sellers. In this case, the scope and content of geographical trade patterns are determined by the company's own production and logistics organization. As such, they often deviate from transactions in free and open competition. One often-cited estimate is that about one third of world trade can be classified as intra-corporate transfers (UNCTAD 2013: 135). However, the definition of a "common group of companies" is not self-evident, and there is an extensive grey-zone of "related" companies that are bound together through various forms of indirect ownership and control. If we adopt a very broad definition, it is possible to claim that 50–70 per cent of the total world trade in goods and services take place between parties that are formally related to each other in some way.

The question of how to look at globally active companies from a trade policy point of view has naturally caught the attention of various interest groups in both home- and host countries for FDI. Ultimately, the issue is about power and control, both domestic and international. It has often been emphasized that multinational companies are more powerful than states because they operate in many countries at the same time, although this assertion can be contested. The discussion about the ultimate power of production lies at the forefront of dispute resolution in terms of how and where a dispute between a foreign company and the host country is settled. Should such disputes be addressed within the framework of bilateral trade and investment agreements through "Investor-State Dispute Settlement" regulations? Alternatively, are they rather settled through a special arbitration procedure via an international, neutral Chamber of Commerce? Will a "Multilateral Investment Court"—an alternative currently being discussed by the EU—handle these issues? The debate about how investment rules should be incorporated in the new and wider trade agreements is relevant and important, even though the ability of the big multinational enterprises to advance their own interests is sometimes exaggerated. The multinational firm has the advantage of being flexible and agile, as it can move production capacity across national borders. In addition, it enjoys control of all or parts of the value chain from upstream suppliers to downstream customers and end-markets. In contrast, the state has the ultimate power over the legal framework and is sovereign in its territory. Ultimately, the state can nationalize a company or, at least, make decisions that affect its profitability or its ability to operate.

As investment agreements are usually bilateral, there is a growing need to agree on a common denominator for the rights and obligations that should apply to foreign companies, and for the coordination of investment and trade policies. The creation of regional or multilateral investment agreements is hampered by the fact that the conditions for such agreements differ significantly between different states. Some countries are typical "home countries" for FDI (i.e. the bulk of the FDI flows have been directed outward through companies' own internationalization processes). Other countries are typical "host countries" (i.e. a large part of the FDI flows has been directed inward owing to the launch of production by foreign companies in these markets). Should regulations primarily protect a country's businesses abroad or primarily ensure that foreign companies do not gain too much power in the host country? In the last few decades, these issues have become more multifaceted owing to the rise of China, which was completely closed to FDI before the 1980s, but became one of the world's largest host countries for inward FDI in the 1990s. It has since evolved into one of the world's largest home countries for outward FDI. Twenty-seven of the EU's 28 member states now have separate investment agreements with China. Attempts have been made at negotiating an EU-wide investment agreement with China that would cover investment protection as well as market access.

The Politicization of Trade Policy: Increasing Interest Among Citizens and the Lack of Confidence in EU Institutions

In recent years, we have also observed a clear move towards a broader interpretation of international trade agreements. As supply chains have become increasingly integrated, not only in terms of goods, services and capital but also with regard to the international mobility of labour, it has become more important to assess trade policy from the wider perspective of labour laws, wage dumping, environmental impacts and human rights. Therefore, trade policy should not be regarded in isolation but as an integrated component in the larger discourse on the ambiguous effects of globalization. On the one hand, the strength of globalization is its ability to enhance economic growth through specialization and the international division of labour. On the other hand, economic growth does not automatically imply increased equality among countries and people, or support ambitions to reach more sustainable social and ecological systems. This imbalance between globalization and equal economic development has been highlighted by a number of scholars who do not oppose trade liberalization as such, but who express concerns regarding its failure to reduce gaps among countries and people (Alvaredo et al. 2017; Collier 2007; Krugman and Venables 1995; Milanovic 2016; Rodrik 2011, 2017; Stiglitz 2017; Williamson 2013).

Therefore, one crucial mission is to raise the level of ambition in the new trade agreements to incorporate a broader set of rules for the conduct of foreign trade. As international trade agreements, labour laws, general principles of human rights and climate agreements have thus far been negotiated in parallel with each other, a need for convergence among these different policy areas in modern trade and economic partnership agreements has emerged (see Zurek in this volume). Which principles should apply in relation to other principles? How should we avoid conflicts among urgent societal goals?

Although there is an aim to incorporate a variety of policy areas into a single comprehensive agreement, this objective has not made it easier to reach a final, balanced conclusion. The more areas covered by a negotiation, the more difficult it is to put the pieces together in a coherent manner. In addition, some negotiation partners may lack the necessary experience in the new fields, which may, for example, lead them to oppose the inclusion of a trade and sustainable development chapter in a broader FTA. At the same time, the broader, more open and more "inclusive" trade agreements become, the more they seem to be criticized for opacity and for their lack of consideration of climate issues, food safety, responsible entrepreneurship and protection against foreign companies' profit interests. Likewise, the more transparent the EU Commission has become by, for instance, publishing negotiation mandates and revealing proposals and reports from negotiation rounds, the louder the criticism has been over the lack of transparency. One possible, although not desirable, result of this discontent could be a return to "less ambitious" FTAs in order to avoid the blocking of more comprehensive agreements. Even seemingly uncontroversial agreements, such as those the EU signed with Canada and Ukraine in 2016 and 2014 respectively, were met with great resistance, on the supranational, national and subnational levels.

In this context, the recent internal discussions on the architecture of the EU's trade agreements are noteworthy. They were the result of competence disputes between the Commission and the Council. After the EU Court of Justice issued its opinion on the division of competences between the EU and its member states in the EU-Singapore FTA in May 2017, the Commission proposed that a distinction should be made between FTAs and investment protection agreements (IPAs) in future negotiations. As a result, the deals with Singapore, Vietnam and Japan were divided into FTAs and IPAs, with the IPA with Japan still being under discussion.

The EU in the New Global Trade Context with a Walled-Off US

The "frozen" TTIP negotiations and the collapse of the original 12-member TPP agreement in early 2017 were the first tangible results of the new, nationalist US trade policy (Evenett and Fritz 2017; Ingelhart and Norris 2017). This shift can be seen as a major setback for the EU's current trade policy and for the general aspirations on the global level to ensure the continued liberalization of economic relations. However, this negative development does not mean that other parts of the world are passive. For example, China now aims to fill the vacuum left by the US's retreat from global leadership in trade policy. In January 2017 (at about the same time the new president of the United States was inaugurated), Chinese President Xi Jinping held a spectacular speech at the World Economic Forum in Davos in which he praised free trade and globalization. Mr. Xi emphasized that "Pursuing protectionism is like locking oneself in a dark room. While wind and rain might be kept outside, that dark room will also block light and air. No one will emerge as a winner in a trade war" (Xi 2017). This ode to globalization was followed a few weeks later with the launch of two new "guidelines" for Chinese foreign policy, which were designed to help China to "guide the international community" and to act as a "guide for the maintenance of national security". These responses can be seen as a powerful move in a proactive direction, as China had previously used the more vague wording of "play an important role" in the design of a new world order.

One key issue throughout the TPP negotiations was China's absence. Was it reasonable to create a large Trans-Pacific trade agreement without including one of the main actors? Did the governments involved hope that China would be forced to join a final agreement or was the tacit intention of the TPP to limit China's influence in the region? South Korea's absence from the negotiations was also remarkable, especially as the country had already concluded a comprehensive bilateral trade agreement with the US (KORUS). The US withdrawal initially left the remaining eleven parties in a vacuum, but a fervent ambition to work towards a TPP-11, which was known as the "Comprehensive and Progressive Agreement for Trans-Pacific Partnership" (CPTPP), soon emerged. The deal was signed in Santiago, Chile in March 2018.

Despite its absence from the TPP and CPTPP negotiations, China has remained far from passive. The Chinese model for regional trade agreements has been evident in the ongoing "Regional Comprehensive Economic Partnership" (RCEP) talks, in which questions regarding labour conditions, human rights and environmental responsibility seem so far to be eclipsed by pure free trade issues. The RCEP, expected to be concluded by the end of 2019, is an interesting initiative, as it excludes the American participants in the TPP, and incorporates all ten countries of the Association of Southeast Asian Nations (ASEAN), including the six that were not in the TPP, as well as Japan, South Korea, India, Australia and New Zealand, as well as China itself. As such, it is a broad trade bloc for Asia and the Pacific, which is consistent with what was previously called "ASEAN+6". The inclusion of Australia and New Zealand means that RCEP uses the sharp border of the International Date Line and builds an Asian rather than a Pacific-based economic community. Notably, Hong Kong SAR and Taiwan (Province of China), which rank 13th and 14th in terms of world trade values and together account for more foreign trade value than Japan, are not participating in the RCEP.

In February 2018, US President Donald Trump launched "a new era in American trade policy" (USTR 2018). The novel feature of this policy was the realization of substantial tariff increases. At the same time, the president launched an aggressive nationalist agenda in many other areas directed at long-term allied trade partners, including its North American Free Trade Agreement (NAFTA) neighbours and the EU, as well as China and the rest of the world. By referring to Section 201 of the Trade Act of

1974, the US imposed global safeguard tariffs on the solar and washing-machine industries in order to "remedy trade disputes and get a fair deal for the American people" (USTR 2018). Furthermore, with reference to Section 232 of the Trade Expansion Act of 1962, the quantities of imported steel and aluminum to the US were argued to threaten national security. Therefore, the US introduced a 25 per cent tariff on steel and a 10 per cent tariff on aluminum imported from the EU, Canada and Mexico as of June 1, 2018. These measures clearly violated the multilateral rules that the US had been instrumental in introducing and maintaining during the entire post-war era. The cases were subsequently brought to the WTO. At the same time, the EU and other US trade partners initiated rebalancing measures (European Commission 2018a).

In the ensuing months, the Trump administration threatened to continue and deepen the conflict by introducing similar barriers in the automotive industry aimed, in particular, at the EU. Even though the acute dispute between the EU and the US was at least temporarily mitigated after a meeting between US President Trump and EU Commission President Juncker in July 2018, after which the main target rather became China, these developments may signal an entirely new era in global trade policy. It should be noted that the US's measures, which supposedly aim at strengthening the competitive edge of American industry and enhancing manufacturing employment, have almost no support from economic research in the US or elsewhere. Moreover, they have found only limited backing from the US's corporate sector or affected trade unions. Instead, they reflect a shift in international trade policy away from solid economic theory, empirical realities and mutual cooperation toward unilateral, inward-looking geopolitics (Obstfeld 2018; Summers 2018; Zoellick 2018).

It is this new trade policy context to which the EU must relate. Should the EU reinforce its global role by more actively using the advantage of its economic and political strength, and take the lead in a reborn multilateral order? Should the member states continue along the regional track and focus on implementing ambitious and broad trade and investment agreements with selected partners regardless of whether the US is involved? Should the EU lower its ambitions and seek improvements in selected sectors and bilateral relations according to the motto of "better one limited agreement than no agreement at all" while prioritizing its own internal market?

The EU's Concluded, Ongoing and Future Free Trade Negotiations

An important policy in line with the "Trade for All" communication (European Commission 2015) has been to conclude bilateral and regional agreements with a wide spectrum of partners. The EU has a large number of FTAs and economic partnership agreements that have entered into force, as well as agreements that have been concluded and have been provisionally applied in anticipation of entry into force. Furthermore, there are a number of ongoing negotiations (some of which are on hold for various reasons), while others are expected to be launched. In addition, there are agreements with EES/EFTA countries, candidate countries and countries with which the EU cooperates on a customs-union basis. In sum, this means that the EU has formalized its economic relationships with a large number of countries around the world and that a growing share of its external trade is regulated under different forms of preferential arrangements.

Although the economic importance of the different country constellations and various forms of agreements varies, the statistics offer an indication of how much weight the EU attaches to different alliances. About 64 per cent (2017) of the EU members' total foreign trade in goods (in terms of value) occurs in transactions within the single internal market. Extra-regional imports and exports (36 per cent of total foreign trade) are distributed across different countries and continents (see Fig. 4.1). The EU's most important relationships (in terms of value) are with "Greater China" (i.e., People's Republic of China, Hong Kong, Taiwan and Macao) and the US, with about 19 and 17 per cent, respectively, of the union's extra-regional foreign trade. From a trade perspective, it would therefore be natural for the EU to intensify its efforts to resume the TTIP negotiations even though the conditions are not the most favourable at present. In addition, comprehensive free trade and investment agreements with China should be trade policy priorities if relative economic importance is the main criterion for considering initiatives. Negotiations for the latter are underway.

The Commission's 2015 trade strategy established that the EU aims to deepen and "balance" the relationship with China in a way that benefits both sides. The "balance" issue requires a more substantial definition to be translated into practical policy. The EU, like the US, runs a major bilateral trade deficit (in goods) with China. The EU's export/import ratio for

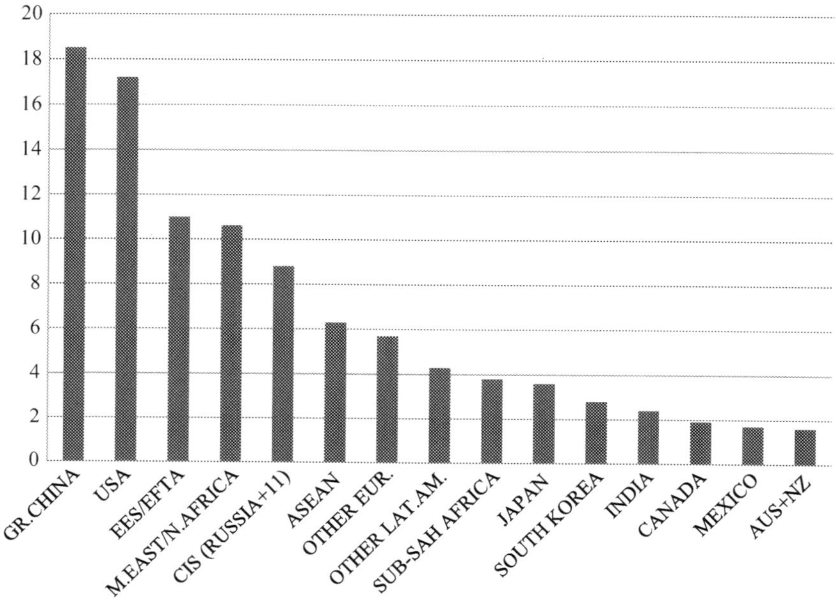

Fig. 4.1 The EU's extra-regional trade in goods (2017). Source: International Monetary Fund, Direction of Trade Statistics Database. The columns represent the percentage of total extra-regional trade in terms of imports and exports of goods, by countries and blocs of countries

China amounted to 0.53 (USD -200 billion) in 2017, while the ratio for the US was 0.26 (USD -375 billion USD) (IMF 2018b). Previously, member states reported a large surplus in outgoing direct investments in China. However, inward direct investments from China have increased dramatically in recent years. Notably, the EU has taken a more pragmatic position regarding its current trade balance deficit than the US. In mainstream economic theory, a bilateral imbalance in trade in goods and services tells us something about how global value chains are built, and about the relationships among consumption, savings and investment in the two partners. It does not indicate whether any "unfair" trade relations, "terrible previous deals" or "currency manipulation" exist, which have been the dominant explanations for the US's new trade policy (USTR 2018). Furthermore, if the net value of exports in goods (i.e., excluding export values that have previously been imported), the trade in services, indirect transactions through Hong Kong and the value of US production in China (which serves as a substitute for exports) were to be included, the US may actually run a commercial surplus with China (Dobozi 2018). Therefore, there is an urgent need to establish a standard that is better able to measure balances in international transactions—a system that can be accepted and used by all parties within the multilateral trading framework.

At the same time, concerns have grown in Europe about Chinese investments in certain key sectors by companies that are state-owned or state-funded. For this reason, in June 2017, the European Council welcomed an initiative from the Commission suggesting that investments from third countries in strategic sectors should be analysed. The EU Commission President therefore presented a proposal in September 2017 for a special mechanism for foreign direct investment screening, which has been discussed by the Council (the Working Party for Trade Questions) in 2018. A new EU framework for the screening of foreign direct investments entered into force in April 2019.

The four EFTA members (Norway, Switzerland, Liechtenstein and Iceland), which together account for 11 per cent of the EU's external foreign trade in goods, are already deeply integrated in the EU, although through different arrangements. Norway is part of the EEA/EES and the Schengen area. In this respect, it is already a functional member of the EU even though it is not part of the customs union. The country has a number of exceptions from the single market, especially in the agricultural, fisheries and food sectors. Norway is also cooperating closely with the UK on oil and gas extraction in the North Sea, an area that has to be renegotiated in conjunction with the UK's exit from the EU. From the EU's perspective, one possible path towards deepening Norway's cooperation with the union would be to gradually eliminate the current exemptions, with the prospect that Norway will eventually join the customs union.

Switzerland, which is deeply integrated with its neighbours for obvious geographical reasons, is not part of the single internal market or the customs union. However, the country is a member of the Schengen area and it has concluded a number of bilateral agreements with the EU. These agreements provide Switzerland with a number of advantages as well as commitments, which generally correspond to status as a functional EU member state. The main agreements concern free movement, the abolition of border controls and public procurement. Like Norway, Switzerland contributes substantial amounts to the EU common budget. The country is also involved in a customs union with Liechtenstein.

Iceland's relationship with the EU is similar to that of Norway. It is a member of the EES and Schengen, but not a part of the customs union. Iceland has a number of exceptions from the EES, especially within the fishing industry. The country applied for EU membership in 2009 and was treated as a candidate country, but it withdrew its application in 2015.

Thus, in the case of all EFTA members, one can speak of a "functional membership" to the extent that these countries are part of extensive trade policy cooperation, albeit with a number of symbolic exceptions, and they pay a non-membership price in the form of limited influence over legislative procedures—the *acquis communautaire*. At the same time, they have the liberty to conclude their own free trade agreements with the outside world—an opportunity that has been used frequently by individual countries and by the common bloc. For example, an FTA was concluded between EFTA and Hong Kong in 2011. Iceland was the first European country to sign a bilateral FTA with the People's Republic of China in 2013. Switzerland followed shortly thereafter and Norway is currently negotiating a similar agreement. From the EU's perspective, the EFTA states' approach to "Greater China" may be viewed as a pilot case for possible future negotiations on a significantly larger scale. In addition, the EFTA agreements are important test cases for China regarding deeper economic cooperation with the EU.

Several Balkan and Southeast European countries have applied for EU membership and are participating in a process that involves closer coordination of trade policy relationships through different degrees of free trade cooperation. These countries can be divided into two groups. The first category consists of EU candidate countries involved in active negotiations: Turkey, Montenegro, Serbia, Albania and FYR (Northern) Macedonia. Turkey, which formally applied for membership in 1987, is already in a customs union with the EU. The second group consists of potential EU member candidates: Bosnia/Herzegovina and Kosovo. The strategic issue from the EU's point of view is whether the enlargement of the union will continue as it has in the past. Tensions among member states have increased in a number of areas, including the common commercial policy. Many of these tensions involve the new members. At the same time, the plans for a renewal of the customs union with Turkey are put on ice, while the approval of Turkey's membership seems further away than ever despite 30 years of negotiation.

In the EU's cooperation with the candidate countries, trade policy issues have become subordinate to a number of major foreign- and security-policy complications. This fact is even more evident in relation to the remaining neighbourhood regions. An external action policy towards the former Soviet republics was initiated within an “Eastern Partnership” under the Swedish EU presidency in 2009. A partnership agreement had already been concluded with Ukraine in 1994. This was replaced twenty years later with an association agreement, in which a “Deep and Comprehensive Free Trade Agreement” (DCFTA) is one of the pillars. The scope of this agreement is similar to that of the EES, as it offers the partner country a high degree of economic integration with the EU. Similar arrangements have been concluded with Moldova and Georgia. These agreements can be seen as precursors to membership. However, given the new geopolitical situation that has emerged in the area since 2014 owing to the Russian occupation of the Crimea and the “frozen war” in eastern Ukraine, these deals have become more sensitive. Nevertheless, the association agreements with Georgia and Moldova entered into force 2016, and the agreement with Ukraine came into effect in September 2017. For its part, Russia has created its own economic bloc through a “Euro-Asian Economic Union” (EAEU) in which Belarus, Kazakhstan, Kyrgyzstan and Armenia participate. This is essentially a customs union that encompasses the same trade policy conditions that existed among the former Soviet republics.

Economic integration continues on a daily basis among the countries in the Eastern Partnership and the EU despite the foreign policy tensions. For instance, one to two million Ukrainian citizens worked in Poland in 2018. Moldova is one of the countries in the world that has a significant share of its citizens employed abroad, mainly in EU member states, and it is therefore highly dependent on remittances sent back home.

The trade policy between the EU and Russia reflects the foreign policy relationship, which is at the lowest point since the end of the Cold War. When the Russian Federation was formed after the collapse of the Soviet Union in 1991, a promising integration process began, which included both foreign trade and foreign direct investment. After the first decade's turbulent economic transformation, which brought great uncertainty about which rules should be applied for trade and investment policy cooperation, the situation stabilized in the early 2000s and the potential for further integration was high. However, since the early 2010s, developments have been negative, and the sanctions that the EU introduced after the Russian occupation of the Crimea further hampered foreign trade relations. Even before that point, there was an extreme imbalance in the bilateral commodity composition. While the EU's exports to Russia are generally similar in content to the union's exports to other countries (i.e., a dominance of advanced industrial goods), Russian exports almost entirely consist of energy and raw materials. Despite a number of foreign direct investments in the Russian manufacturing industry, the country's exports have not been upgraded. It is striking that the value of Russian exports of advanced industrial goods, in absolute terms, is at about the same level as that of Portugal. The EU's dependence on Russian oil and gas is still high, and the unity among member states regarding additional sanctions is fragile. Notably, the newest EU members have the most to lose from deteriorating trade relations and continuing sanctions.

The "Southern Neighbourhood" is no less complicated. The old colonial relations of the North African countries with Europe, especially France, have given rise to some benefits in the sense that these countries have enjoyed some trade preferences. However, these benefits have been diluted over time. The southern EU member states have pushed for closer economic and political integration across the Mediterranean Sea, but more substantial results have been modest. A broad "Euro-Mediterranean Partnership" in the Middle East and North Africa (MENA) that would act as an extended free trade agreement across the southern and eastern Mediterranean (including Turkey but excluding Libya and Syria) still exists only as a long-term vision. Furthermore, the existing FTAs with these countries are largely under-utilized by EU exporters (Kommerskollegium 2018b). The EU's general trade policy strategy is to wait for a coherent geographical framework consisting of various types of free trade and association agreements with individual countries. The EU is currently negotiating DCFTAs with Tunisia and Morocco, and it has also engaged in a dialogue with Egypt, with which an association agreement already exists.

When the US, Greater China, the European neighbourhood and the MENA countries are excluded, about 30 per cent of the total EU external trade in goods remains. The bulk of the EU's FTAs concern Asian countries, which is the area the union has prioritised. In line with the "Global Europe" strategy, negotiations were launched for an ambitious interregional agreement with ASEAN in 2007. This is Asia's largest regional trading bloc with 10 member countries and 650 million inhabitants. These negotiations were halted in 2009 when it became difficult to achieve progress, partly due to different ambitions. Therefore, the EU initiated bilateral negotiations with individual ASEAN countries. It concluded negotiations with Singapore in 2014 (Alvstam et al. 2017) and another with Vietnam in late 2015. Negotiations are also ongoing with the Philippines and Indonesia, as are discussions on the resumption of the paused negotiations with Malaysia. Negotiations with Thailand and the Philippines have been on hold for some time, due to the domestic political situations in these countries. The long-term goal is to return to negotiations for an interregional agreement with the entire ASEAN area. Thailand, which has traditionally been one of the EU's most important partners in the region, presents a special case. The country's domestic-policy trend has not been positive in recent years, which resulted in a break in the negotiations in 2014. A complication when it comes to creating a comprehensive, ambitious interregional agreement with ASEAN has been the significant economic differences among its members. While Singapore enjoys prosperity equal to the European level, Cambodia, Laos and Myanmar are among the poorest countries in the world. However, this latter group is already exempt from EU tariffs on all goods except weapons in accordance with the policy of "Everything But Arms" (EBA). There have also been negotiations for an investment agreement with Myanmar.

In 2007, negotiations were launched on a free trade agreement with India, but these talks have progressed very slowly. However, negotiations with South Korea, which were also initiated in 2007, were a success. This FTA was applied provisionally as of July 2011 and came into force in December 2015. Furthermore, negotiations on an ambitious agreement with Japan began in 2013 and the agreement was successfully completed in 2017. The EU-Japan Economic Partnership Agreement entered into force in February 2019. Negotiations on investment protection and the EU's new model for dispute settlement (Investment Court System) have continued. These two latter agreements are particularly interesting in light of Japan's relationship with the US after the latter's withdrawal from the TPP agreement. South Korea did not participate in the TPP, but it has its own bilateral agreement with the US (KORUS), which was renegotiated in 2018 owing to pressure from President Trump. For Japan, which had a lot of prestige riding on participation in the TPP and which was forced into far-reaching domestic-policy compromises (especially in the "sacred" agricultural sector), the message that the US would pull out of the TPP was a major disappointment. The Japanese government thereafter struggled to decide whether to try proceeding with a "TPP minus 1" or to provide a cautiously positive response to US signals of the possibility of a bilateral agreement. It decided to go for the first option, with the eleven remaining member states signing the CPTPP in March 2018. About one year later, in April 2019, negotiations were kicked off for a bilateral trade agreement between the US and Japan.

Japan is the largest Asian trading partner for the US within the TPP. The US's informal proposal regarding a bilateral trade agreement with Japan as a substitute for the TPP is highly improbable, as the US's motivation for leaving the TPP was that the agreement was "unfair". A side-effect of the collapse of the TPP agreement and the "frozen" TTIP negotiations was the intensification of bilateral negotiations between the EU and Japan—the political prestige associated with completing a comprehensive FTA had increased significantly on both sides. In July 2018, the two parties signed an "EU-Japan Economic Partnership Agreement", after which negotiations on investment protection and the EU's new model for dispute resolution (Investment Court System, ICS) continued.

For two other "leftover" parties in the TPP collapse—Australia and New Zealand—the US retreat resulted in a push to deepen commercial policy relations with the EU. The two countries are also involved in the RCEP negotiations. At the same time, they have deep, historical links with Europe in general and with the UK in particular. After extensive discussions in the Council on the mandates for the two parallel but separate negotiations on broad and ambitious FTAs, negotiations were launched in June 2018. However, in both cases, the UK's withdrawal will have negative consequences. The UK accounts for 20 per cent of Australia's and New Zealand's total EU trade, and it is no coincidence that the UK's post-Brexit trade policy will prioritize the UK's own bilateral agreements with these two countries.

This is also true for Canada. In 2009, the EU started talks with Canada on a Comprehensive Economic and Trade Agreement (CETA). This agreement, which became the most ambitious FTA at the time, was signed by the two parties in October 2016. Significant discontent was expressed by various interest groups, which either thought that the agreement did not adequately take a number of important issues into account or that the agreement was too far-reaching. In particular, the EU's system for investment protection and dispute resolution (ICS) was criticized, although the ICS sought to address concerns regarding the previous model (Investor-to-State Dispute Settlement, ISDS). When the UK leaves the EU, Canada will lose an important partner in the CETA, as trade with the UK accounts for about 25 per cent of Canada's EU trade in goods. Moreover, the UK is overrepresented in all other areas of cooperation, such as services and foreign direct investments. As the CETA agreement has already been provisionally applied, it should be an important objective for all parties involved to ensure that any bilateral agreement between the UK and Canada after the UK's exit is nearly identical to the CETA.

Canada's interest in further deepening its economic relationships with the EU has also been dependent on the "renegotiation" of the NAFTA agreement among the US, Canada and Mexico. A new agreement, "The United States-Mexico-Canada Agreement" (USMCA), was signed in November 2018, but remains to be ratified. This revision had, in fact, already been finalized within the framework of the TPP negotiations. Trade with the US is fundamental for Canada in the same way as trade with the EU is fundamental for the UK. About two thirds of Canada's foreign trade take place with the US, and supply chains between the two countries could hardly be more connected. Nevertheless, this historically deep economic relationship is currently at stake owing to the US's aggressive and unpredictable trade policy, which could result in Canada seeking to reduce its dependence on the US and aiming to broaden its relationships with Europe and Asia.

A corresponding situation is evident in Mexico, which is also a country that has historically been dependent on the US. In fact, the US represents approximately two thirds of Mexico's foreign trade turnover. The two countries share closely connected supply chains. The EU and Mexico entered into a "Global Agreement" in 1997 and the trade provisions from that agreement were developed into an FTA in 2000. Renegotiations for a far-reaching and modernized agreement on trade and investment started in 2016. An agreement in principle was reached on the trade part in April 2018. Mexico is currently prioritizing reducing its dependence on the US and continuing to develop relationships with Asia, Europe and the rest of Latin America. Even though there is no doubt about which partner has been the strongest in the 25-year-old NAFTA, the US has been loud and aggressive about the alleged negative effects of the agreement from the US perspective. The US Secretary of Commerce, Wilbur Ross, stated in the spring of 2017 that a renegotiation should aim at achieving a "NAFFTA"—"North American Free *and Fair* Trade Agreement" (Ross 2017).

From the EU perspective, the countries of Latin America can be categorized into at least four different groups. The first group consists of the larger South American economies within the Mercosur bloc: Argentina, Brazil, Paraguay and Uruguay (Venezuela has, in reality, left the bloc). Wide-ranging free trade negotiations are ongoing with this group. These negotiations were initially launched in 1999 and have been idle at times, but they have intensified since 2015 and may be concluded in 2018. Second, the EU has an old bilateral relationship with Chile, with which it has had an association agreement that covers free trade since 2003. Negotiations are underway to modernize the trade part of the agreement in order for it to better correspond to the EU's more ambitious model for FTAs. Third, negotiations have been concluded on a trade agreement with countries in the Andean Community. Since 2013, an agreement with Colombia and Peru has been applied, which Ecuador joined in 2017. Peru and Chile are now also part of the CPTPP. Fourth, the EU has an association agreement with the Central American countries (from Guatemala in the north to Panama in the south), which was established in 2012.

With regard to the countries in Africa, the Caribbean and the Pacific (ACP), the Lomé Agreement was concluded in the 1970s. It can be viewed as a fusion of various agreements previously created within the framework of economic relations between European countries and their colonies. This agreement provided full access to the European market and supported close cooperation in several other fields. In 2000, it was transformed into the Cotonou Agreement, which covers 79 countries as of 2018. Following a number of revisions and modernizations, the majority of the ACP countries are now involved in different types of economic partnership agreements (EPAs).

The EU's Post-Brexit Trade Policy

The United Kingdom's decision to leave the EU after almost 45 years of membership came as a shock to its close economic and political partners, including the EU. The UK accounts for 13 per cent of the EU's total trade in goods and 18 per cent of its total trade in services. After Brexit, the EU27 will remain the most important partner for the UK, accounting for about 50 per cent of the country's foreign trade in goods and about 45 per cent of its trade in services. The UK automatically remains as part of all of the EU's existing trade agreements until its formal exodus.

The exit negotiations have been complicated. Several possible strategies have been tested. The negotiations within the UK government seem to have been at least as difficult as the negotiations between the UK and the EU. The Council signed the withdrawal agreement in January 2019, whereupon it has been turned down by the British Parliament. Following the subsequent stalemate, the exit could not take place on March 29, following the Article 50 schedule. The EU leaders agreed therefore on April 10 to extend the exit until the end of October 2019. From a commercial policy point of view, the best solution for all parties would be for the UK to remain in the internal market and in the customs union. In reality, such a "soft" Brexit would not imply any drastic changes on either side. After its exit, the UK would be able to participate in all new free trade agreements that the EU27 concludes with other countries and *de facto* remain in the existing agreements as part of the customs union. Continued participation in the customs union would also mean that the administrative costs of continued foreign trade within and outside the EU would be significantly lower than in a "hard" Brexit, as the latter would require introduction of customs-clearance procedures as well as trade documentation and control.

However, this does not seem to be a politically viable solution for either the EU or the UK, which is why the opposite scenario must also be considered. A "hard" Brexit would entail the UK leaving both the single internal market and the customs union, such that it would trade with the EU27 based on the same rules that apply to WTO members in general. Customs tariffs and various non-tariff barriers must then be restored (e.g., between Northern Ireland and the Republic of Ireland, and between Gibraltar and Spain). The same is true for document management. All rules and regulations that were coordinated and simplified during the UK's decades of membership will have to be revised. The total socio-economic costs of such a scenario are impossible to estimate. There is an impressive amount of theoretical and empirical academic literature on how to form a customs union with regard to both internal and external foreign trade, but there are no examples (with the exception of the Greenland case) of a country leaving a deeply integrated union, such as the EU. The UK's strategy could be to raise tariffs towards the EU to the EU's current external level (i.e., the applied WTO level) or it could maintain free trade with the EU but introduce a separate external tariff level. In the latter case, the UK would actually form a comprehensive free trade area with the EU. One option in this regard could be what is sometimes labelled "CETA++", which is a broad FTA modelled on the EU's agreement with Canada, but even more ambitious and far-reaching in its regulatory and market access provisions. Thereafter, the UK can maintain the same external tariff level as the EU27, possibly with some minor (but spectacular) exceptions within the consumption goods sector.

Another option would be to launch an ambitious liberalization policy, which would mean that the UK's external tariffs would be lower than the EU's. Such a policy would be in line with the UK's self-image of being more liberal in foreign trade issues than the rest of the EU. It could also stimulate the formation of bilateral agreements with other countries in the world. Such a "free trade and investment haven" policy would also have some disadvantages, such as extensive bureaucracy around the maintenance of rules of origin. If the UK were to place a lower duty on a good from a third country than the EU27's common external tariff, it could not re-export that good duty-free to the EU with an unchanged origin. On the other hand, a good imported from a third country could undergo further processing that would change its country of origin to the UK. In that case, when re-exported to the EU, that good would be subject to any rules negotiated in a possible free trade agreement. To ensure proper customs clearance for importers and exporters, an extensive, time-consuming and costly documentation procedure would be necessary.

Another aspect of the UK's exit has to do with the EU's attraction as a bilateral/regional trading partner, which will decrease after the UK's exit. The free internal market will shrink, because one of the most important member states, as seen from the partner perspective (especially in the areas of services, direct investments and, more generally, market access) will disappear. Again, we see two potential alternatives: the UK may remain in the customs union and follow the EU's external trade policy, or it may establish parallel agreements with all existing and new free trade partners if it relaunches its sovereign external trade policy. The UK could also begin to compete with the EU through a more liberal trade and investment policy. The latter strategy, although unlikely, could be beneficial for all parties in the long term because it could force the EU toward an even more liberal trade policy.

Regardless of the strategies that are chosen, the UK's exit requires a long and energy-consuming negotiation process, which is not beneficial to either party, at least in the short run. The long-lasting uncertainty about the new shape of the EU's cooperation with the UK could be very negative for Europe in general and for the UK in particular.

The EU in a Fragmented World Order: Multilateral Cooperation Needs to Be Strengthened

The EU is highly dependent on a well-functioning and healthy world trade order. As the fastest development within the international economy is still likely to occur outside of Europe, it is even more important for the EU to take a more active role in safeguarding the progress made in the seven decades that have passed since the end of World War II toward reducing the physical and technical barriers across national borders. The EU's explicit objective should be to work towards a more equal allocation of resources, production and welfare among countries. It is not enough to maintain the status quo. The world economy is undergoing minor and major changes, which must be addressed and incorporated into a continuously modernized and agile trade policy strategy.

In this chapter, we have pointed out a number of structural changes, each of which contributes to a new trade policy map and the need for reconsideration of the EU's trade policy. The EU28 is the world's largest economic-political bloc. Its total foreign trade in goods represents one third of world trade. If we exclude intra-EU trade, the EU's external foreign trade still accounts for around 15 per cent of world trade, which puts the EU ahead of both China and the US. This position entails significant responsibility, especially as the US, with its new nationalist foreign trade policy, appears ready to renounce its leadership role in continued trade liberalization efforts while it initiates "trade wars" with its closest political allies. At the same time, China is emerging as an increasingly important actor with its own agenda. The challenges facing global free trade are not necessarily a matter of tariff barriers—they consist of more subtle issues, such as how to deal with new forms of service transactions, the integration of trade and foreign direct investment, and regulatory competition. In addition, dramatic technological changes in production and distribution, including the emergence of the digital economy and data-sharing issues (Baldwin 2017), as well as the role of foreign trade in a globally sustainable social and political system, should be addressed.

While the EU, as the largest trading bloc in the world, has the right to defend its interests through retaliatory measures, it should continue to abide by the multilateral system and seek partners that share these values. Therefore, the EU should primarily work toward restoration of the stalled multilateral trading system and vigorously support the reforms necessary to "Make the WTO Great Again". The major challenges of the global economy can only be addressed on a multilateral level. A similar call for active participation in WTO reforms has also been made by the EU Trade Commissioner (Malmström 2018) and the EU has already contributed ideas along these lines in Geneva. At the same time, work should continue on developing ambitious and broad bilateral and regional agreements with the outside world. Such agreements can be seen as complements to and, in favourable cases, as leverage for deeper, more effective multilateral cooperation. Therefore, despite the current crisis in Trans-Atlantic relations, it is important to work towards a resumption of trade talks between the EU and the US. If such talks are not possible, the focus should shift towards bilateral sectoral agreements. While full TTIP negotiations do not seem to be likely at the moment, it remains to be seen whether the vision in the joint US-EU statement from July 2018 and the subsequent mandates on the two sides will translate into more limited sectoral negotiations. Moreover, it is essential to enter into a dialogue with China regarding how to liberalize its bilateral trade and investment relations. Such talks must also cover the need to strengthen the protection of intellectual property rights and to ensure equal treatment of domestic and foreign companies.

In his annual speech on The State of the Union, held in September 2017, EU Commission President Juncker presented a "Roadmap for a more united, stronger and more democratic Union". One area he highlighted was the increased use of a qualified majority, rather than consensus, when voting in the Council. Such a discussion should also include the common commercial policy and is partly a result of the perceived risks that individual member states, or even individual regional parliaments, delay EU agreements, despite the fact that trade policy is an exclusive EU competence. Furthermore, the emphasis on multilateral cooperation was further emphasized in the State of the Union speech in September 2018 (European Commission 2018b).

The great internal challenge to a proactive multilateral, regional and bilateral trade policy in the EU lies in its democratic legitimacy, which is also the key challenge with the consensus principle. The liberalization of trade and investments has sometimes been connected with increased inequality, uneven economic development, lack of consumer protection, deteriorated working conditions and environmental degradation. These critiques have been widespread, although the basic reason for unequal resource allocation is not free trade itself but the general economic policies carried out in individual countries. It is imperative to not only preach free trade as a rhetorical credo or as something that can be perceived as a project for the economic elite. Rather, the advantageous impacts of free trade on welfare and equality must be made more visible and real to all citizens. The positive effects of an FTA must also be shared with the other party in an agreement. Such "rope tricks" sound difficult to master, but they are nevertheless necessary in order to avoid a negative trend towards nationalism, protectionism and isolationism. A nationalist agenda is regrettably a classic strategy for political leaders, as it appears to offer a universal solution to perceived frustrations and fears among citizens related to complex and sometimes painful societal transformations at the local and global levels.

References

Ahnlid, A., Alvstam, C. G., & Lindberg, L. (2011). A World Without Verona Walls: New Challenges for the External Trade Policy of the EU in a Resilient Global Economy – With Special Focus on Asia. In C. G. Alvstam, B. Jännebring, & D. Naurin (Eds.), *I Europamissionens tjänst*. Gothenburg: Centre for European Research at the University of Gothenburg.

Alvaredo, F., Chancel, L., Piketty, T., Saez, E., & Zucman, G. (2017). Global Inequality Dynamics: New Findings from WID.world. *American Economic Review, 107*(5), 404–409.

Alvstam, C. G., Kettunen, E., & Ström, P. (2017). The Service Sector in the Free Trade Agreement Between the EU and Singapore. *Asia Europe Journal, 15*(1), 75–105.

Baldwin, R. (2014). Trade and Industrialization After Globalization's Second Unbundling: How Building and Joining a Supply Chain Are Different and Why It Matters. In R. C. Feenstra & A. M. Taylor (Eds.), *Globalization in an Age of Crisis: Multilateral Economic Cooperation in the Twenty-First Century*. Chicago: Chicago University Press.

Baldwin, R. (2017). *The Great Convergence: Information Technology and the New Globalization*. Cambridge, MA: The Belknap Press of Harvard University Press.

Baldwin, R., & Robert-Nicoud, F. (2014). Trade-in-Goods and Trade-in-Tasks: An Integrating Framework. *Journal of International Economics, 92*(1), 51–62.

Baldwin, R., Evenett, S., & Low, P. (2009). Beyond Tariffs: Multilateralizing Non-Tariff RTA Commitments. In R. Baldwin & P. Low (Eds.), *Multilateralizing Regionalism: Challenges for the Global Trade System*. Geneva: World Trade Organization.

Bhagwati, J. N. (2008). *Termites in the Trading System: How Preferential Agreements Undermine Free Trade*. Oxford: Oxford University Press.

Bremmer, I. (2018). *Us vs. Them: The Failures of Globalism*. New York: Portfolio Penguin.

Collier, P. (2007). *The Bottom Billion: Why the Poorest Countries Are Failing and What Can Be Done About It?* Oxford: Oxford University Press.

Cuervo-Cazurra, A., Mudambi, R., & Pedersen, T. (2017). Globalization: Rising Skepticism. *Global Strategy Journal, 7*(2), 155–158.

Dobozi, I. (2018, July 10). Trade Relationship Is Much More Balanced. *Financial Times*.

European Commission. (2010). Trade, Growth and World Affairs. Retrieved October 2, 2018, from http://trade.ec.europa.eu/doclib/docs/2010/november/tradoc_146955.pdf.

European Commission. (2015). Trade for All: Towards a Responsible Trade and Investment Policy. Retrieved October 2, 2018, from http://trade.ec.europa.eu/doclib/docs/2015/october/tradoc_153846.pdf.

European Commission. (2017). Reflection Paper on Harnessing Globalisation. Retrieved October 2, 2018, from https://ec.europa.eu/commission/sites/beta-political/files/reflection-paper-globalisation_en.pdf.

European Commission. (2018a). EU Adopts Rebalancing Measures in Reaction to US Steel and Aluminium Tariffs. Retrieved October 2, 2018, from http://trade.ec.europa.eu/doclib/press/index.cfm?id=1868.

European Commission. (2018b). The Hour of European Sovereignty. State of the Union 2018. Retrieved October 2, 2018, from https://ec.europa.eu/commission/sites/beta-political/files/soteu2018-speech_en_0.pdf.

Evenett, S. J., & Fritz, J. (2017). *Will Awe Trump Rules? The 21st Global Trade Alert Report*. London: Centre for Economic Policy Research Press.

IMF. (2018a). *World Economic Outlook April 2018*. Washington, DC: International Monetary Fund.

IMF. (2018b). *Direction of Trade Statistics, Quarterly 06/18*. Washington, DC: International Monetary Fund.

Ingelhart, D., & Norris, P. (2017). Trump and the Populist Authoritarian Parties: The Silent Revolution in Reverse. *Perspectives on Politics, 15*, 443–454.

Kobrin, S. J. (2017). Bricks and Mortar in a Borderless World; Globalization, the Backlash, and the Multinational Enterprise. *Global Strategy Journal, 7*(2), 159–171.

Kommerskollegium. (2018a). *Regional Integration Works: The Trade Effects of Regional Trade Agreements*. Stockholm: National Board of Trade.

Kommerskollegium. (2018b). *The Use of the EUs Free Trade Agreements: Exporter and Importer Utilization of Preferential Tariffs*. Stockholm and Geneva: National Board of Trade and United Nations Conference on Trade and Development.

Krugman, P., & Venables, A. (1995). Globalization and the Inequality of Nations. *Quarterly Journal of Economics, 110*(4), 857–880.
Laplume, A. O., Petersen, B., & Pierce, J. M. (2016). Global Value Chains from a 3D Printing Perspective. *Journal of International Business Studies, 47*(5), 595–609.
Lindberg, L., & Alvstam, C. G. (2012a). The Ambiguous Role of the WTO in Times of Stalled Multilateral Negotiations and Proliferating FTAs in Asia. *International Negotiation, 17*(1), 165–189.
Lindberg, L., & Alvstam, C. G. (2012b). Interregional Trade Facing Repolarization: The EU Trade Negotiations with ASEAN Countries. In L. Oxelheim (Ed.), *EU-Asia in the Age of Repolarization of the Global Economy*. Singapore: World Scientific Press.
Malmström, C. (2018, July 27). Reform Rules-Based Trade Before It Is too Late. *Financial Times.*
Meyer, K. E. (2017). International Business in an Era of Anti-Globalization. *Multinational Business Review, 25*(2), 78–90.
Milanovic, B. (2016). *Global Inequality: A New Approach for the Era of Globalization*. Cambridge, MA: The Belknap Press of Harvard University Press.
Obstfeld, M. (2018, April 23). Targeting Specific Trade Deficits Is a Game of Whack-a-Mole. *Financial Times.*
Rodrik, D. (2011). *The Globalization Paradox*. Oxford: Oxford University Press.
Rodrik, D. (2017). *Straight Talk on Trade: Ideas for a Sane World Economy.* Princeton, NJ: Princeton University Press.
Ross, W. (2017, April 4). Donald Trump Will Make Trade Fair Again. *Financial Times.*
Stiglitz, J. E. (2017). *Globalization and Its Discontents Revisited: Anti-Globalization in the Era of Trump*. New York: WW Norton & Co.
Summers, L. (2018, June 5). US Trade Policy Violates Every Rule of Strategy. *Financial Times.*
Teigland, R., Holmberg, H., & Felländer, A. (2018). The Importance of Trust in a Digital Europe: Reflections on the Sharing Economy and Blockchains. In A. Bakardijeva Engelbrekt, N. Bremberg, A. Michalski, & L. Oxelheim (Eds.), *Trust in the European Union in Challenging Times*. Cham: Palgrave.
The Economist. (2017, January 28). The Retreat of the Global Company.
UNCTAD. (2013). *World Investment Report 2013, Global Value Chains: Investment and Trade for Development*. New York and Geneva: United Nations Conference on Trade and Development.
USTR. (2018). 2018 *Trade Policy Agenda and the 2017 Annual Report.* Washington, DC: Office of the United States Trade Representative. Retrieved October 2, 2018, from https://ustr.gov/about-us/policy-offices/press-office/reports-and-publications/2018/2018-trade-policy-agenda-and-2017.

Vahlne, J.-E., Ivarsson, I., & Alvstam, C. G. (2018). Are Multinational Enterprises in Retreat? The Internationalization and Globalization Process of Swedish MNEs Continues Unabatedly. *Multinational Business Review, 26*(2), 94–110.

Williamson, J. G. (2013). *Trade and Poverty: When the Third World Fell Behind*. Cambridge, MA: MIT Press.

Xi, J. P. (2017). Full Text of Xi Jinping's Keynote Speech at the World Economic Forum. Retrieved August 15, 2018, from http://www.china.org.cn/node_7247529/content_40569136.htm.

Zoellick, R. (2018, May 25). America Will Be the Loser from Trump's Focus on Trade Deficits. *Financial Times*.

Zurek, K. (2019). From "Trade and Sustainability" to "Trade for Sustainability" in EUExternal Trade Policy. In A. Bakardijeva Engelbrekt, N. Bremberg, A. Michalski, & L. Oxelheim (Eds.), *The European Union in a Changing World Order*. Cham: Palgrave.

CHAPTER 5

From "Trade *and* Sustainability" to "Trade *for* Sustainability" in EU External Trade Policy

Karolina Zurek

Introduction

Contemporary free trade agreements (FTAs) have developed to cover much more than traditional trade issues such as tariffs and quotas. As increasingly more areas are identified as trade-relevant, FTAs grow broader and broader. This can, on the one hand, be seen as a response to the complexity of contemporary trade reality. On the other, it is also a reflection of developments within trade policy itself. Trade is increasingly looked upon as a tool to generate inclusive economic growth and contribute to global sustainable development, and not least as a response to growing tendencies towards protectionism and the backlash against globalisation.

Since the 1990s, sustainable development has been an established element of EU's trade agenda, not the least with regard to free trade agreements. Ambitious chapters on trade and sustainable development (TSD chapters) recognise the socioeconomic and environmental implications of

K. Zurek (✉)
National Board of Trade in Sweden, Stockholm, Sweden
e-mail: Karolina.Zurek@kommers.se

A. Bakardjieva Engelbrekt et al. (eds.), *The European Union in a Changing World Order*,
https://doi.org/10.1007/978-3-030-18001-0_5

trade relations and aim to use trade relations between the parties to promote the implementation and enforcement of their international commitments in the field of labour and the environment. The European Commission's trade and investment strategy encompasses not only trade with goods and services, but also the idea of spreading European values, such as respect for human rights and the rule of law, through trade policy (European Commission 2015b). Having established sustainability as an indispensable objective of both trade policy and specific trade instruments, the focus has shifted in recent years from *inclusion* to *implementation* and *enforcement* of the EU's sustainable development commitments.

This broadening of the EU's trade agenda, and inclusion of a growing number of areas and concerns in their trade instruments, raised doubts about competence regarding the new "deep and comprehensive" free trade agreements. The question has arisen of whether they can still be considered covered by the EU's exclusive competence over the Common Commercial Policy, or if the new complexity and breadth of these agreements should imply the shared competence of the EU and the Member States. The debate was additionally sharpened by the unexpected outburst of popular resistance in many Member States towards the Transatlantic Trade and Investment Partnership agreement with the USA (TTIP), as well as the negative vote by Wallonia's regional parliament on the comprehensive trade agreements with Canada (CETA). As a result, the competence question has been put to the test by the Commission's request for an opinion from the Court of Justice of the European Union (CJEU) about competence required to enter into an FTA with the Republic of Singapore. In December 2016, the Advocate General delivered her opinion, which stated that the negotiated FTA between the EU and Singapore requires ratification by both the EU and all the Member States, as some of the chapters of the agreement, including the TSD chapter, go beyond the EU's exclusive trade competence. Half a year later, the CJEU confirmed the conclusion that national ratification was necessary. Interestingly, however, the Court's assessment of competence over the TSD chapter did not follow the Advocate General's argumentation. The Court judged that the TSD chapter falls under the EU's exclusive competence. This raises a question as to the consequences this may have for the future development of TSD chapters in FTAs, in terms of both their scope and implementation. It will also be interesting to observe whether the EU will be able to retain its high level of ambition with regard to trade and sustainability, especially with reference to the constantly changing world order.

The objective of this chapter is to explore the EU's ambitious sustainability agenda in the field of trade policy and to address questions of its implementation and enforcement. The chapter opens with an overview of connections between trade and sustainable development, and discusses their relevance in the contemporary trade reality and the changing world order. It then traces the development of EU engagement with sustainable development in the field of trade policy, with a special focus on sustainability provisions in FTAs. Furthermore, the chapter approaches questions of competence over trade policy and sustainability issues. It analyses the problem of the implementation and enforcement of TSD chapters in the EU's FTAs, and assesses the Commission's reform proposal and the efforts towards improvement already undertaken. The CJEU opinion of the EU-Singapore FTA is analysed, with an emphasis on the implications it may have for the future of sustainability agenda in EU FTAs. The chapter closes with a discussion on the challenges, and possibilities for improvement of the implementation and enforcement of sustainability provisions. A preliminary assessment of recent developments and a number of recommendations are offered to address some of the identified shortcomings. These are juxtaposed with the Commission's recent action plan for TSD implementation.

Links Between Trade and Sustainable Development

As demonstrated by Alvstam and Lindberg in this volume, the nature of trade and trade policies have significantly altered during the last decade. A number of parallel trends can be identified. Firstly, the emergence of global value chains and the geographical fragmentation of production processes have changed the character of trade flows and patterns of exchanges. Secondly, increasing "servicification" and digitalisation require a broadening of regulatory approaches to trade. Thirdly, the growing influence of business on trade patterns and trade rules has led to a certain degree of privatisation of trade regulation. Finally, as the socio-economic and geopolitical significance of trade has become clearer, trade issues have gained unprecedented attention from the media, NGOs and society at large. This has brought about a new type of awareness of the intended and the unintended effects of trade, and a call for increased transparency in trade policy and trade regulation. Furthermore, popular interest in the socio-economic and environmental implications of trade agreements requires a renewed commitment to responsible trade policy.

These changes are not the only reasons for the demand to link trade and sustainable development more closely. A similar message was sent in 2015 by the UN's new Sustainable Development Goals (SDGs), and the 2030 Agenda. The Agenda identifies trade as an important instrument with which to achieve sustainable development in all its three dimensions: economic, social and environmental. Trade is perceived as a tool to generate inclusive economic growth and poverty reduction, which in its turn contributes, directly or indirectly, to attaining all 17 goals and 169 targets. Trade is, however, not only recognised as an instrument in the Agenda, but also as a goal in itself. Goal 17, pertaining to implementation and cooperation, includes three directly trade-related targets, facilitating trade's sustainability promoting function. The SDGs and the 2030 Agenda can be seen as a paradigm shift for the relationship between trade and sustainable development. The focus has shifted from tackling the social and environmental consequences of economic growth, to having sustainability as a central objective for all policy areas, including trade policy. The relationship between the two policy areas has thus graduated to become more conditional and intertwined, in essence this entails a shift from "trade *and* sustainable development" to "trade *for* sustainable development".

The 2030 Agenda builds on the assumption that liberalising and regulating trade at the multilateral level is the best method to guarantee its contribution to sustainable development. Contemporary trade reality, however, does not necessarily follow this scenario. The regulation of global trade is indeed primarily based on the system developed under the umbrella of the World Trade Organisation (WTO). This system, however, is complemented by a large number of trade instruments adopted at plurilateral, regional, bilateral and unilateral levels. Trade liberalisation and regulation is happening simultaneously at all these levels, which on the one hand complicates the trade-policy context in which the Agenda is meant to be implemented, but on the other hand offers alternative opportunities to promote sustainable development through trade instruments. In the face of a slow-down of development within the WTO and the unclear future of the Doha Round, the majority of transnational trade regulation is today conducted through regional and bilateral trade agreements. At the same time, the modern FTAs incorporate an increasingly broader number of areas, such as labour, environment, transparency, intellectual property or public procurement. This creates much wider opportunities for trade to act as the engine of sustainable development compared to the options currently available within the WTO.

One of the methods developed to facilitate trade's contribution to sustainable development was the inclusion of sustainability provisions in trade agreements. In recent years, the number of FTAs which contain references to sustainable development issues has increased significantly. For example, the incidence of substantive environmental provisions in FTAs rose from 30 percent in 2010 to nearly 70 percent in 2012 (George 2014). Similarly, the number of trade agreements which include labour provisions grew from four in 1995, to 21 in 2005, to reach 58 in June 2013 (ILO 2016).

In terms of modes of incorporation of sustainability provisions in FTAs, a variety of approaches have been applied. In some FTAs, particularly the early ones, sustainability is merely mentioned in the preamble to the agreement. Some FTAs use separate side-agreements to address environmental or labour issues. An increasing number of FTAs, however, devote individual sections to sustainable development. The latter can take a form of separate articles or separate chapters on environment and labour, or in the case of the latest EU FTAs, one joint chapter on "Trade and Sustainable Development", the TSD chapter, which combines both environmental and labour provisions with common horizontal provisions.

Sustainability provisions in FTAs also vary significantly in terms of substance, ranging from declaratory clauses, through cooperation provisions, to actual commitments. It is primarily the latter that give rise to discussions on implementation and enforcement, although the interpretative relevance of the softer alternatives should not be dismissed (National Board of Trade 2016).

Last, but not least, sustainability provisions are of a significantly different character than other provisions of FTAs, which have the objective of trade liberalisation. Unlike the core FTA provisions, sustainability articles do not have the same primary objective of trade liberalisation, and consequently do not follow the same logic as the core trade liberalisation provisions of the agreement. Moreover, the commitments they lay down do not always resemble those of the other FTA provisions. As a result, the implementation, monitoring and evaluation of compliance with sustainability provisions can be more challenging, and may require specific tailor-made enforcement structures (National Board of Trade 2016).

Trade and Sustainable Development in EU FTAs: Policy and Practice

In the EU, the practice of including sustainability provisions in FTAs is a recent, yet well-established element of the common commercial policy (CCP). Early references to sustainable development in EU agreements, in the form of human rights clauses, date back to the early 1990s. The inclusion of substantive provisions in the body of the agreement, came, however, much later (Bartels 2013). The first sustainable development chapter was included in the 2008 EU-Cariforum Economic Partnership Agreement, and since then such chapters have become a systematic element of all EU trade agreements, and are present in all EU FTAs currently in force, namely with Cariforum, Central America, Georgia, Moldova, Columbia, Peru and Ecuador, South Korea and Japan. Sustainability chapters are also included in finalised, but not yet ratified, agreements with Singapore and Vietnam. Equivalent provisions, but divided into two chapters pertaining to labour and environment, are included in the Comprehensive Economic and Trade Agreement with Canada (CETA). Finally, all FTAs currently negotiated by the EU include a proposal for a sustainability chapter.

The overarching objective of TSD chapters is to engage the partner countries in a cooperative process involving civil society in strengthening the national implementation and enforcement of international labour and environmental standards. Through this cooperation, partner countries can use their trade relationships to reinforce their sustainability commitments, and to promote dialogue and involvement. Moreover, the inclusion of environmental and social provisions in a trade agreement is a clear signal that sustainability issues are on an equal footing with economic aspects of the parties' trade relationships, and are therefore to be treated with the same importance and engagement.

The EU's modern TSD chapters include, as a rule, the following components: (1) confirmation of the parties' commitments to respect and implement multilateral agreements in the field of labour and environmental protection; (2) the parties' rights to regulate domestic levels of protection; (3) a commitment not to use sustainability provisions in a protectionist manner and not to use a lowering of levels of protection in order to attract trade and investments; (4) specific commitments and cooperation areas in the field of labour and the environment, which are of relevance to the trade relationship between the FTA partners; (5) a commitment to promote trade and investments favouring sustainable development, such as trade with environmental goods and services, or the promotion of voluntary, incentive-based mechanisms and systems that promote the objective of sustainable development, including corporate social responsibility (CSR); (6) institutional structures to facilitate the implementation of TSD provisions, system of procedures, including the involvement of civil society, and a dedicated dispute settlement mechanism that does not involve the use of trade sanctions, and which differs from the dispute settlement system applicable to the other parts of the FTA.

In terms of substantive content, the provisions of sustainability chapters are built on references to existing rights and obligations as foreseen in international legal instruments on labour and the environment, mainly the regulatory heritage of the International Labour Organisation and multilateral environmental agreements, to which the trade partners are parties. The objective of sustainability chapters is, thus, not to create new obligations or commitments, but rather to promote cooperation between the parties in the implementation of their existing international commitments under multilateral labour and environmental law, in the areas which are of relevance to trade between those parties.

The EU Commission uses impact assessments as a means to facilitate the identification of the sustainability areas that are relevant to trade relationships between the parties, either in order to preclude their potentially negative implications or to encourage the positive contribution of increased trade between the parties to sustainable development. Before initiating new FTA negotiations, the Commission prepares an internally developed impact assessment (IA), which assesses the potential economic, social and environmental implications of the proposed agreement. In 1999, the Commission's trade directorate (DG Trade) developed a new, more advanced tool for assessing the sustainability consequences of trade agreements, the Sustainability Impact Assessment (SIA) (European Commission 2016). The SIA is initiated simultaneously with FTA negotiations, after the adoption of a negotiations mandate. It is developed by independent consultants and combines the use of various analytical tools, both quantitative and qualitative, and broad consultations with relevant stakeholders. The objective of SIA is to assess potential sustainability implications of the negotiated agreement in more detail, in terms of its economic, social and environmental impact, for both the EU and its future trade partner(s). The SIA's conclusions are meant to support the negotiations process, so as to allow the future agreement to adequately address the potential negative and positive sustainability impacts. To that effect, SIAs often include suggestions for complementary measures to minimise the foreseen negative consequences of trade liberalisation, and to maximise its positive effects and synergy potential. SIAs thus function as support tools in the negotiation process and in developing the future agreement, in particular the TSD chapter, facilitating the identification of focus areas for future cooperation between the parties (European Commission 2016). Since 2015, the SIA has included a specific assessment of the FTA's potential effects on human rights situations in partner countries (European Commission 2015a).

One of the major challenges of assessing the impact of TSD provisions, which was recently highlighted by researchers in the field of international environmental law, is the complexity of interdependencies (Harrison et al. 2016). It is, namely, difficult to analyse the actual effects of TSD provisions on labour and environmental situations in partner countries, separating their impact from the impact of other reforms both domestic and international, and from general global developments in the fields of trade and of the various dimensions of sustainability. It is therefore recommended that greater focus is placed on impact analysis *ex-post*, when the trade agreement has already entered into force and is being implemented, aiming to assess whether the TSD provisions are used effectively and if they work adequately together with the EU's trade related technical assistance (Harrison et al. 2016).

Competence Over EU Trade Policy After the Lisbon Treaty

Before beginning a detailed discussion about effectiveness, however, a brief look at the common commercial policy and the changes introduced through the Lisbon Treaty revision is called for. The CCP belongs, in line with Article 3(1)(e) TFEU, to the EU's exclusive competences. Pursuant to Article 207 TFEU, following the Lisbon Treaty revision, "the CCP shall be based on uniform principles, particularly with regard to tariff rates, the conclusion of tariff and trade agreements relating to trade in goods and services (…). The common commercial policy shall be conducted in the context of the principles and objectives of the Union's external action." The exercise of this competence shall, however, not affect the delimitation of competences between the European Union and Member States. One of the major changes brought about by the Lisbon Treaty, was embedding the EU trade policy into the Union's overall principles and objectives, in particular those that refer to external action. Consequently, the EU's trade competence ought to be exercised within the framework of the Treaties' general external objectives, which include sustainable development, free and fair trade and the promotion of human rights (Cremona 2017).

The Commission, which plays a strategic and major role in the exercise of the CCP, gave a clear signal that this normative framework is taken seriously, not the least with its 2015 strategy "Trade for All: towards a more responsible trade and investment policy" (European Commission 2015b). In the foreword to the strategy, EU trade commissioner Cecilia Malmström announces a trade policy that "will not only project our interests, but also our values" and which "involves trade agreements and trade preference programmes as levers to promote, around the world, values like sustainable development, human rights, fair and ethical trade and the fight against corruption". This approach is developed in a dedicated chapter of the strategy entitled "A trade and investment policy based on values", which on the one hand, presents a more responsive approach to the public's expectations of regulations and investment, and on the other, a trade agenda to promote sustainable development, human rights and good governance. In the context of FTAs, the strategy confirms that the aim of the systematic inclusion of provisions on trade and sustainable development is to maximise the potential of increased trade and investment for decent work and environmental protection, including the fight against climate change, and to engage with partner countries in a cooperative process fostering transparency and civil society involvement. As FTAs come into force, the EU needs to work on implementation and the effective use of sustainability provisions, including by offering the appropriate support through development cooperation (European Commission 2015b).

One of the Commission's main commitments is to focus on the implementation of the sustainable development dimension of FTAs, making it a core component of the enhanced partnership with the Member States, the European Parliament and stakeholders, and of dialogue with civil society. This requires prioritisation of the effective implementation of the core labour standards and health and safety at work, and prioritisation of work on the sustainable management and conservation of natural resources and the fight against climate change. This commitment will be exercised through the promotion of ambitious and innovative sustainable development chapters in all trade and investment agreements, which contain far reaching commitments on core labour standards, occupational health and safety and decent work in accordance with the ILO agenda, as well as far reaching commitments to environmental protection in relation to multilateral environmental agreements. It will furthermore be supported by offering improved connections between trade policy instruments and development aid action in order to assist trade partners in achieving the required levels of protection (European Commission 2015b).

The "Trade for All" strategy can, therefore, be seen as the Commission embracing the extension of the CCP competence introduced by the Lisbon Treaty. Submitting the CCP to the general external policy principles and objectives, including sustainable development, has amplified the role of non-economic policy objectives in the pursuit of the aim of gradual liberalisation of trade. This strengthened the EU's mandate to pursue a more value-driven trade policy in the framework of its exclusive CCP competence, as confirmed by the CJEU in its Singapore opinion which will be analysed below.

TSD Chapters in FTAs: From Inclusion to Implementation

Having established the inclusion of sustainability provisions in FTAs as a norm rather than an exception, and having the European Commission outspokenly committed to implementation, current debate turns towards an inquiry into the effectiveness of these sustainability provisions and their actual impact on labour and environment in the partner countries. With an ambitious role as the driver of sustainable development assigned to trade by the Sustainable Development Goals and the Commission's "Trade for All" strategy, these questions have increasing political significance.

In the context of international law *enforcement*, compliance scholarship has been divided between the proponents of two models: the managerial model and the sanction-oriented model. The *managerial model* advocates a cooperative, problem-solving approach to promoting compliance with international law (Chayes and Handler Chayes 1998). Compliance strategies should, here, focus on the actual causes of non-compliance and "manage" these through positive means, consisting of a blend of transparency, dispute settlement and capacity building (ibid). Departing from an assumption of growing international interdependence, the theory argues that states can now only realise their sovereignty through participation in various international regimes, which makes them rationally prone to comply in order to retain a good standing as a member of the international system (Brunnée 2006). The *sanction model*, is based on the assumption that in cases where treaties require states to depart significantly from what they would have done in the absence of the treaty, there is a strong incentive for non-compliance, and cooperation can only be ensured by sanctions that encompass a broad range of measures which create costs and remove benefits (Downs et al. 1996; Downs 1998). States and international organisations have built enforcement systems applicable to sustainability provisions in FTAs based on one of the two models.

The EU has developed an implementation system based on the managerial model, focusing on incentivising partner countries to work together with the Union on sustainability issues. Following this logic, TSD chapters are not linked to the FTA's general dispute settlement mechanism, which foresees the possibility of imposing trade sanctions in cases of violations of rules of the agreement, but build their own implementation and enforcement structures. The implementation of sustainability provisions is addressed through structured dialogues on sensitive issues, in joint projects and enhanced interaction with international bodies and civil society (Bartels 2013).

Firstly, EU FTAs provide for the development of a dedicated *institutional infrastructure* in order to facilitate coordinated activities, and to exercise management and oversight over the development of the relationships between the parties. They typically establish *contact points* whose main purpose is to facilitate communication between the parties in the implementation of the TSD chapters; and *committees* composed of senior government representatives of the relevant national authorities, which oversee the implementation of the relevant chapters, provide periodic reports and function as a forum to discuss and review cooperative activities and possible conflicts (National Board of Trade 2016).

Secondly, EU FTAs foresee various forms of *cooperation* between the parties, with the aim of achieving the objectives of the agreement, including those relevant to sustainability. This cooperation can include the development of common actions, the exchange of information and experts, the joint organisation of events and the facilitation of partnership, including with the private sector. FTAs can also establish increased cooperation under other international agreements, such as multilateral environmental agreements (MEAs), or with international institutions with acknowledged expertise and experience in the specific sustainability area, such as the International Labour Organisation (ILO).

Thirdly, FTAs provide for *public participation* in the implementation processes of sustainability provisions. To that effect, EU FTAs create specific institutional structures for public participation, such as Domestic Advisory Groups or Civil Society Dialogue mechanisms, the latter involving civil society organisations from both parties. Civil society's alternatives for involvement in FTAs can, thus, include both domestic and transnational mechanisms (National Board of Trade 2016).

Fourthly, EU FTAs use sustainability provisions that include *concrete commitments* or obligations, which require parties to recognise or implement certain rules, or abstain from certain actions, such as a provision where the parties commit to not weakening their environmental laws in order to secure trade advantage, or a commitment not to use environmental standards as disguised barriers to trade. FTAs also commonly contain commitments to implement multilateral agreements in the fields of the environment or labour, often specifying concrete agreements or addressing specific issues.

Fifthly, FTAs include provisions on *promoting voluntary instruments* and schemes that have the objective of enhancing sustainability performance. This may include voluntary auditing and reporting, market-based incentives, the voluntary sharing of information and expertise, and public-private partnerships, which can contribute to the achievement and maintenance of high levels of protection and complement domestic regulatory measures. In order to guarantee that such schemes are designed in a manner that maximises their environmental or social benefit and avoids the creation of unnecessary barriers to trade, FTAs can include specific criteria that such mechanisms should fulfil or contain references to internationally recognised standards and guidelines. As an example, modern EU FTAs contain provisions mobilising the parties to encourage enterprises to voluntarily adopt corporate social responsibility (CSR) initiatives addressing labour and environmental issues. Such provisions contain references to internationally recognised standards and guidelines in the field of CSR, including concrete international schemes.

Sixthly, FTAs typically include provisions for the monitoring and assessment of their sustainability implications. In the EU, they have so far primarily focused on *ex-ante* assessment for the purpose of facilitating preparation of the agreement, in the form of the SIA described in the previous section of this chapter. Although less attention has so far been given to the *ex-post* assessment of FTAs' sustainability impacts, we are now experiencing a move towards increased and more structured *ex-post* monitoring. References to *ex-post* assessment are, for example, included in the new "Handbook for trade sustainability impact assessment" issued by the Commission in 2016 (European Commission 2016).

Finally, TSD chapters in EU FTAs contain rules and *mechanisms for the resolution of conflicts* between the parties, which pertain to sustainability provisions. These mechanisms are primarily based on consultations, conciliatory activities and non-binding institutional arrangements, and on recourse to expertise, such as through the engagement of a panel of experts (National Board of Trade 2016).

TSD Chapter Put to the Test: Implementation Debate and Reform Proposals

Due to the limited history of the inclusion of TSD chapters in EU FTAs, a full-fledged evaluation of their effectiveness would be premature. This is amplified by the fact that the managerial model for the implementation of sustainable provisions relies on the idea of building a long-term relationship of trust and cooperation, and thus focuses on achieving long-term progress, rather than quick fixes. The ambition of addressing structural problems, requiring complex reforms and gradual implementation process, makes quantitative assessment on a short term basis rather difficult. Still, some progress is visible and is being reported, as discussed for example in Harrison's research (Harrison et al. 2016). Moreover, as substantive sustainability provisions in EU FTAs are primarily based on references to international agreements and their implementation is linked with institutional and procedural structures developed by those agreements, it is often hard to assess which portion of the aggregate sustainability gain can be assigned to the provisions in FTAs. This can be explained by the fact that the actual implementation of commitments in other international agreements, in the field of labour or the environment, is primarily executed by institutional structures specific to these agreements. For example, where a provision in a TSD chapter contains a commitment to cooperation to effectively implement a specific ILO convention, this implementation is going to take effect under the ILO structures. The role of the relevant TSD provision in a trade agreement is to additionally strengthen, support and facilitate this process in the framework of the trade relationship between the parties (National Board of Trade 2017).

Through this approach, EU FTAs contribute to strengthening the existing multilateral governance structures without creating a parallel set of bilateral rules on labour and the environment. Other notable outcomes include establishing or strengthening civil society structures, which is especially significant in the partner countries where the tradition of civil society involvement has been very weak, in particular in terms of involvement in trade matters. A number of implementation activities should also be mentioned, including work with non-discrimination in the labour market in EU-Korea, ILO projects in El Salvador and Guatemala on implementing fundamental conventions on the freedom of association, collective bargaining and non-discrimination, a dialogue with Colombia on the implementation of the Convention on International Trade in Endangered Species of Wild Fauna and Flora (CITES), and projects in cooperation with the ILO and OECD on corporate social responsibility in Asia and Latin America (European Commission 2017a).

Despite progress in the short implementation period of EU TSD chapters, there has been criticism of the effectiveness of the EU's trade and sustainability agenda. The main source of criticism is that the current system, where TSD provisions are not linked to the general dispute settlement mechanisms and trade sanctions, does not include the ability to punish partner countries that do not live up to their sustainability commitments. Thus, EU TSD chapters are perceived as lacking "teeth," especially when compared to the solutions applied by other strong negotiating partners (Young 2015). This critique, and the heated debate that followed, evolved during negotiations of the Transatlantic Trade and Investment Partnership (TTIP) (a trade agreement negotiated between the EU and the US). Unlike the EU, the US applies a sanctions-based model for implementing sustainability provisions, and the meeting of the two at the same negotiating table led to the recognition and vivid discussion on the consequences of this discrepancy. With a transparency policy applied by the Commission for the first time in trade negotiations, and the inclusive model of stakeholder involvement, the TTIP negotiations have received unprecedented popular attention and media coverage. The main objects of criticism from civil society were the system for investment protection and the provisions for sustainable development.

Before moving on to discussing the Commission's response to the TTIP challenge, a few words about the US model are called for. The logic behind the US system of TSD implementation is significantly different from that applied by the EU. TSD provisions in US FTAs are primarily focused on ensuring that domestic producers do not suffer the economic consequences of lower labour and environmental standards in partner countries, rather than on strengthening existing international regulations in the field of sustainability in order to guarantee a level playing field. As a consequence, substantive TSD provisions in US FTAs emphasise upholding domestic regulation of labour and the environment, and a prohibition to lower domestic levels of protection (Ebert and Posthuma 2011). The provisions refer to fundamental labour standards and to selected environmental agreements. The overarching assumption in the US system is that partner countries will be more prone to uphold the levels of protection and strengthen domestic implementation of labour and environmental provisions if there is a risk of negative economic consequences in cases of non-compliance. In contrast, the EU can be said to have a more balanced approach where the parties, on the one hand, confirm their individual right to regulate the levels of labour and environmental protection. On the other hand, the parties commit to uphold their levels of protection and not use their lowering as a means to achieve competitive advantage, in terms of trade and investments.

A fully-fledged analysis of the effectiveness of the sanctions-based model goes beyond the scope of this chapter, but it can, however, be established that the empirical evidence so far is rather limited and ambiguous. Until now, a breach of labour or environmental commitments by a US trade partner has never led to the application of trade sanctions (Ebert and Posthuma 2011). Although the US has raised a number of relevant complaints against trade partners such as Guatemala, Bahrain, Honduras, the Dominican Republic, Mexico and Paraguay, a dispute settlement panel has only been established in one case (with Guatemala). The panel, established in 2011, concluded in its final report delivered in June 2017 that it was not possible to establish a failure by Guatemala to implement the labour provisions of the FTA. One of the main reasons for this conclusion was that it was impossible to establish that Guatemala's failure to effectively implement domestic labour regulation affected trade between Guatemala and the US. Since the link between the breach of labour regulation and trade between the parties could not be established, trade sanctions could not be applied.

Despite the fact that the TTIP negotiations have now been indefinitely postponed, the Commission was required to confront the criticism and address the issue of the effectiveness of TSD chapters in both existing and future FTAs in a constructive way. The Commission's reply was twofold: an effort was made to assess the state of the art in the implementation of the existing agreements; and conceptual work and broad discussion on possible improvements to TSD implementation were initiated.

In order to support its first effort, the Commission established an expert group on trade and sustainable development (TSD-expert group) composed of representatives of all Member States, in order to improve the exchange of information and coordination of activities between the EU institutions and national administrations. The group's work began by developing a broad inventory of activities in the field of trade and sustainability, ongoing and planned by the Commission and Member States with the EU's trade partner countries. During quarterly meetings of the group, the inventory is updated and discussed in order to guarantee coordination and facilitate cooperation, streamlining the use of both the EU's and national resources, and efforts. The meetings also provide an opportunity for the Commission to update the Member State representatives on current developments in negotiations of TSD chapters in future FTAs and in the implementation of the TSD chapters already in force. Moreover, the priorities, plans and activities of both the Commission and Member States in a number of sustainability areas, such as gender, CSR, or fair and ethical trade are discussed. The group was also the main forum for the debate on the effectiveness of TSD chapters and on reforming their implementation and enforcement process. The debate was initiated in July 2017 by issuing a non-paper on the TSD chapters in FTAs (European Commission 2017). In the document, the Commission attempts to assess the current implementation system and its functioning so far. It juxtaposes the ongoing activities, achievements and developments with the criticism of the EU's model. Finally the Commission puts forward two reform options: (1) a more assertive partnership on TSD, and (2) a model with sanctions.

According to the first option, the EU should continue with, and build on the current TSD implementation model, with ambitious content in the TSD chapters, and strengthening its implementation in a number of available ways. The Commission identified a need to strengthen collaboration with the ILO and MEA international bodies with the aim of a closer and better-structured cooperation for the increased monitoring and implementation of commitments. Second, it called for improved action to react to allegations of non-compliance by enhancing the transparency of the complaint mechanism and clarifying the steps of the procedure. It has to be pointed out that the fully-fledged application of the dispute settlement system under the TSD chapter has not been tested yet, which in the absence of praxis, drives the need for a better understanding of its functioning, its components and its potential effects, at least in theory. Third, the Commission foresees the need for a greater focusing on TSD implementation. This can be done by developing individual partner country strategies, and identifying priority areas in the context of each concrete trade relation. This should be strengthened by enhanced efforts of awareness raising and training on TSD commitments, which will facilitate the identification of possible shortcomings at an early stage.

Fourth, the non-paper recommends the improved monitoring and follow-up of all TSD issues raised at the government level, involving all other relevant sources, such as the SDG reporting mechanism and other UN reporting instruments. This should be facilitated by a more result-oriented regular dialogue with partner countries to define and address specific priority areas and shortcomings in terms of TSD commitments. Early and continuous engagement to achieve ratification of the fundamental ILO conventions is specifically emphasised. Fifth, more assertive use of all existing TSD tools, including dispute settlement, is anticipated. Sixth, the paper highlights the need for increased partnership, both with the Member States and with civil society. The Commission also wishes to enhance partnership with Member States and their embassies, as well as cooperation with EU delegations in order to streamline and more effectively use the resources available for TSD implementation. The Commission wishes to enhance the advisory role of civil society by improving the functioning of the Domestic Advisory Groups and the Joint Civil Society Forums under EU FTAs.

The second alternative put forward by the Commission in the non-paper builds on the sanctions-based model currently applied by, for example, the US and Canada (European Commission 2017). In accordance with this alternative model, the sustainability chapter is linked directly to the agreement's general dispute settlement system, which offers the potential to apply trade sanctions in cases of non-compliance, whenever the breach affects trade between the parties. The reasoning given by the Commission, when introducing this option, does not focus on the model itself, but rather on its suitability for the EU's established approach to tackling sustainability issues in trade agreements. The Commission observes that the majority of complaints regarding the implementation and enforcement of TSD provisions in FTAs concerns breaches which are relevant in the context of trade, but which do not have a direct and measurable impact on the bilateral trade exchange between the parties. In accordance with the logic of the sanctions-based model, they would rarely lead to a dispute settlement procedure, and even more seldom, to the actual application of trade sanctions.

Moreover, the Commission argues that it can be difficult to apply the sanctions system to the EU-type of TSD provisions, which refer to and anchor the obligations in other sources of international law, such as the ILO conventions and MEAs, rather than national labour or environmental regulation. Such a reform would probably require a revision of how the international institutions that have a monitoring role with regard to these international legal instruments should be involved in the process of enforcing TSD provisions. Finally, the Commission raises a concern that the introduction of sanctions can jeopardise long-term relationships with trade partners, which in turn is the basis for EU TSD strategy based on promoting trust and dialogue, generating incentives and cooperation, and on capacity building (European Commission 2017).

The Commission's non-paper was presented for discussion in the European Parliament, the Trade Policy Committee (TPC), which is the Council's body for trade policy issues, for the European Economic and Social Committee (EESC), and for representatives of civil society. Finally the non-paper was discussed within the new TSD expert group, where all Member States were given an opportunity to react and comment on the Commission's proposal. Based on the reactions received, the Commission issued another non-paper in February 2018, "Trade and Sustainable Development chapters in EU Free Trade Agreements" developing and defining the way forward (European Commission 2018). It builds on the consensus that the implementation of TSD chapters should be increased and improved, retaining the current broad and ambitious approach. In the absence of consensus on a sanctions-based model, the Commission proposed a set of 15 concrete and practical actions to substantially strengthen and improve TSD implementation, categorised under four broad headings: (1) Working Together; (2) Enabling Civil Society and Social Partners to Play a Greater Role in Implementation; (3) Delivering; and (4) Transparency and Communication. The Commission also emphasises that this list is not exhaustive and that further measures and actions can be undertaken. The idea is that developments with TSD implementation should be analysed on a continuous basis and, based on this analysis, additional measures be proposed if required. The needs assessment should be undertaken within five years at the latest (European Commission 2018).

The proposed measures include, for example, closer partnership with the European Parliament and with international organisations, empowering civil society and facilitating its participation in implementation, and broadening the scope of its engagement beyond the TSD chapter. The non-paper proposes streamlining TSD implementation activities to fit individual country priorities, while at the same time enhancing the scope of support measures including regular reviews, an implantation handbook, and making funding available to facilitate domestic reforms by trade partners. Finally, under the heading "Assertive Enforcement," the Commission is committing to take all possible action to improve compliance, including the use of a dispute settlement mechanism with a panel of experts, which has not yet been tested in practice in the framework of TSD implementation (European Commission 2018). Some of these proposals will be discussed further below.

Meanwhile, propelled by the timely and bumpy CETA ratification process, with an unexpected "no" vote from the Belgian region of Wallonia, which could in fact jeopardise the entry into force of the entire agreement and nullify the many years of negotiations effort, the question of the competence to enter into EU FTAs returned to the agenda. The debate culminated with the CJEU decision on the trade agreement between the EU and its Member States with the Republic of Singapore of May 2017, the so called Singapore Opinion (Opinion 2/15), which will be analysed in more detail below.

The CJEU's Opinion on the EU-Singapore FTA and Its Implications for the Future of the Sustainability Agenda in EU Trade Agreements

On the 16th of May 2017, the CJEU delivered its long awaited opinion on whether the EU had the requisite competence to sign and conclude the Free Trade Agreement with Singapore, which belongs to the "new generation" of deep and comprehensive FTAs. More specifically, the Court was asked by the Commission to establish which provisions of the agreement fall within the Union's exclusive competence, which provisions of the agreement fall within the Union's shared competence, and whether any provision in the agreement falls within the exclusive competence of the Member States. If the Court found that some provisions fell under shared or Member State exclusive competence, the FTA would require ratification by all Member States as a mixed agreement.

The Court examined the agreement chapter by chapter, and established that the agreement fell within the scope of the EU's exclusive competence, with the exception of provisions pertaining to investments and investment protection, insofar as they relate to non-direct investment between the European Union and the Republic of Singapore, the provisions on Investor-State Dispute Settlement, and selected provisions of other chapters related thereto. This means that, according to the Court, the provisions of the TSD chapter fall within the EU's exclusive competence (Cremona 2018; Lavranos 2017).

The Court's analysis of the TSD chapter follows two lines of reasoning. On the one hand, the Court examined the relevant Treaty provisions which define competence over the common commercial policy and their relationship to other policy areas. On the other hand, it reviewed individual TSD provisions, scrutinised their relationship to trade between the parties, and clarified their relevance for the entire agreement.

The Court based its reasoning on the significance of the Lisbon Treaty reform for the definition and anchoring of the common commercial policy (CCP), which differs considerably from the relevant provisions of its predecessor—the Treaty establishing the European Communities (TEC). In accordance with Article 207 (1) TFEU the CCP "shall be conducted in the context of the principles and the objectives of the Union's external action". These principles and objectives as stipulated in Articles 21 and 22 TEU, include, among others, fostering sustainable economic, social and environmental development, which includes preserving and improving the quality of the environment and the sustainable management of global natural resources, and the universality and indivisibility of human rights and fundamental freedoms, respect for human dignity, the principles of equality and solidarity. Furthermore, the Court considered Articles 9 and 11 TFEU, which require that "in defining and implementing its policies and activities, the Union shall take into account requirements linked to the promotion of a high level of employment, the guarantee of adequate social protection, the fight against social exclusion, and a high level of education, training and protection of human health", and that "environmental protection requirements must be integrated into the definition and implementation of the Union's policies and activities, in particular with a view to promoting sustainable development". Moreover, the Court referred to Article 3.5 TFEU: "in its relations with the wider world, the Union shall uphold and promote its values and interests and contribute to the protection of its citizens [and] contribute to peace, security, the sustainable development of the Earth, solidarity and mutual respect among peoples, free and fair trade, eradication of poverty and the protection of human rights...". Based on this reasoning the Court concluded that the objective of sustainable development forms an integral part of the common commercial policy.

With regard to the substance of the chapter, the Court, after careful consideration of its individual provisions, concluded that the TSD chapter governs trade between the EU and Singapore "by ensuring that it takes place in compliance with those agreements and that no measure adopted under them is applied so as to create arbitrary or unjustifiable discrimination or a disguised restriction on such trade." The TSD chapter must therefore be considered to have direct and immediate effects on that trade.

In accordance with the Court it would therefore "not be coherent to hold that the provisions liberalising trade between the European Union and a third State fall within the common commercial policy and that those which are designed to ensure that the requirements of sustainable development are met when that liberalisation of trade takes place fall outside it".

Before moving on to the reasoning about the potential future implications of the CJEU opinion, it is important to add that the Court's interpretation of competence over the TSD chapter went against the submission of Advocate General on the case. Advocate General Eleanor Sharpston built her reasoning on juxtaposing the trade and non-trade objectives of EU external action. She concluded that some components of the TSD chapter, namely the provisions concerning labour protection standards and environmental protection standards, clearly fall outside the scope of EU exclusive CCP competence, and should be handled under shared competence (Kleimann 2017).

Advocate General Sharpston argues that "despite the Parties' stated intention not to harmonise labour or environmental standards, a significant number of provisions in Chapter Thirteen neither *impose a form of trade conditionality* (by enabling the other Party to adopt trade sanctions in case of non-compliance or by making a specific trade benefit dependent on compliance with labour and environmental standards) nor *otherwise regulate the use of commercial policy instruments* as a means to promote sustainable development". These TSD provisions must, therefore, be understood as essentially seeking to achieve minimum standards of (respectively) labour protection and environmental protection in the EU and Singapore, *in isolation* from their possible effects on trade. Those provisions thus clearly fall outside the scope of the CCP.

This discrepancy between the opinion of the Advocate General and that of the Court could have significant consequences for the future interpretation and application of the Court's judgement. It has to be emphasised that this kind of disagreement between the Advocate General and the Court happens relatively seldomly, and rarely remains unnoticed. It may, therefore, contribute to certain degree of caution about relying on the Court's verdict, as the establishment of the EU's exclusive competence over TSD questions by the Court may be seen as somewhat dubious or weaker. As a result, decision makers may be more reserved about relying on the opinion, in order not to risk opening Pandora's Box and provoking another revision of the competence question (Kleimann 2017).

What does the Singapore Opinion mean for the future of sustainability work in EU FTAs? Such a clear signal from the Court that sustainable development provisions fall under the CCP, making the EU a sole master thereof, might contribute to the strengthening of the Commission's mandate with regard to this area. This may support the Commission's efforts to pursue an ambitious sustainability agenda and facilitate support for the actions undertaken to that affect. (Van der Loo 2017).

On the other hand, however, a significant proportion of implementation effort is made by the Member States. The Court's interpretation of competence division may be read as releasing Member States from their responsibility for sustainability work, including their participation in the implementation of TSD chapter in partner countries. This could significantly weaken the implementation potential that has been communally built over the last couple of years.

The Singapore Opinion could also potentially have negative consequences on the future development of TSD chapters in EU FTAs. It is possible to imagine that the TSD chapter as agreed in the Singapore-EU FTA will be treated as an acknowledged standard, and will establish a ceiling for future FTAs. This would make it more difficult to raise the level of ambition for TSD provisions in the future, both in terms of their depth and their width. Areas not covered by the Singapore-EU FTA could be difficult to introduce into future FTAs, as they could be considered as not having received the Court's competence clearance. This issue may gain importance now that the EU is to begin negotiations with trade partners expressing high sustainability ambitions and wishing to include in their FTA provisions in areas which were not previously explicitly included in EU FTAs, such as gender equality. It may also be of relevance for the ongoing discussion on strengthening the implementation and enforcement of TSD chapters, where one of the options discussed would require a complete amendment of the implementation structure and the introduction of provisions linking the TSD chapter to the dispute settlement chapter, allowing for recourse to trade sanctions in case of a breach of sustainability provisions by any of the parties to the agreement. Some of these limitations could possibly be by-passed by recourse to side-agreements on the subject areas going beyond the Singapore model, but the extent to which this would be practical is rather uncertain.

Last, but not least, the significance of the Court's statement in paragraph 161 of the opinion should be considered, where the Court holds the following: "… the link which the provisions of Chapter 13 of the envisaged agreement display with trade between the European Union and the Republic of Singapore is also specific in nature because a breach of the provisions concerning social protection of workers and environmental protection, set out in that chapter, authorises the other Party—in accordance with the rule of customary international law codified in Article 60 (1) of the Convention on the law of treaties, signed in Vienna on 23 May 1969, which applies in relations between the EU and third states—to terminate or suspend the liberalisation, provided for in the other provisions of the envisaged agreement, of that trade". It is the first such direct and open acknowledgement of the potential for sanctioning a breach of sustainability provisions in FTAs, which is not stated in the text of the agreement but stems from the general principles of public international law, in this case the Vienna Convention. Moreover, it goes against the assessment of the Advocate General, who draws a dividing line between the essential element clause on human rights and democratic principles on the one hand, and the provisions of the TSD chapter on the other. She argues that as the breach of the essential element clause explicitly authorises a party to suspend or terminate the agreement in accordance with Article 44 par. 4 (b) of the Partnership and Cooperation Agreement between the European Union and its Member States, of the one part, and the Republic of Singapore, of the other part (PCA), while a breach of any of the provisions of Chapter 13 does not automatically give rise to such a possibility. This was in fact one of the arguments of the Advocate General's decision on the competence over the TSD chapter which differs from that of the Court.

She argues that this is an indication of the fact that, unlike the essential element clause, the provisions of the TSD chapter seek to achieve minimum standards of labour protection and environmental protection in the EU and Singapore, in isolation from their possible effect on trade, and thus clearly fall outside the common commercial policy.

Paragraph 161 of the Court's opinion can be read as a reply to the popular criticism of the EU logic of TSD chapters in FTAs, in particular the claim that sustainability provisions in EU FTAs lack enforcement potential as they are not linked to the general dispute settlement systems and the possibility it offers to apply trade sanctions (Cremona 2018). Circumventing this system and connecting a breach of sustainability provisions directly to responsibility under public international law can have a range of interesting consequences. Firstly and paradoxically, this can make actual enforcement of serious breaches of sustainability commitments easier, as it would not require a proof of its effect on trade, which is otherwise necessary if trade sanctions are to be considered, and which, as demonstrated by the US-Guatemala dispute, is very difficult to successfully argue. Secondly, however, it can make the enforcement of TSD provisions as political as that of the essential element clauses. The suspension or termination of the agreement is a serious consequence and that would surely only be considered in cases of the most severe breaches. Nevertheless, it rhymes with the general logic of the EU's approach to sustainability provisions in FTAs, according to which cooperation and incentive creation should be the primary form of implementation, while any form of sanctioning should be treated as a last resort for particularly grave breaches. It can also be seen as an important message to the public, which has recently been particularly vocal about the shortcomings of a system which does not seem to offer sanctions in cases of serious breaches.

Conclusions: Stepping Up Monitoring and Strategic Partnerships

This concluding section revisits the central questions posed at the beginning of the chapter, building upon the assessment of developments traced above. How can the enforcement of the EU's TSD chapters be strengthened? Can the EU retain its ambitious trade and sustainability agenda in the increasingly turbulent world order? On the one hand, high levels of sustainability ambition can make EU FTAs progressively more complex and difficult to conclude. On the other hand, it would be hard and undesirable for the EU to scale down, especially given the current negative global developments, with rising protectionism and "minimalist" trade policy conducted by some of the strongest economic actors, not the least the US. The question, thus, remains, how to guarantee that these ambitious commitments are put into action and realised.

In my view, the process should begin with the European Commission undertaking a serious overview of activities pertaining to TSD implementation, delivered or pending delivery by the EU and the Member States. A number of attempts at such an overview have been undertaken, but neither the activity list prepared regularly by the Commission services and presented to the TSD expert group, nor the recent Report on Implementation of Free Trade Agreements, seem to give an overarching picture of the actual implementation effort (European Commission 2017a). Seen from a long-term perspective, the institutionalisation of a comprehensive *ex-post* assessment would be advisable, which would entail an analysis of the agreement's factual impact on environment and labour. Such an exercise would significantly facilitate the identification of loopholes and challenges, and an assessment of the effectiveness of various practices and methodologies applied, enabling the creation of a catalogue of successful practices to be prioritised in future implementation efforts. Moreover, it would make it possible to address some of the most common criticisms of the EU implementation model, namely insufficient information about TSD implantation and its tangible results, facilitating constructive communication about the enforcement and effects of the EU TSD agenda.

Secondly, there seems to be significant potential for improvement in terms of communication. There is a need to be more transparent and report comprehensively on the actual activities undertaken in the course of TSD implementation and on the tangible results achieved. It is, above all, necessary to be open about the logic, possibilities and limitations of the EU TSD model. The specificity of this model, based on references to other international agreements and institutional dependency resulting therefrom, may require clarification. It is also necessary to clearly articulate the need for establishing a long-term relationship between the parties, in order to contribute to sustainable change through open dialogue and credible commitment. It would make it easier to avoid creating an unrealistic expectation on the part of some stakeholders that FTAs will bring positive change overnight and address all challenging areas at once.

Thirdly, much more effort should be put into establishing the explicit and direct involvement of the ILO and the MEA institutions in TSD implementation and monitoring. Arguably, a great deal has already been achieved to harness cooperation with the ILO, for example by engaging their specific expertise and knowledge of labour-related challenges with concrete partner countries in monitoring and implementation, including through joint technical assistance projects. Moreover, although the Commission acknowledges this need, it proposes a rather abstract commitment to closer cooperation with other international organisations (European Commission 2018). What would be worth considering is a number of concrete alliances. Possible examples of strengthening cooperation with relevant international institutions include direct references to their role in TSD implementation, participation in implementation activities, and systematic partnership in technical assistance projects. Introducing a form of co-responsibility for implementation, enforcement and monitoring could further reduce the risk of undermining the multilateral structures and at the same strengthen the legitimacy of TSD implementation.

Fourthly, although the Commission's action plan devotes more than one of the proposed commitments to strengthening the role of civil society in TSD implementation and monitoring, it still does not see the need to establish a specific procedure for addressing complaints from stakeholders. One of the most commonly recurring points of criticism of the current TSD setup was precisely the lack of a formal structured complaint mechanism, which would make civil society's role in TSD monitoring more explicit and more effective. A clear procedure for the acknowledgement of complaints, an institutional framework for their processing and time framework for various stages of the procedure would significantly strengthen the transparency and legitimacy of the process, additionally creating pressure on the party in question to adequately address the contested issue (National Board of Trade 2018).

Last, but not least, the role of the private sector in TSD implementation has still not been sufficiently acknowledged and put into use in the EU FTA context. Globally, in the framework of the SDGs and the 2030 Agenda, the private sector is seen as a crucial actor in the implementation effort. At the EU level, the updated "Aid for Trade" strategy makes direct reference to the need to engage the private sector in supporting trade and productive capacity (European Commission 2017b). In the framework of TSD implementation, the challenge is to make this role concrete. The private sector's financing and expertise could be used to support the implementation of necessary reforms, especially in partner countries with significant sustainability challenges. Acknowledging their different roles, capacities and fields of activity, measures undertaken by public and private actors can be better streamlined to support efforts in challenging sectors. Parallels, here, can be drawn with ongoing public-private initiatives in the field of trade and sustainable development, such as the Bangladesh Sustainability Compact (Joint Statement 2013). Such cooperation has the potential to bring mutual benefits. Private sector actors with advanced sustainability policies, who engage in in-depth due diligence and apply private codes of conduct, tend to have a great deal of knowledge and expertise, not only about the sustainability challenges at stake, but also about ways of addressing them in a value chain. This expertise and capacity can be used to support action at the government level in increasing levels of protection, and to implement national regulations for labour and environmental protection. This can benefit the private sector as well, through strengthening a business friendly environment and encouraging reforms that facilitate their business activities, particularly in complex markets. The business community needs to be better informed about the relevance of TSD provisions in FTAs and their relevance for establishing and maintaining a business friendly environment, and a level playing field for all actors. This would also make it easier for the private sector to see their own role in TSD implementation and, hopefully, to generate their support for necessary reforms.

References

Bartels, L. (2013). Human Rights and Sustainable Development Obligations in EU Free Trade Agreements. *Legal Issues of Economic Integration, 40*(4), 297–314.

Brunnée, J. (2006). Enforcement Mechanisms in International Law and International Environmental Law. In U. Beyerlin, P. T. Stoll, & R. Wolfrum (Eds.), *Ensuring Compliance with Multilateral Environmental Agreements. A Dialogue Between Practitioners and Academia*. Leiden: Brill.

Chayes, A., & Handler Chayes, A. (1998). *The New Sovereignty: Compliance with International Regulatory Agreements*. Cambridge: Harvard University Press.

Cremona, M. (2017). *A Quiet Revolution: The Common Commercial Policy Six Years After the Treaty of Lisbon*. Stockholm: Swedish Institute of European Policy Studies.

Cremona, M. (2018). Shaping EU Trade Policy Post-Lisbon: Opinion 2/15 of 16 May 2017. *European Constitutional Law Review, 14*, 231–259.

Downs, G. W. (1998). Enforcement and the Evolution of Cooperation. *Michigan Journal of International Law, 19*, 319–344.
Downs, G. W., Rocke, D. M., & Barsoom, P. N. (1996). Is the Good News About Compliance Good News About Cooperation? *International Organisation, 50*(3), 379–406.
Ebert, F. C., & Posthuma, A. (2011). *Labour Provisions in Trade Arrangements: Current Trends and Perspectives.* Geneva: ILO/IILS.
European Commission. (2015a). Guidelines on the Analysis of Human Rights Impacts in Impact Assessments of Trade-related Policy Initiatives. Retrieved August 31, 2018, from http://trade.ec.europa.eu/doclib/docs/2015/july/tradoc_153591.pdf.
European Commission. (2015b). Trade for All: Towards a More Responsible Trade and Investment Policy. Retrieved August 31, 2018, from http://trade.ec.europa.eu/doclib/docs/2015/october/tradoc_153846.pdf.
European Commission. (2016). Handbook for Trade and Sustainability Impact Assessment. 2nd edition. Retrieved August 31, 2018, from http://trade.ec.europa.eu/doclib/docs/2016/april/tradoc_154464.PDF.
European Commission. (2017, July 11). Non-paper of the Commission Services on "Trade and Sustainable Development (TSD) Chapters in EU Free Trade Agreements (FTAs)". WK 8022/2017 INIT. Brussels.
European Commission. (2017a, November 9). Report from the Commission to the European Parliament, the Council, the European Economic Committee and the Committee of the Regions on *Implementation of Free Trade Agreements*, 1 January 2016–31 December 2016, COM(2017) 654 final.
European Commission. (2017b, November 13). Communication from the Commission to the European Parliament, the Council, the European Economic Committee and the Committee of the Regions *Achieving Prosperity through Trade and Investment. Updating the 2007 Joint EU Strategy on Aid for Trade*, COM(2017) 667 final.
European Commission. (2018, February 26). Non-paper of the Commission services on "Trade and Sustainable Development (TSD) chapters in EU Free Trade Agreements (FTAs)". WK 2419/2018 INIT. Brussels.
George, C. (2014). Environmental and Regional Trade Agreements. Emerging Trends and Policy Drivers. *OECD Trade and Environment Working Papers 2014/02.* Retrieved August 31, 2018, from https://www.oecd-ilibrary.org/trade/environment-and-regional-trade-agreements_5jz0v4q45g6h-en.
Harrison, J., Campling, L., Richardson, B., & Smith, A. (2016). Can Labour Provisions Work Beyond Border? Evaluating the Effects of EU Free Trade Agreements. *International Labour Review, 155*(3), 357–382.
International Labour Organisation. (2016). *Assessment of Labour Provisions in Trade and Investment Agreements.* Geneva: ILO.

Joint statement. (2013, July 8). *Staying Engaged: A Sustainability Compact for Continuous Improvements in Labour Rights and Factory Safety in the Ready-Made Garment and Knitwear Industry in Bangladesh.* Geneva. Retrieved August 31, 2018, from http://trade.ec.europa.eu/doclib/docs/2013/july/tradoc_151601.pdf.

Kleimann, D. (2017). Reading Opinion 2/15: Standards of Analysis, the Court's Discretion and the Legal View of the Advocate General. EUI Working Paper RSCAS 2017/23. Retrieved August 31, 2018, from http://cadmus.eui.eu/bitstream/handle/1814/46104/RSCAS_2017_23REVISED.pdf?sequence=4.

Lavranos, N. (2017). Mixed Exclusivity: The CJEU's Opinion on the EU-Singapore FTA. *European Investment Law and Arbitration Review, 2*, 3–34.

National Board of Trade Sweden. (2016). Implementation and Enforcement of Sustainable Development Provisions in Free Trade Agreements – Options for Improvement. Retrieved August 31, 2018, from https://www.kommers.se/publikationer/Rapporter/2016/Implementation-and-enforcement-of-sustainable-development-provisions-in-free-trade-agreements%2D%2Doptions-for-improvement/.

National Board of Trade Sweden. (2017). Trade and Social Sustainability. An Overview and Analysis. 2017: 2. Retrieved August 31, 2018, from https://www.kommers.se/publikationer/Rapporter/2017/Trade-and-social-sustainability/.

National Board of Trade Sweden. (2018). Possible Tools for Strengthened Implementation of Sustainable Development Provisions in Free Trade Agreements (FTAs). Retrieved August 31, 2018, from https://www.kommers.se/publikationer/Rapporter/2017/Possible-tools-for-strengthened-implementation-of-sustinable-development-provisions-in-free-trade-agreements-FTAs/.

Van der Loo, G. (2017). The Court's Opinion on the EU-Singapore FTA: Throwing off the Shackles of Mixity? *CEPS Policy Insights.* 17. Retrieved August 31, 2018, from https://www.ceps.eu/system/files/PI2017-17Gvdl_SingaporeJudgement.pdf.

Young, A. R. (2015). Liberalizing Trade, Not Exporting Rules: The Limits to Regulatory Co-ordination in the EU's "New Generation" Preferential Trade Agreements. *Journal of European Public Policy, 22*(9), 1253–1275.

CHAPTER 6

EU Climate Policy in a Changing World Order

Sverker C. Jagers, Frida Nilsson, and Thomas Sterner

Introduction

The UN Intergovernmental Panel on Climate Change (IPCC) presented its first report in 1990, which summarised current research and determined that global warming exists and constitutes a grave threat to world communities. The report was the basis for the United Nations Framework Convention on Climate Change (UNFCCC) adopted at the 1992 UN Conference on Environment and Development in Rio. This agreement later resulted in the Kyoto Protocol, which entailed binding emission reductions for industrialised countries during the first commitment period of 2008–2012. World leaders met once again in December 2015 to reach consensus on further commitments that must be made—and complied with—to prevent global warming from rising beyond unacceptable levels. The conference was held in Paris and was the largest gathering of world leaders ever. It resulted in the Paris Agreement, which became legally binding within only about a year after 55 countries responsible for at least 55 percent of global emissions had ratified the agreement. The rapid

S. C. Jagers • F. Nilsson • T. Sterner (✉)
University of Gothenburg, Gothenburg, Sweden
e-mail: sverker.jagers@pol.gu.se; frida.nilsson.2@gu.se;
thomas.sterner@economics.gu.se

A. Bakardjieva Engelbrekt et al. (eds.), *The European Union in a Changing World Order*,
https://doi.org/10.1007/978-3-030-18001-0_6

"success" of the Paris process cannot be directly compared to the "failure" of Copenhagen (2009) in any simple way. One of the reasons for this is that the attempted agreements were very different in character with that of Copenhagen being more ambitious in terms of details concerning individual country commitments.

Europe has historically played a key role in environmental and climate policy, closely linked to the region's strong economic position. In parallel with the increasing urgency to take forceful climate action, Europe is stagnating economically, and other regions are advancing. This shift, along with the advent of the Paris Agreement, brings several interesting and important problems to the fore. What role has the EU played in global climate policy, and what role might it play in the future? What opportunities do EU Member States have to actually contribute to reducing global CO_2 emissions, especially when the countries have chosen to act under the EU's common emissions umbrella? Do the conditions exist for a joint EU policy that can promote these reductions, or are there factors indicating that the individual Member States should instead seek unique measures and solutions?

Proceeding from these problem statements, this chapter analyses the European relationship to climate policy in the light of the past, present and future economic context. The chapter is arranged as follows. We first describe Europe's historical role in terms of emissions and reductions of GHG in relation to other countries (primarily the US). We thereafter take a closer look at EU climate policy as it is currently pursued and show that there is wide variation among the Member States as to both measures taken and public attitudes towards a more ambitious climate policy. We then seek to explain why we see such large differences in level of ambition and attitudes towards climate policy instruments that we do within and between EU countries. Based on this, we finally discuss whether—and, if so, how—the EU can continue to play a key role in climate policy that is increasingly global and diversified. Due to the large differences we see in the factors at the individual and contextual levels in EU Member States, we have concluded that in the future we are most likely to see not only a changed position for Europe as an actor in global climate negotiations, but also a development in partially divergent directions for EU countries as regards climate policy action. Rather than "EU climate policy", we can and should think more in terms of a European climate policy spectrum now that the Paris Agreement is to be implemented in the Member States. The chapter ends with a discussion of recommended actions for the EU based on the premise that instruments aimed at reducing CO_2 emissions must not only be cost effective, but also designed with consideration to the characteristics of the Member States and opportunities to coordinate the instruments within the Union.

Europe and the Climate from a Historical Perspective

It was in Europe, chiefly Great Britain, that the Industrial Revolution began. Beginning in the late eighteenth century, the British created the wave of technical progress that would be the source of rapidly growing material prosperity and climate change. It has been argued that high British wages in relation to the low cost of coal was an important economic catalyst of the British breakthrough. This state of affairs generated strong incentives to develop technology driven by cheap coal instead of expensive labour, and because coal was so inexpensive there was no reluctance to test new technologies that were not fully developed. In this way, Britain evolved into an environment strongly characterised by experimentation and innovation, which in turn further spurred on development (Allen 2009). The innovations, the prosperity and the emissions they brought eventually spread, as we know, to nearby countries in Europe. During much of the Age of Industrialism, Europe was the leader in technology for the engineering industry, chemical industry and several other sectors intimately connected to fossil energy. This eventually developed into a general technological advantage that has in recent years also made Europe a leader in renewable energy and related industries.

Thanks to its head start in the industrialisation race, Europe quickly became the first and the foremost source of GHG emissions caused by human activity. A review of CO_2 emission levels in the mid-1800s and a little over a century later clearly indicates how well people managed to increase energy use and how this later spread to other countries (see Table 6.1). In 1850, the group of countries that today make up the European Union accounted for a full 89 percent of global emissions. By 1900, these countries had more than quintupled their emissions, but by then accounted for "only" 55 percent of global emissions. The US in particular had sharply increased its emissions and by 1960, the US had run away in no uncertain terms, with emissions figures that then topped Europe's by 75 percent. In 1960, other parts of the world were lagging

Table 6.1 CO_2 emissions 1850–1960 (megatons carbon)

	1850	*1900*	*1960*
Europe (EU 28)	48,251	296,132	451,094
USA	5402	180,878	788,300
China	–	–	212,906
India	–	3562	32,883
World	54,000	534,000	2,569,000

Source: Carbon Dioxide Information Analysis Center (2011)

behind: China's emissions were less than half of Europe's, while India's had not even risen to the levels Europe was producing around 1850. When the newly established IPCC published its first report in 1990, today's EU countries produced 19.5 percent of total global emissions, compared to 22 percent for the US.

According to Gupta (2010), the pre-1990 period was characterised above all by the attempt to frame the climate problem as serious, but also by strong emphasis on the differentiation between rich Annex I countries and poorer Annex II countries and their respective commitments. This differentiation gained general acceptance and this reasoning was the basis of the opinion that the rich countries in particular should commit to reducing emissions and lead the way as good examples. Among Annex I countries, those in Europe went the furthest by advocating binding targets. The US had previously been strong drivers of the Montreal Protocol on the ozone layer in the 1980s, for example, but wanted to keep emissions reduction targets more open. When the UNFCCC went into effect in 1994 it contained only extremely vaguely worded emissions targets, bowing to US pressure. The European countries had some success with their binding targets agenda with the Kyoto Protocol of 1997. This European ideal of acting as leaders in the context of climate talks can be said to have been further solidified after the US chose to withdraw from the Kyoto Protocol in 2001 (Bäckstrand and Elgström 2013). Through total emissions reductions of 22 percent in 2015 compared to 1990 levels and by outperforming targets according to the commitments made in the Kyoto Protocol, the EU countries have, by and large, also delivered in practice.

If one were to speculate as to why Europe has traditionally been a more evident leader than the US in the climate area, one could, for example, talk about the strong lobbying for fossil fuels in the US, based partially on the country's abundant coal, oil and gas resources. This in turn is based on geological conditions provided by nature, but also legal conditions. In the US, oil and mineral finds belong to the landowner; consequently, millions of Americans support or sympathise with oil and gas extraction that generates income for them. Such is rarely the case in Europe.

Is the EU Still a Heavyweight Global Climate Actor?

EU CO_2 emissions in 2015 accounted for 9.6 percent of the global total, which can and should be compared to the much higher 19.5 percent the EU produced as late as 1990 and the 89 percent these countries generated around 1850. Naturally, the percentage reduction is not explained entirely, or even close to it, by the EU's own efforts; the decline is largely due to the increasing rate of emissions in pace with accelerating economic growth in the US and elsewhere. After peak levels around 2005, US emissions have declined somewhat in recent years, but nevertheless are still higher than 1990 levels. China and India in particular, but certain other countries as well, have grown at breakneck speed in recent decades. China's CO_2 emissions exceeded those of the US in 2005, coming close to the US position in 1960 (30.7 percent). In 2009, the BASIC countries (Brazil, South Africa, India and China) generated 25 percent of world GDP and more than 25 percent of GHG emissions. These macroeconomic shifts are contributing to the sharp decline in the European share of emissions. This is supported by goal-oriented climate policy where countries in Europe have been much more radical than in many other regions.

Taken as a whole, these factors mean that the EU will probably meet its target of reducing emissions from the 1990 baseline by 20 percent by 2020 by a healthy margin. As mentioned previously, in 2015 emissions had already been reduced by 22 percent compared to 1990. It has been estimated that these reductions will have increased to between 23 and 24 percent by 2020 and 26 percent by 2030, based on actions already implemented. This would put the EU share of global emissions well below 10 percent. According to the EU's own target for 2030, it will have achieved even greater reductions—of 40 percent compared to 1990—by that time, which would entail a further substantial reduction in the EU's share (see Table 6.2).

Table 6.2 Population, GDP and CO_2 emissions 1990–2015

	1990	*2005*	*2015*
EU 28			
Population Billions	0.48	0.5	0.51
GDP USD trillions, current value	7.6	14.4	16.3
Emissions Gton CO_2	4.4	4.2	3.5
USA			
Population Billions	0.25	0.3	0.32
GDP USD trillions, current value	6	13.1	18
Emissions Gton CO_2	5	5.9	5.2
China			
Population Billions	1.1	1.3	1.4
GDP USD trillions, current value	0.4	2.3	11.1
Emissions Gton CO_2	2.3	6.2	10.6
India			
Population Billions	0.8	1.1	1.3
GDP USD trillions, current value	0.3	0.8	2.1
Emissions Gton CO_2	0.65	1.3	2.5
World			
Population Billions	5.3	6.5	7.4
GDP USD trillions, current value	22.6	47.4	74.5
Emissions Gton CO_2	22.5	30	36

Source: Emissions Database for Global Atmospheric Research (EDGAR) and the World Bank

Is the EU United on Climate Policy?

Notably, European environmental and energy policy seems to have undergone a gradual harmonisation over a very long time (Angelier and Sterner 1990). This is an important consideration from an international perspective and particularly in relation to the latest developments in global climate policy. As mentioned, the Paris Agreement was adopted in November 2015. It is worth noting that the Paris Agreement differs from the Kyoto Protocol in several respects. Firstly, under the Paris Agreement, every country in the world makes commitments to reduce or limit GHG, thus not only the industrialised countries. The agreements are also structured differently. The Kyoto Protocol was a typical "top-down" agreement where a united group forced individual industrial nations to accept specific percentages of emissions reductions compared to those countries' emissions levels in 1990 (e.g., US -7 percent and EU -8 percent). In contrast, the Paris Agreement is a "bottom-up" agreement with *one common objective*—to limit global warming to less than 2 degrees Celsius by 2100 compared with pre-industrialism temperatures, but preferably to cap warming to a maximum of 1.5 degrees—and where most individual states have formulated their own unique "Intended Nationally Determined Contributions" (INDC).

The Paris Agreement is a unique occurrence in many respects. Some have called it a major diplomatic victory and a turning point of comparable importance to the "Fall of the Wall" in the late 1980s. Some have chosen to go so far as to interpret the Paris Agreement as meaning that the global community has opened the door to a new world order. There is, however, reason to be cautious in the interpretation. Certainly, the Paris Agreement is innovative, but it is nonetheless a very weak agreement in many respects, with no clear rules or consequences for non-compliance. One can note that the countries of the world have found a negotiating format that makes it possible to achieve major global changes that do not rely on compulsory, top-down solutions, as was the case with Kyoto. And yet the question remains: is this a strength or a weakness?

The interesting aspect here is that the EU countries did not submit separate INDCs, referring instead to the EU's joint INDC, which presently calls for a 40 percent reduction of emissions in the Union by 2030 compared to 1990 levels. The EU thus acted in a highly coordinated manner in the Paris Agreement. In many respects, the INDCs are the central policy instruments and the most concrete content of the entire Paris

Agreement, as this is where each country specifies their commitments. The INDCs thus serve only as guidelines and there are no sanctions whatsoever for non-compliance. The strength of the Paris Agreement is that each country formulates its own INDC and the process has diverged considerably from, for example, efforts prior to the Copenhagen Summit, which was still characterised by a top-down process in which the parties negotiated about how to allocate a specific emissions reduction requirement.

This was viewed as a cost or burden, and attention was directed exclusively at the allocation and implicit (un)fairness of the allocation. There were certain advantages to this process, including the genuine attempt to achieve a specific, collective reduction in emissions. The drawback was the focus on how each country was to try and negotiate the "best agreement" possible for itself, meaning the smallest possible burden and reduction. In the Paris Agreement process, the negotiators were not the only ones who had a say. To a certain extent, a hearing was given to all of the groups and voices in each country that could, in a somewhat visionary sense, answer the question: How can we contribute? In some cases, extremely bold and innovative proposals were presented. Ethiopia's INDC, for example, promises rapid economic development to reach middle-income status *with zero increases in GHG emissions.* Instead, Ethiopia proposes vigorous investments in reforestation and renewable energy. Two additional COP sessions have been held since Paris, in Marrakech (2016) and Bonn (2017), which clearly continued along the path laid out in Paris. The parties worked partly with specific matters like water in Marrakech, along with attempts to create institutions to generate pressure on the countries to meet their obligations. Discussions about putting a price on CO_2 have also continued without so far having led to any decisive breakthrough.

It is thus in the INDC process where each country defines its positive visions for a climate-friendly future that the EU has behaved as a united actor and submitted only a joint INDC. No other economic bloc in the world has done anything like it and we believe this is evidence of fairly strong political coordination in the area on the part of the EU. According to one proposal put forth in the summer of 2017 within the framework of the Paris Agreement, there may be talk of a new EU regulation that will set out provisions for national emissions reductions in the sectors not covered by the EU Emission Trading System, ETS. In such case, the extent of reductions would vary and be based on a country's assessed potential to implement reductions. For a country like Sweden, which is assessed as having the potential to achieve the highest possible reduction targets, this proposal would, for example, entail reductions of 40 percent by 2030 compared to a 2005 baseline. Because the application of EU legislation would make a regulation binding in all Member States as soon as it enters into force, the proposal would mean that EU countries would be allotted obligatory emissions reductions with no scope for national legislation in the area.

As we have seen, the EU is presenting a single climate position in several respects vis-à-vis other countries and regional cooperative organisations, and the entire EU has been gradually harmonised so that all countries have relatively high taxes on petrol (with Luxembourg the glaring exception). With the ETS, the EU also has harmonised and central policy instruments for large and heavy industry. Nevertheless, European policy is not entirely homogeneous and the conditions for EU countries vary widely. As for the EU ETS, while there is indeed a single price and a single set of rules for all, this applies only to major installations in heavy industry. There is no common policy on the private consumption of petrol and other energy sources, and consequently the authorities in each country carefully monitor all new proposals for supranational coordination at the EU level. There are also important practical policy differences among EU countries. Some are still heavily dependent on coal power, while others have developed nuclear power or renewable energy. Some have heavily centralised systems, while others are more decentralised. Even when there are certain common elements to policy, such as an ambition to solve the climate problem, there are distinct national characteristics. In Fig. 6.1 below, we show what the relationship looks like between the parts of EU climate policy that are

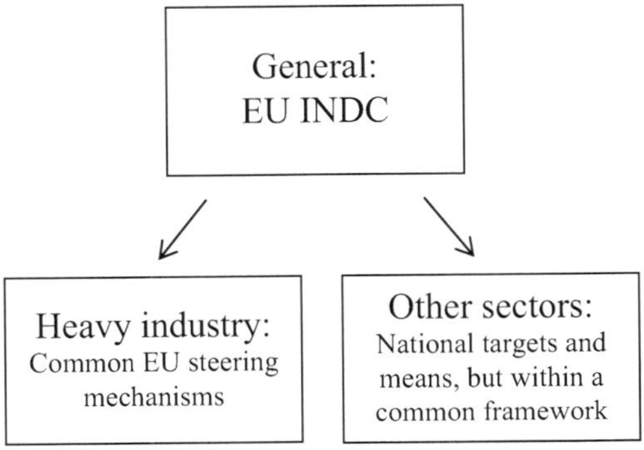

Fig. 6.1 EU climate policy

common to all Member States of the Union (INDC and joint policy instruments for heavy industry) and the sectors in which there are national variations.

If we take a closer look at the differences between Member States, Germany has its *Energiewende* (energy transition) for example, whose objective is not only to achieve a climate transition, but also to phase out nuclear power (Quitzow et al. 2016). The German policy seems to be driven by the conviction that this is a technical problem and as such Germany, with its stellar history of technical and engineering expertise, is in a unique position to play a key role in finding a solution. The country has made substantial and consistent investments in long-term and stable support for renewable energy, especially wind and solar power.

France, on the other hand, seems convinced that the best way to solve the climate problem is through major, systematic investments in nuclear power. But in recent years—and in preparation for the summit in Paris—French policy has diversified and the country is now using numerous policy instruments, among which nuclear power is assigned a more modest (but still important) role. Actions taken in France include the introduction of a bonus-malus system for vehicle purchases (from the Latin for good-bad, meaning that vehicles with low CO_2 emissions carry a bonus at the time of purchase, while vehicles with higher emissions are taxed at a higher rate for a period), but the country has also managed (on the third try), to enact on a heavy carbon tax that starts at €44.60 per metric ton of CO_2 and will gradually increase over the period of 2018–2022 (Grantham Research Institute on Climate Change and the Environment 2017).

The French carbon tax is large and significant, but still moderate compared to carbon tax in Sweden, which is the highest in the world (about SEK 1100/ton). Considering that economic theorists (Somanathan et al. 2009; Sterner 2007; Hammar et al. 2004) usually mention a general (and sufficiently high) carbon tax as the ideal, but perhaps the most politically difficult to implement policy instrument, it is interesting to note that Sweden has managed to establish this instrument with the stated levels. The background includes high trust in public institutions and especially in taxes in Sweden, but also historically high taxes in general (along with a high level of welfare services and a large public sector). In the 1980s, high taxes combined with a certain level of progressivity had led to unacceptably high marginal taxes that became a hot political issue.

As a result of a cross-party political consensus, Sweden implemented its major tax reform in 1991, including the repeal of wealth and capital taxes and inheritance taxes, as well as reductions in income and marginal taxes. This became a historic opportunity to implement a high carbon tax as a component of the financing (Agell et al. 1996; Sterner 1994). Other factors that probably helped make the increase politically viable was the strong position of the Center Party at the time, along with widespread coverage of environmental issues in the late 1980s. The Green Party won seats in the *Riksdag* for the first time in the 1988 election, which indicates the growing public concern about the environment at the time. The absence of strong fossil-fuel lobbyists in Sweden, which has no domestic oil or coal resources, probably also made a difference.

The UK is also an interesting forerunner in terms of climate policy instruments. In 2008, the country passed the first Climate Change Act (CCA) in the world, with binding targets for emissions reductions by 2050, employing a series of "carbon budgets" to consider along the way. This thus entails a national climate act that requires the sitting government, regardless of political ideology, to pursue a policy that is beneficial to the global climate system. In parallel with the CCA, the UK established a Committee on Climate Change, tasked with independently monitoring and analysing progress. Assisted by these two instruments, the British successfully realised the wish for stability and predictability in UK climate policy that decision-makers and other actors in the area had often called for but had not managed to push through in many EU Member States. The climate laws in Austria, Denmark and Finland, as well as Sweden's new climate policy framework that went into effect on 1 January 2018, are successors of similar structure and similar ambitions to achieve stability.

A Variety of Factors Explains Differences Among EU Member States

There are wide variations among EU countries about public attitudes towards the climate problem as such, but also towards various climate policy actions. Data taken from the Eurobarometer, for example, shows clear differences among citizens in different EU countries in relation to worry about the climate and how urgent people believe it is for the EU to take climate action (Jagers 2008). There are, of course, also differences between people and actors in the same country. How can this variation be explained? Somewhat simplistically, the explanatory factors can be categorised as contextual and individual-specific. Let us begin with the first category.

When comparing the success of different countries in pursuing effective environmental and natural resources policies, it has been found that the degree of democracy and the maturity of democracies affect whether or not countries are able to protect their environments. The quality of public institutions also matters, in that countries with a high level of corruption and dysfunctional administrative systems tend to be poorer stewards of their natural resources (Povitkina 2018). These factors also have some impact on people's attitudes towards the climate problem as such (for example, whether they believe climate change is real and whether they believe it is caused by human activity) and, above all, the opinions people hold about various environmental policy actions. The following contextual factors are among those that seem to matter for these opinions.

First, there is political culture. Although the EU project has done very well at harmonising the Member States in several respects, there are still major differences concerning things like views on political authority and the powers such authority should be given. There is generally strong trust in government and political institutions in the Scandinavian countries, manifest for example in a higher degree of acceptance for political control than is the norm in countries like the UK and several of the eastern European Member States. This is also reflected in public acceptance of climate policy actions, where support for a carbon tax in Sweden is high, for example, and has thus been established since the early 1990s, while such taxes on individual consumption of fossil fuels have been considered more or less unthinkable in other countries (Jagers and Matti 2018).

Another factor usually designated "social norms" and which has primarily been the preoccupation of psychological research involves the rules of conduct that are shared in a social context (such as the population of a country). We find large differences between the countries of Europe here as well. National identity is a closely related phenomenon. In Sweden, for example, we have historically had a self-image/identity of being a generous country. This is also accompanied by, or is the root of, common rules of conduct dictating that we Swedes should help others in need by for example being at the head of the class in reducing the quantity of GHG in the atmosphere (Matti 2015).

Another contextual factor is usually called path dependency. Put in other words, this has to do with how countries tend to paint themselves into a corner, meaning that they have made decisions in the past that make it increasingly difficult to change directions and thus also to decide to do so. The country goes down these paths and the longer they are travelled, the more problematic and often costly it becomes to break the pattern (Kirk et al. 2007). In the US, for example, most cities were planned based on the assumption that the car is and will remain the main mode of travel. Once the infrastructure is in place and where jobs, shops, schools and fitness centres are accessible only by car, breaking this pattern is no easy task. Such path dependency obviously affects people's attitudes towards climate policy actions aimed at changing ingrained and firmly established patterns and persuading people to start walking or cycling to the gym or the preschool or to ride public transportation (which in many cases might not be available at all).

It has also been observed that people who live in countries with a high degree of corruption have different preferences for environmental policy instruments than people in countries where there are fewer problems with corruption and otherwise dysfunctional public administrative systems. The patterns found are that people in highly corrupt societies want law, order and more punitive instruments rather than monetary and market-based instruments, while people in societies where corruption is low have stronger preferences for market-based instruments and prefer opportunities for freedom of choice that are largely absent from legal instruments (Harring 2014).

When one thinks about it, these results are perhaps not unexpected. Market-based instruments are often preferable because they are cost-effective, tend to produce results for the environment and provide some scope for freedom of choice. At the same time, if such an instrument is implemented in and by a corrupt political and administrative system, people are likely to assume that the revenues generated will be used in an improper manner. People simply do not trust the system—and they probably do not trust other people either. Are they really going to pay if I do, or are they going to try to free-ride and pay less because, after all, they must in order to maintain the corruption in other sectors of society? In this case, it seems that people prefer a system where legal instruments exist and are clear-cut in terms of both what they dictate and what happens if people try to get around them.

As regards the category of individual-specific factors, these can, as mentioned, differ among individuals in different countries, in part because contextual factors like social norms and the quality of the political system interact with individual-level factors. Weak political governance impacts people's trust in other people and in political government, for example. Likewise, it seems that most of the individual-specific factors discussed below seem to be relatively stable among people in different countries.

People's fundamental values are a factor that affects their attitudes towards environmental policy management. If people have strong preferences for the environment and nature and have high regard for authorities (such as the state), they are generally considerably more accepting of political management aimed at improving the status of the environment (Dunlap and York 2008). Although values control people's acceptance of policy instruments to a great extent, this is cold comfort in most cases because values are often resistant to change, sometimes evolving only over as long as an entire lifetime. Changing people's values is thus not a quick fix for politicians looking to increase acceptance, but may very well be a strategy for getting future generations to be more accepting of new directions in climate policy.

If someone believes that environmental problems exist, or there is risk that these problems will directly affect them or others whom they care about and, above all, if the person believes these environmental threats are *worrying*, this strongly increases the likelihood that they will accept the implementation of environmental policy actions. Thus, several studies have shown that people who are seriously worried or even suffering from "climate anxiety" have a strong tendency to accept the introduction or strengthening of instruments such as carbon taxes (Tjernström and Tietenberg 2008). This correlation is addressed in greater depth in Jagers (2008). Interestingly enough, however, such anxiety can also produce the opposite effect, causing people to abandon hope and believe there is no point in taking action because the game is over anyway (Smith and Leiserowitz 2013).

A long series of environmental psychology studies have shown that people's tendencies to act green and accept political measures aimed at improving the environment are controlled to a great extent by the personal norms they bear, by their internalised norms that prescribe how they should behave in a particular situation. In a person with strong personal environmental norms, these tend to trump other things that people often care about, such as low fuel prices (Steg et al. 2005).

Another result of many studies generally accepted among political scientists, economists and psychologists is that people's opinions about environmental policy actions are informed by their beliefs about fairness. If people are strongly convinced that political decisions should "impact" people equally, a carbon tax (which, after all, only affects people who buy petrol and diesel), is probably not a particularly viable action. If, on the other hand, people believe that folks should get what they deserve, including punishments, such a tax might seem considerably more attractive than a government subsidy of alternative fuels that everyone in society must help finance (Hammar and Jagers 2007).

As noted earlier, it has been found in recent years that people's trust in other people and in public institutions is strongly correlated with attitudes towards climate policy instruments. Simply put: the higher the trust, the more favourable the attitude. We who have been preoccupied with this correlation tend to explain the effect in two ways. If I trust other people in general, it probably also means that I also believe they will comply with the policy instruments that are introduced. They will do their bit, just like me. This reinforces my own inclination to accept the instruments. Surely, it can go the other way too (although this is rarely shown in the empirical results), where if I trust others to act green, that is good enough and the policy instruments are thus unnecessary, so I choose to accept them to a lesser extent. That institutional and political trust correlates with acceptance of control mechanisms is probably less surprising (and is something we addressed when we discussed corruption above). If people do not trust the institutions that devise the environmental policy measures, they will probably also be unwilling to accept their actual implementation (Jagers and Robertson 2018).

Finally, we would like to bring up a factor that has also been shown to govern people's inclination to accept the implementation of or changes to existing instruments: beliefs about the actual instrument as such. In many cases, it can be that while I have strong environmental preferences and otherwise evince all the driving forces that should make me approve of an environmental policy action I still disapprove strongly of the action. It turns out that this often depends upon my having strongly negative opinions about the actual instrument that the government has chosen to implement. An environmental tax is a good example here. Some people think that such taxes affect people unfairly, for example by disproportionately hurting people with the lowest incomes or the greatest need to drive (such as rural people who have no viable alternatives to the car). Others do not believe that the chosen instrument is effective and therefore disapprove of it (consider, for example, the ongoing debate about air travel tax in Sweden), while others may be deeply committed to the environment, but still prefer other instruments because a tax in particular is perceived as a strong encroachment on personal liberty (Kallbekken and Saelen 2011).

The Role of the EU Going Forward

As shown, the framing of climate change as a global problem in recent years has undergone profound changes. The steep increases in both economic growth and emissions, divided among more actors than before, has seriously redrawn the climate policy map. This has brought the issue of fair allocation of necessary emission reductions to a head. The macroeconomic changes also mean that the EU's once so large space in global climate policy as a dominant emitter and economic powerhouse, has become less obvious.

Following tremendous difficulties concluding a climate agreement with binding targets, a sort of compromise came about with the Paris Agreement in 2015 as regards burden sharing, in that the point of departure for the talks was shifted and instead proceeded from the voluntary efforts of the parties. This turnabout when it comes to commitments is an entirely new way for the countries of the world to approach climate policy. Beyond the new climate policy reality in which the EU must act while seeking influence in the global arena, the Paris Agreement also changed somewhat the conditions under which the EU countries are meant to implement their commitments.

In a way, these new conditions could diminish the significance and power of Europe. If the large-scale emitters of the world are gathered together, the EU is a lightweight in the sense that even if the EU drastically reduces its emissions in that situation, it will have no major effect on global emissions. On the other hand, one can easily argue the opposite and say that the EU is holding all the trump cards. If the world must reduce its emissions, there stands the EU in a place of much higher moral authority, as long as it has maintained employment and welfare while reducing its emissions. In a positive scenario, this could also mean that EU countries will be in a position to sell the necessary technology to other countries that must achieve a rapid transition. Here, one might find a simile with the dawn of industrialism when coal paved the way to technological leadership and faster economic growth in Europe. In the future, there might once again be a European lead in technology, this time in renewable energy that takes us out of the epoch of fossil fuels and into the next Industrial Revolution.

The US situation is interesting in this context. If the US continues to ignore the needs for climate policy and, in the extreme case, withdraws from the Paris Agreement and takes only limited action at home, the EU will naturally assume a leadership role. Signs of this can be discerned in expanded cooperation between the EU and China and India, respectively, and for that matter with California and other regions, cities and large corporations in the US that are opposed to the current federal policy under President Donald Trump. Outside the context of formal climate talks, there are already established collaborations between cities and regions, and these new, smaller actors could conceivably become increasingly significant if their strategies and results are spread and can become politically relevant at the national level. Regions are already working as active parties in collaborative efforts related to climate commitments. At about the same time that President Trump declared that the US will be withdrawing from the Paris Agreement, representatives of California and China met to discuss California's experiences with emission trading. The Under2 Coalition started as a collaboration between California and Baden-Württemberg, Germany, but has now evolved into a coalition of 177 local and regional governments endeavouring to reduce their GHG emissions by 80–95 percent compared to 1990 levels. Naturally, the mandates these actors have to make independent decisions in line with their ambitions varies between different national contexts and in many cases, they are ultimately dependent upon getting national legislation on their side. It is however clear that even before the advent of the Paris Agreement, bottom-up processes have been ongoing elsewhere in the absence of globally binding agreements.

If we continue along the track of the structure of the Paris Agreement, the EU's joint INDC along with all of the differences between the Member States that we can already see as regards both the chosen instruments and contextual and more individual-related factors that affect opportunities to implement various policy instrument strategies, there are indications that it may be less relevant in the future to talk about EU climate policy, but rather the spectrum of climate policies pursued in the EU policy arena. This may at least be the case in the category we call "other sectors" above—the parts of society not considered heavy industry.

If EU Member States are to design further climate policy measures and hope to achieve the greatest possible acceptance of them among as many social actors as possible, it would be wise to consider some of the challenges and opportunities that we have identified in this chapter. If a carbon tax is to gain sufficient popular support and be enacted by a national parliament, it must be designed so that it optimally aligns with such things as people's values, norms and perceptions of fairness. Otherwise, the measure will probably be only a paper tiger (Carlsson and Johansson-Stenman 2012). If we also add all of the contextual factors discussed earlier, we understand even more clearly what a delicate task it is for politicians to design instruments that simultaneously meet sufficient demands for effectiveness, comply with the individual countries' climate commitments in accordance with the EU INDC and are not perceived as so repugnant that they will never been accepted or decided.

In the light of the wide variation we find among EU Member States concerning everything from degree of corruption and path dependency to political culture, it seems difficult to find a one-size-fits-all common policy instrument. It is more likely that several different policy instruments will have to be applied in concert, although in different countries, and countries should perhaps also think in terms of combinations of instruments. If for example the intent of one instrument is to be environmentally effective and cost-effective, another might instead be more compensatory and serve to mitigate the perceived injustices that the first instrument may be at risk of causing.

EU Climate Policy Instruments in the Light of the Paris Agreement: Cost-Efficiency and Legitimacy Will Be Key Issues to Address

To sum up our message in terms of recommended actions, we can put it as follows: it is important to analyse (1) what types of instruments can most successfully contribute to drastic reductions of current GHG emissions levels, and this in the (2) most cost-effective way possible, while these instruments (3) are designed so that they are "sensitive" to the unique characteristics of each Member State and can also (4) be coordinated within the EU.

As things stand, continued and more successful management going forward of other sectors in the EU that have impact on the global climate will require governments to seek the most cost-effective instruments possible while meeting demands for legitimacy and acceptance among the actors concerned. In this context, it is important to emphasise that political acceptance is often more dependent upon distributional fairness than on general effectiveness.

Considering that governments often have multiple and relatively separate objectives at the same time, a successful path forward might be to think more in terms of a policy package, that is, combinations of instruments. This might, for example, involve a combination of a carbon tax aligned with tax switching of some kind and, not least importantly, preceding this with information campaigns that explain the reasons for the chosen policy instruments. Instruments like taxes are usually the most effective, but often enjoy low acceptance, partly because they challenge powerful economic interests. In this case, there may be reason to also use instruments that expressly align with new technologies. Once these technologies have grown powerful, it can sometimes be easier, for example, to raise taxes on older, more polluting technologies or raw materials.

Finally, more countries could learn from the UK about the enactment of a climate act by designing their policy packages with some kind of law that ties the hands of sitting and future governments to guarantee continuity regardless of which party is in power.

References

Agell, J., Englund, P., & Södersten, J. (1996). Tax Reform of the Century: The Swedish Experiment. *National Tax Journal, 49*(4), 643–664.

Allen, R. C. (2009). *The British Industrial Revolution in Global Perspective.* Cambridge: Cambridge University Press.

Angelier, J. P., & Sterner, T. (1990). Tax Harmonization for Petroleum Products in the EC. *Energy Policy, 18*(6), 500–505.

Bäckstrand, K., & Elgström, O. (2013). The EU's Role in Climate Change Negotiations: From Leader to 'Leadiator'. *Journal of European Public Policy, 20*(10), 1369–1386.

Carlsson, F., & Johansson-Stenman, O. (2012). Behavioral Economics and Environmental Policy. *Annual Review of Resource Economics., 4*, 75–99.

Dunlap, R. E., & York, R. (2008). The Globalization of Environmental Concern and the Limits of the Postmaterialist Values Explanation: Evidence from Four Multinational Surveys. *The Sociological Quarterly, 49*, 529–563.

Grantham Research Institute on Climate Change and the Environment. (2017). Finance Law 2018 and Second Rectifying Finance Law for 2017. Retrieved July 17, 2018, from http://www.lse.ac.uk/GranthamInstitute/law/finance-law-2018-second-rectifying-finance-law-2017/.

Gupta, J. (2010). A History of International Climate Change Policy. *Wiley Interdisciplinary Reviews: Climate Change, 1*, 636–653.

Hammar, H., & Jagers, S. C. (2007). What Is a Fair CO2 Tax Increase? On Fair Emission Reductions in the Transport Sector. *Ecological Economics, 61*(2–3), 377–387.

Hammar, H., Löfgren, Å., & Sterner, T. (2004). Political Economy Obstacles to Fuel Taxation. *The Energy Journal, 25*(3), 1–17.

Harring, N. (2014). The Multiple Dilemmas of Environmental Protection: The Effects of Generalized and Political Trust on the Acceptance of Environmental Policy Instruments. *Dissertation*. Department of Political Science, University of Gothenburg.

Jagers, S. (2008). Människors oro – ett medel för radikal klimatpolitik? In P. Cramér, S. Gustavsson, & L. Oxelheim (Eds.), *Europaperspektiv 2008: EU och den globala klimatfrågan*. Stockholm: Santérus förlag.

Jagers, S. C., & Matti, S. (2018). Climate Policy Support in a Comparative Perspective: Exploring the Meaning and Significance of Political-Economic Contexts. *Environmental Politics* (Forthcoming).

Jagers, S. C., & Robertson, F. (2018). The Role of Trust in Large-Scale Collective Action. Journal of Social Medicine (*forthcoming, in Swedish*).

Kallbekken, S., & Saelen, H. (2011). Public Acceptance for Environmental Taxes: Self-interest, Environmental and Distributional Concerns. *Energy Policy, 39*, 2966–2973.

Kirk, E. A., Reeves, A. D., & Blackstock, K. L. (2007). Path Dependency and the Implementation of Environmental Regulation. *Environment and Planning C: Politics and Space, 25*(2), 250–268.

Matti, S. (2015). Climate Policy Instruments. In K. Bäckstrand & E. Lövbrand (Eds.), *Research Handbook of Climate Governance*. Edward Elgar Publishing.

Povitkina, M. (2018). The Limits of Democracy in Tackling Climate Change. *Environmental Politics, 27*(3), 411–432.

Quitzow, L., Canzler, W., Grundmann, P., Leibenath, M., Moss, T., & Tilmann, R. (2016). The German *Energiewende* – What's Happening? Introducing the Special Issue. *Utilities Policy, 41*, 163–171.

Smith, N., & Leiserowitz, A. (2013). The Role of Emotion in Global Warming Policy Support and Opposition. *Risk Analysis, 34*(5), 937–948.

Somanathan, E., Sterner, T., Sugiyama, T., Chimanikire, D., Essandoh-Yeddu, J., Fifita, S., Goulder, L., Jaffe, A., Labandeira, X., Managi, S., Mitchell, C., Montero, J. P., Steg, F., & Vlek, C. (2009). Encouraging Pro-environmental Behaviour: An Integrative Review and Research Agenda. *Journal of Environmental Psychology, 29*, 309–317.

Steg, L., Dreijerink, L., & Abrahamse, W. (2005). Factors Influencing the Acceptability of Energy Policies: A Test of VBN Theory. *Journal of Environmental Psychology, 25*(4), 415–425.

Sterner, T. (1994). Environmental Tax Reform: The Swedish Experience. *European Environment, 4*(6), 20–25.
Sterner, T. (2007). Fuel Taxes: An Important Instrument for Climate Policy. *Energy Policy, 35*(6), 3194–3202.
Tjernström, E., & Tietenberg, T. (2008). Do Differences in Attitudes Explain Differences in National Climate Change Policies? *Ecological Economics, 65*(2), 315–324.

CHAPTER 7

Migration and the European Welfare State in a Changing World Order

Johan E. Eklund and Pontus Braunerhjelm

Introduction

Why do individuals migrate? The standard reasons referred to are either economically (i.e. a wish to achieve a more decent standard of living) or to escape war and oppression. The former reason led to the major waves of emigrants from Europe to the United States in the late nineteenth century. Now Europe is experiencing a mix of large-scale refugee and migration flows and there is reason to expect this will bring significant economic and social upheavals, especially for well-established and extensive welfare states in western and northern Europe. It is easy to understand and get behind the drivers of the increased migration, still the conditions for

J. E. Eklund (✉)
Blekinge Institute of Technology, Karlskrona, Sweden

Swedish Entrepreneurship Forum, Stockholm, Sweden
e-mail: johan.eklund@entreprenorskapsforum.se

P. Braunerhjelm

Swedish Entrepreneurship Forum, Stockholm, Sweden

Swedish Royal Institute of Technology, Stockholm, Sweden
e-mail: pontus.braunerhjelm@indek.kth.se

A. Bakardjieva Engelbrekt et al. (eds.), *The European Union in a Changing World Order*,
https://doi.org/10.1007/978-3-030-18001-0_7

successful establishment in the host country vary among countries as well as different groups of immigrants. Moreover, the scope of the welfare state also differs even though countries are relatively similar in a large part of Europe, implying different economic outcomes at the country level but also between migrant groups.

In this chapter we examine the expected economic consequences of migration for the European welfare state. We discuss the design of the welfare state from the perspective of the refugee crisis that Europe has experienced in recent years and the large-scale reception of asylum-seekers, particularly in Sweden and Germany. Our aim is thus to shed light on the economic costs and benefits that migration can generate, considering the welfare policy ambitions and distribution policy systems in many European countries. We emphasize that an effective integration policy is going to be critical to national economic outcome of immigration, as well as to the future scope and design of the welfare state. There is consequently room for policy to shape the ultimate outcome of higher immigration.

The analysis is confined to the questions above and we have no ambition to provide an exhaustive overview of the vast economic literature on immigration and its economic consequences. Nor do we address issues such as social problems, criminality or declines in social trust that have followed in the wake of failed integration. The issues are politically controversial, but it is important to objectively illuminate and analyze the effects of large-scale immigration and identify the barriers to successful integration. We will consistently use Sweden to illustrate the challenges that European welfare states are confronting. The combination of universal welfare policy ambitions and high refugee immigration makes Swedish experiences particularly relevant from the European perspective. The future challenges in this respect will be less onerous from the outset for countries with more limited welfare ambitions.

The chapter is divided into nine sections. Initially a brief account of the extent of European immigration and public attitudes towards immigration is given, followed by a description of how increased immigration can be expected to affect the welfare state. The next section discusses the heterogeneity of migrant groups, especially in terms of education and its impact on opportunities for successful economic integration in the recipient country. In section "Immigrants: A Heterogeneous Group", covers the potential consequences of migration on the welfare state according to earlier research findings. This lays the foundation for arguments concerning the consequences on the welfare state discussed thereafter. The following, seventh, section stresses the exigency of an efficient labor market. Section

"A Divided Labor Market in Europe with Dysfunctional Economic Integration" focuses on the importance of human capital to successful integration. Finally, the results are summarized and a few general recommendations are presented for how the economic costs of immigration, refugee immigration in particular, could be reduced.

Migration to Europe: An Overview

Undeniably, issues related to migration divide opinion not only within many European countries, but also sow discord between nations. One well-known cleavage, for example, runs between northern and western Europe on one side and central and eastern Europe on the other, where the latter group of countries have more restrictive migration and asylum policies. Migration in recent years, particularly refugee-driven migration, is expected to affect all of Europe for the foreseeable future. Intra-European and extra-European migration to the UK, for example, impacted the British vote in favor of Brexit in the 2016 referendum. Likewise, both the German and French elections in 2017 were also influenced by these issues.

Just how many people are in flight globally and have been forced to leave their homes due to armed conflict is uncertain. The UN estimates that about 65 million people have been displaced globally and the outlook for quickly improving the situation is dire. Added to this number are migrants moving within Europe for other reasons and migrants coming to Europe from other regions in the world. In 2015 alone, an estimated 1.3 million refugees made their way to Europe. Of all European countries, Sweden received the highest share of refugees measured as a percentage of the population during the period of 2014–2016 (163,000 refugees arrived in 2015 alone). In absolute numbers, only Germany has received more; per capita, Sweden has accepted about ten times the average for EU Member States (see Fig. 7.1).

Many EU countries that have received relatively high numbers of refugees can be defined as welfare states but vary in terms of distribution policy ambitions and scope of social protection. The differences between the central and eastern parts of Europe and northern and western Europe are particularly stark. In relation to asylum applications granted, Hungary is an outlier with the highest share of asylum seekers per capita in Europe in 2015, but few of these applicants have been granted asylum, which reflects a more negative view of immigration compared to Germany and Sweden. Family reunification immigrants and people granted residence permits for family reasons are included in the group of asylum seekers, which has

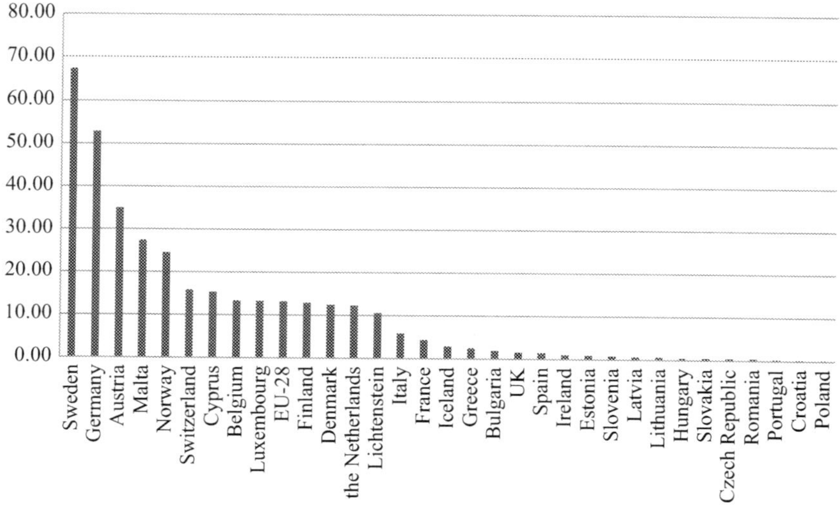

Fig. 7.1 Number of asylum applications granted in 2016 per 10,000 inhabitants in the EU. Source: Eurostat

grown in several European countries. In the Swedish case, about 22,000 residence permits were granted based on family ties compared to 17,000 based on asylum status during the first half of 2017.

As regards attitudes towards immigration, the emergence of the Islamic State (ISIS) and a string of terrorist attacks with religious overtones have affected views on various immigrant groups. In the United States, President Trump has succeeded in halting entry to the US from a few selected Muslim countries. According to Chatham House, many Europeans are also opposed to immigration from Muslim countries, regardless of whether due to war, disaster or other reasons. Of the ten countries included in the study (Austria, Belgium, France, Greece, Hungary, Italy, Poland, Spain and the UK), the percentage of people who disagreed with the statement "All further migration from mainly Muslim countries should be stopped" was lower than 50 percent in only two (Spain and the UK). Both countries also have a long history with a relatively large percentage of Muslims in the population. For the other eight countries, the percentage of respondents who agree with the statement is above 50 percent and by a wide margin in Austria, Belgium, Hungary and Poland, showing that it is not only eastern European countries who oppose Muslim immigration.

For all countries, opposition is especially intense among men, people with low education and older age cohorts. Overall, across all ten countries included in the study, 55 percent agreed with the statement, while 20 percent disagreed (and 25 percent were undecided) (Chatham House 2017). These religious and ethnic antagonisms are exploited by various populist parties in Europe and are exacerbating tensions (see Blombäck in this volume). One of the possible consequences is that irrespective of skills. Muslim immigrant will find it particularly difficult to find a foothold in recipient countries.

The Debate on Migration and the Welfare State

The long-term political, economic and social consequences of the large-scale immigration that the EU has witnessed in recent years are highly uncertain, not least for welfare states. Social debate in Europe has also been affected, and some pundits consider migration a threat not only to the survival of the welfare state, but the very survival of the nation state and fundamental European values. Others consider migration the solution to some of the challenges of the welfare state, such as aging populations and their associated challenges, as well as a source of renewal and innovative processes. Differing perspectives on these issues are, naturally, a strong contributing factor to the discord between and within the countries of Europe on the issue of migration, as discussed above.

The issues are also current beyond the borders of Europe. In the US, fears of "welfare arbitrage" have resulted in national welfare transfers being restricted to US citizens. Sweden is an interesting example in a European context, considering the scope of the welfare state and the generous reception of asylum seekers. In the wake of large-scale asylum migration, a debate has also ensued on issues including which parts of the welfare system should be immediately available to immigrants and what requirements should be imposed on immigrants in particular, but also other citizens, to automatically have the right to use the system. Basically this issue boils down to whether the welfare system should be differentiated instead of universal. Other points of contention have involved the distribution of refugees among countries and regions and where and how it should be possible to apply for asylum.

Immigration to Europe is not a new phenomenon, of course, but its nature has changed and it is now more widespread than ever before and to a larger extent characterized by refugee migration rather than labor force immigration, as in the past. The migrants also come from entirely different countries today. Net immigration to Sweden in 2016 corresponded to 1.17 percent of the population, which may seem like a modest figure, but that can be compared, for example, to the mass immigration wave to the US between 1880 and 1890, which then corresponded to 0.67 percent of the US population. How immigration and asylum reception are affecting the welfare state and, especially, the sustainability of welfare systems is thus an urgent research question in the light of the situation in Europe for the past several years. One important aspect has to do with the extent to which migration issues can and should be managed at the national level or the EU level. Is institutional competition in this area a good thing, or do the systems need to be harmonized to a greater extent?[1]

In other words, asylum reception can have profound distribution policy consequences in Europe and its Member States, but also enhance the resiliency of European welfare systems. We will argue that integration policy is critical to the long-term outcome. If everything else remains unchanged, increased welfare transfers to immigrants will mean that more people will have to enter the workforce to maintain the average level of welfare. Rapid integration thus lightens the economic costs that are undoubtedly generated in the short term. At the same time, successful integration can produce economic opportunities, such as eliminating labor shortages and skills provision problems. If, on the other hand, it takes too long for immigrants to become established in the labor market, the burden of support for those who work in the host country increases, which may over time have consequences on both public finances and distribution policy.

The Scope of the Welfare State and the Significance of Economic Integration

The welfare state is a political idea, or a social contract, based on the principle that the state, not the individual, is responsible for the welfare of its citizens and for ensuring that all citizens enjoy a minimum standard of living. In other words, the welfare state can be defined based on ambitious distribution policies rather than any absolute level, such as GDP per capita. Although the scope varies, most countries in Europe are considered welfare states, at least when measured as the share of public spending allocated to distribution policy objectives.

[1] On institutional competition in the EU, see Wihlborg and Khoury (2018).

Table 7.1 below provides an overview of the scope of public spending in a selection of European countries and the US. Public spending as a percentage of GDP is slightly below 50 percent in Sweden. Similarly high levels can be observed for most other European countries, although they are slightly lower in the UK. If we consider the composition of public spending, it becomes clear that social protection (mainly health, unemployment and parental insurance, as well as pensions and long-term care for the elderly) is the largest expenditure item by far, the exception being the US. In Europe, Finland tops the list with a cost share of 25 percent of GDP, or slightly more than 50 percent of public expenditure. Combined with education and health, these three welfare transfer areas correspond to about 60–80 percent of public spending in the EU countries. There is thus no doubt that Europe has much more comprehensive welfare states compared to the US, but also that there are relatively wide differences between many European countries.

Distribution policy is not, however, limited to outright transfers. Other distribution policy instruments, such as regulations and norms can be added to direct public spending. These also vary among EU Member States. Evidently, the Swedish model (like that of several other countries)

Table 7.1 Public spending as a percentage of GDP distributed by expenditure area

	Total	*Defense, public order and safety*	*Social protection*	*Education*	*Health*
Finland	57.0	2.6	25.6	6.2	7.2
France	56.6	3.3	24.4	5.4	8.1
Sweden	50.2	2.4	20.9	6.5	6.9
Germany	44.0	2.8	19.0	4.2	7.2
Spain	43.8	3.1	17.1	4.1	6.2
Greece	55.4	4.8	20.5	4.3	4.5
United States	37.7	5.3	7.8	6.1	9.1
United Kingdom	42.8	4.1	16.4	5.1	7.6
Netherlands	44.7	2.9	16.4	5.4	7.9
Italy	50.3	3.1	21.4	4.0	7.1
OECD average	43.8	3.1	16.5	5.3	6.5

Source: OECD (2018). The expenditure areas are defined according to the *Classification of Function of Government* (COFOG). Expenditure areas not included are general public services, economic affairs, environmental protection, housing and community amenities and recreation, culture and religion

is based not only on a comprehensive social safety net and free education, but also other such policy measures (e.g. rent control, housing subsidies, transport subsidies, child allowance, student financial aid, municipal tax equalization, housing allowance, etc.) and a compressed wage structure with high minimum wages. This combination of direct welfare transfers of various kinds (both within and between generations) and various forms of regulations and institutional structures based on distribution policy aims implies complex systems that obscure the consequences of migration. The differences, not least with regard to incentives, can also affect which countries migrants choose to immigrate to within the EU, thereby affecting the speed and effectiveness of integration.

It is important to remember that distribution policy instruments that do not function via direct transfers but are instead based on various forms of regulation also generate large economic costs. These are not immediately apparent in public finances, e.g. barriers to rapid inclusion in the labor market or wage formation structures that obstruct opportunities for rapid entry to the labor market. For example, Sweden has the most compressed wage structure in the OECD, and the third-lowest percentage of unskilled jobs after Norway and Switzerland. This can be expected to affect how well and how quickly immigrants can be integrated into the Swedish economy and become established in the labor market.

The European welfare states are thus based on diversified and separated structures that are difficult to penetrate. It is particularly difficult to gain a comprehensive view of all consequences of migration on the sustainability of various welfare state transfer systems. The outcomes are, of course, dependent upon immigrant and incentives to economic integration. In other words, one can say that outcomes are dependent upon both individual circumstances and policy design. Conditions also differ considerably between migrants from different countries.

Immigrants: A Heterogeneous Group

It was mentioned at the beginning of this chapter that immigrants as a group are composed of individuals who are quite different from each other and whose reasons for migrating vary widely. The lowest common denominator is, of course, a desire achieve higher welfare in economic terms and in living conditions more generally. In addition, out of the some 1.3 million refugees who came to Europe in 2015, the overwhelming majority were 35 or younger, most coming from Syria, Afghanistan and Iraq.

Refugee immigrants and family reunification immigrants make up the dominant group. This differs from immigration in the past, when volumes were considerably smaller and labor force immigration was dominant. During the postwar period and up to the 1970s and 1980s, immigration to Sweden was dominated by labor force immigration. Since then, immigration has increasingly shifted to refugee immigration.

It is noteworthy that asylum and family reunification immigration is larger than labor force immigration, a situation that was exacerbated in 2015 in particular. The composition of migration to Sweden has obviously changed in the 2000s. A corresponding pattern can be observed for other European countries. A larger number of guest workers came to Germany from Turkey in the 1970s, for example.

Refugee immigrants thus constitute a large group of all immigrants who come to Europe. However, in addition to this group there are immigrants who are driven by more purely economic reasons. The vice president of the European Commission, Frans Timmermans, claims for example that six out of ten migrants to Europe are economic migrants, not refugees (NOS 2016). Similar arguments could be made with regard to Sweden. Many immigrants who apply for asylum are assessed as lacking grounds for asylum status and should be regarded as welfare or economic immigrants: they are driven by economic motives, not war and oppression.

The size of the group comprising economic migrants is uncertain. One indicator is that the share of migrants whose applications for asylum are rejected is about 50 percent in the EU as a whole, and roughly the same in Sweden. During the first half of 2017, 44 percent of applications were rejected. A small group of labor force migrants can be added to this group. The scope of intra-European migration is also unknown. There is, of course, a problem in demarcating these groups of migrants, but according to the Swedish Migration Agency, about 16,000 residence permits were granted in 2014 for labor market reasons, of which about 11,000 applicants were from Asia and about 2300 from Europe. Over the period of 2000–2014, 201,399 people were granted residence permits for labor market reasons. It is likely that circumstances are similar in other European countries that have received a high number of refugees.

Labor force migration has thus declined. An interesting question that should be further explored is how the labor force migrators are composed and their skill structure, i.e. the percentage share having academic qualifications. Concerning migration to Sweden, we can presume that qualified labor force migration is a marginal phenomenon in the greater scheme of things (in 2016, only 838 applications for expert tax relief were received). Qualifications and skills, such as an academic background, are a critical factor in the success and effectiveness of economic integration. It follows that group composition can be presumed highly important to the overall economic outcome for the recipient country, where a higher percentage of qualified labor immigration will improve the economic outcome.

The Economic Consequences of Immigration

The economic consequences of immigration differ between a welfare state and states with more limited distribution policy ambitions. Asylum reception in Europe is based primarily on humanitarian grounds, meaning that European countries, Sweden in particular, are facing significant economic challenges—but also economic opportunities. One opportunity is the influx of workers in an era when many developed economies are confronting demographic challenges in the form of an aging population. The challenge, naturally, lies in creating the conditions to reap the potential economic advantages.

There are several arguments based on economic theory for how labor force migration can impact an economy. An early model by Brezis and Krugman shows how the impacts can be expected to differ over the short and long runs (Brezis and Krugman 1996). In the short-run perspective, there may be upward pressure on unemployment and downward pressure on real wages. But this is not a predetermined outcome, rather it depends on how capital investments are affected and adjusted to a change in the labor supply. Likewise, a large population may improve the effects of immigration due to economies of scale at both the industrial and national levels, with falling prices as a result and higher real wages. Brezis and Krugman conclude that over the long run, immigration leads to an increase in real wage development (ibid). However, their model is based on several strong assumptions, for instance, all migrants are employable and that only certain products are traded internationally.

International trade theory explains how labor mobility is expected to lead to better global allocation of various skills and also help to reduce the income gap within as well as between countries. This is especially clear in service industries where the corresponding equalization cannot occur through international trade (see Alvstam and Lindberg in this volume). Nonetheless, this means that certain groups are going to see their incomes decline, at least in the short-run. Correspondingly, major changes in a country's set of production factors can affect its specialization.

An influx of workers can however also be expected to contribute to novel and complementary ideas, wider dissemination of knowledge and better understanding of other markets in other countries. Likewise, shortages in the labor market can be relieved, which can contribute to better market dynamics and more efficient use of both capital and labor. The OECD estimates that in recent decades, immigration has accounted for about 47 percent of labor supply growth in the US and up to 70 percent in Europe (OECD 2010).

Lazear recently showed in a theoretical model how the rationing of immigration slots affects the educational or skills attainment profile of recent arrivals. The larger the quotas, the lower the average educational attainment of the immigrants. Correspondingly, the size of the countries of origin will have a positive impact on the average educational level of immigrants. Taken as a whole, the combination of low quotas and large source countries should generate the highest educational attainment among immigrants. A relatively large number of countries also have quotas linked to education and skills requirements, and Lazear also finds empirical support for his model using American data (Lazear 2017).

The effects of immigration in the above models are often based on relatively far-reaching assumptions about, for example, labor market participation. One point of departure for many models and analyses is that migration consists of workers and that these workers go from employment in the source country to employment in the recipient country. This assumption is usually not accurate and must, on the contrary, be considered unrealistic in most European countries. Nevertheless, these analyses provide key insights into the effects of migration. Workers who move between countries are usually associated with an aggregate positive net effect, but there may be distribution effects, such as redistribution of income through wage competition. The magnitude of these effects is ultimately an empirical question.

Borjas estimates that immigrants to the US increased GDP by approximately 11 percent (Borjas 2013). The economic contribution of immigration has, however, had relatively little impact on native workers because about 98 percent of the increase accrued to the immigrants themselves in the form of wages and benefits. Borjas estimates the net gain for native workers at a modest 0.2 percent of the estimated GDP increase generated by immigrants (ibid). In addition, there is a significant distribution effect, where Borjas estimates that immigrant workers, via increased competition, reduce wages for native workers in the US by 2 percent if immigration increases by 10 percent (ibid). In parallel, the profits of those who employ the immigrants increase.

In other words, these results align with what we would theoretically expect to happen when immigration occur, at least over the short to medium term. It should be emphasized, however, that analyses and figures must be interpreted with some caution, since they usually do not include dynamic effects. If a corresponding study were to be done for a European country, it is likely the results would be affected by the magnitude of the redistribution and by the success, or lack thereof, of economic integration. In a country like Sweden, it would probably entail a somewhat larger redistribution from the native-born population, at least in the short run.

The results of the empirical research are, however, far from clear-cut and, especially, earlier results that have found a negative correlation have come under increasing fire. For example, Peri and Sparber conclude that the influx of immigrants to the US from the 1970s onwards has had no negative impact (or very modest impact during certain periods) on American wages, regardless of geographical region or level of education (Peri and Sparber 2009). Instead, a small positive effect can be found, and also that immigration has moderated the widening gap in income distribution in the US. The effects may differ somewhat from one decade to the next, however, and the negative impact of immigration on wage development is clearest during the period of 1990–2000. However, immigration to the US is dominated by labor force immigration of mainly well-educated workers. According to these studies, immigrants seldom compete with native workers, regardless of educational attainment. Foged and Peri find similar results in a recent study on immigration to Denmark (Foged and Peri 2016).

A relatively large share of immigrants to the US have also contributed to innovative and successful entrepreneurship in high value-added sectors. This is particularly evident in times of recessions. Immigrant entrepreneurs are over-represented among owners of new firms in the high-tech industries, patents and innovation, and have more venture capital invested in their firms. Through these firms, they have made a significant contribution to creating jobs in technologically advanced industries, according to economists like William Kerr and William Lincoln (Kerr and Lincoln 2010). In general, the research shows positive impacts of migration on business ownership and entrepreneurship, although dissenting results have also been presented. It also seems easier for immigrants to the US to improve their wages over time, compared to immigrants to Europe. Viewed from a longer perspective where the period is extended to the end of the nineteenth century, analyses of mainly the US show almost unambiguously significant and positive effects. This applies whether one studies income trends, productivity, educational attainment or innovation and the dissemination of knowledge.

Differences Between the US and Europe

It is impossible to draw conclusions for Europe or Sweden based on studies of the United States. What we can conclude is that the outcome will be affected by how quickly immigrants enter the labor market and by how dependent immigrants are on transfers. It is obvious that immigrants and refugees who are swiftly integrated (in an economic sense) and become self-supporting will make a positive contribution to public finances, while the reverse applies to the immigrants and refugees who remain dependent upon public transfers.

As discussed above, the analysis is made more difficult in the European welfare state by numerous distribution policy effects that are difficult to survey and yet must be factored in. Theoretically, it is entirely possible that an individual who is in work and economically active is nevertheless a net benefits recipient. The economic contribution during the years the person is working and economically productive must exceed the total redistribution they receive. Hence, depending upon the outcome of economic integration and how much wealth is redistributed via transfers and welfare structures migration can either constitute a gradually accumulating burden or a factor that increases welfare in the recipient country.

To fully understand the economic consequences of migration in a European-style welfare state, a "life-cycle income" perspective should be adopted. Briefly, the life-cycle income theory is based on the understanding that income and earning capacity are spread across the entire life cycle. In the early years of life before the labor market is entered and in later years when exit from the labor market takes place, individuals have zero earnings capacity. If there is no redistribution, incomes must compensate for the negative savings that arise. This may be accomplished voluntarily, through private pension savings for example. Education is another form of investment, if it results in higher productive and value-creating skills, which entails negative savings (paid by the individual or society).

In a welfare state, this life cycle income is affected by redistribution between individuals and between generations. The life cycle perspective enables a few general conclusions concerning factors that influence the economic effects of migration: 1) age at migration and remaining years in the labor market; 2) level of capacity and human capital at migration; 3) size of redistribution in welfare systems. These factors will also vary among different migrant groups. Overall, the economic outcome of refugee migration and asylum seekers will primarily depend upon how quickly migrants enter productive employment and transition from being net benefits recipients to net contributors. It makes sense to expect that more qualified immigrants will make a greater contribution by becoming quickly established in the labor market, delivering higher productivity and generating greater knowledge dissemination effects. It is thus possible to understand the impacts of migration by studying labor market outcomes.

A Divided Labor Market in Europe with Dysfunctional Economic Integration

There are several signs that the economic integration of migrants is not working well in Europe, although there are significant differences between countries. We refer to economic integration as becoming employed or some form of business activity or entrepreneurship. The time it takes to become established in the labor market varies among different groups, countries of origin, age and educational attainment. As an example, it takes a relatively long time for refugees to get established in the labor market in Sweden. Historically, it has taken eight years for 50 percent of immigrants to have secured a job, which can be compared to Germany, where the corresponding time span is five years. In comparison with the US integration seems to be relatively ineffective. Dysfunctional labor market integration is also apparent in Swedish employment statistics, where the employment rate for foreign-born workers was 64 percent in 2015, compared to 84 percent for native-born workers.

The figures for immigrants with low educational attainment are particularly depressing. For those having only pre-secondary education, the majority remain outside the regular labor market ten years after arriving in Sweden. A thorough analysis by economists Lina Aldén and Mats Hammarstedt shows that 35–40 percent of refugees were in work after five years in Sweden and only about 50 percent after seven years. The authors emphasize that there are significant differences among refugees as a group:

> The percentage of people in work among refugees from Iraq and Syria was somewhat lower than among the total number of refugees. We found the lowest percentage of people in work among refugees from Somalia. In this group, only 25 to 30 percent of refugees were in work five years after immigrating to Sweden. Only 35 percent of refugees from Somalia were in work seven years after immigrating to Sweden. (Aldén and Hammarstedt 2016: 6)

As regards migrants from Somalia, a number of comparative studies have been made between North America and European countries. The results show that both the percentage of employed people and business owners was significantly lower in the European countries compared to the US and Canada. According to earlier research the percentage of Somalis in work in Sweden in the 2000s was 22 to 35 percent and the percentage declined between 2000 and 2010. Roughly equivalent figures can be noted for Denmark and Finland. The statistics look considerably better in the US (2010) where the employment rate was 54 percent and also in Canada (2006) where the corresponding figure was 46 percent. Similarly, the employment gap was 13 percentage points in the US, 27 in Canada and but a striking 52 in Sweden. Business ownership was about ten times higher in the North American countries. Some of these differences, but far from all, are related to the level of education, time in the country and the size of the Somali immigrant groups. Accordingly, there should be lessons to be learnt from how other countries have managed immigration.

The large percentage of migrants with low educational attainment is thus a challenge for EU. Many lack the skills required to gain a foothold in the European labor market and this is the primary cause of low employment among immigrants. Language skills are particularly important, and it has been shown that refugees to Germany who are able to communicate relatively well have an employment rate about 35 percentage points higher than those with little or no German language skills. To an increasing degree, even unskilled jobs require language proficiency. As for Sweden, more than one third of immigrants had deficient reading and mathematics comprehension in 2015, while the corresponding figure for the native-born population was five percent.

It is important to emphasize the economic advantages that immigrants can bring. Immigrants can (beyond the addition to the labor force) contribute in several ways to economic renewal. Historically, immigrants have in many cases become entrepreneurs and had significant impact on economic growth. Economists Andreas Hatzigeorgiou and Magnus Lodefalk point out that immigrants are making a positive contribution to the internationalization of Swedish enterprise (Hatzigeorgiou and Lodefalk 2015). In line with this, the OECD has also argued that immigration can spur social renewal and innovation and bring new ideas (OECD 2010). It is, however, reasonable to expect these economically positive impacts will be linked mainly to labor force migration and migrants with high human capital.

From the perspective of the percentages of migrants who are integrated policies in Europe must be considered a failure that has preventing the realization of the potential benefits of immigration. To reap the economic benefits associated with immigration, economic integration has to happen fast and at a low cost to the public purse. Important in that regard are the labor market institutions and what the framework conditions look like for entering the labor market with low education. Looking at the employment gap between native and foreign-born workers, we can observe significant variations among countries in Europe. This statistic also indicates a large—and growing over time—employment gap between native and foreign-born workers. This is linked to the reduction in labor force immigration and the increase in refugee immigration.

The Importance of Human Capital

Beyond their reasons for migration, immigrants are a heterogeneous group in terms of human capital, that is, the knowledge and skills that equip them for the labor market. Human capital should not be considered synonymous with education: it includes all the value-adding and productive capacities, skills and knowledge that an individual possesses. Nonetheless, educational attainment provides an approximate picture of the level of human capital. As a whole, a report from the Swedish Entrepreneurship Forum indicates that the migrants Sweden has received have low educational attainment on average, thereby lowering the likelihood of successful establishment in the labor market (Eklund 2016). Conditions in Europe for migrants with low qualifications to become established in the labor market vary widely across Europe. After Norway and Switzerland, Sweden has the lowest share of unskilled jobs that requires no or little education (see Fig. 7.2).

Statistics from Eurostat also show that a lower share of unskilled jobs results in a wider employment gap (see Fig. 7.3). Compared to other countries, only the Netherlands demonstrates poorer integration and a wider employment gap between the native-born and foreign-born populations than Sweden. In other words, it is reasonable to deduce a connection between a compressed wage structure (high minimum wages) and dysfunctional economic integration.

There is obviously risk that failed economic integration will result in persistent and costly dependency on benefits. We have previously mentioned the long delay between arrival and labor market entry that can be observed in both Germany and Sweden. This is accompanied by the considerable public costs generated in connection with failed integration and the problems that economist Tino Sanandaji has pointed to (Sanandaji 2016). An interesting observation that can be made in the context is the "positive" employment gap (that is, when immigrants have a higher employment rate than native-born workers), as seen in Hungary for example. This indicates that the migration that Hungary accepts is driven by labor market reasons or that Hungary only accepts migrants with strong potential to secure jobs.

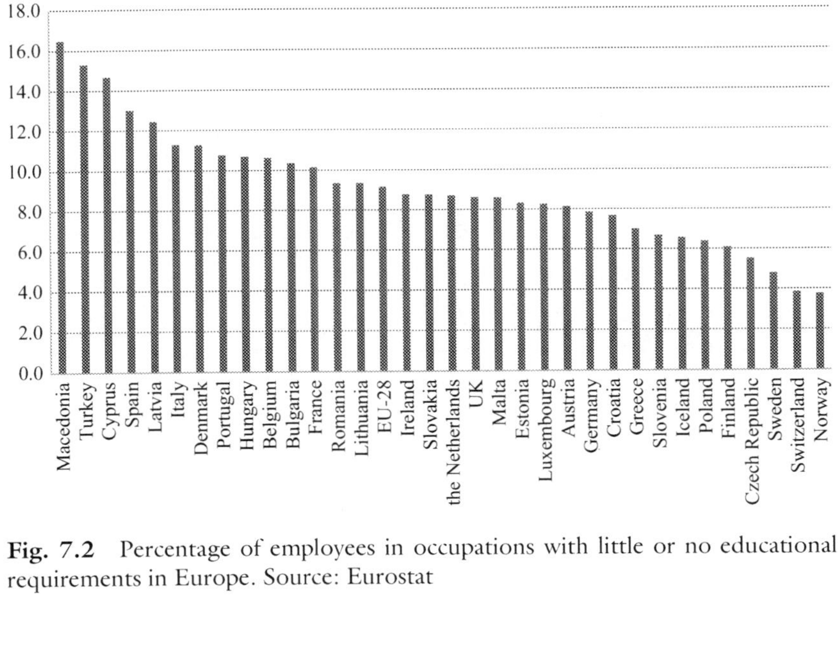

Fig. 7.2 Percentage of employees in occupations with little or no educational requirements in Europe. Source: Eurostat

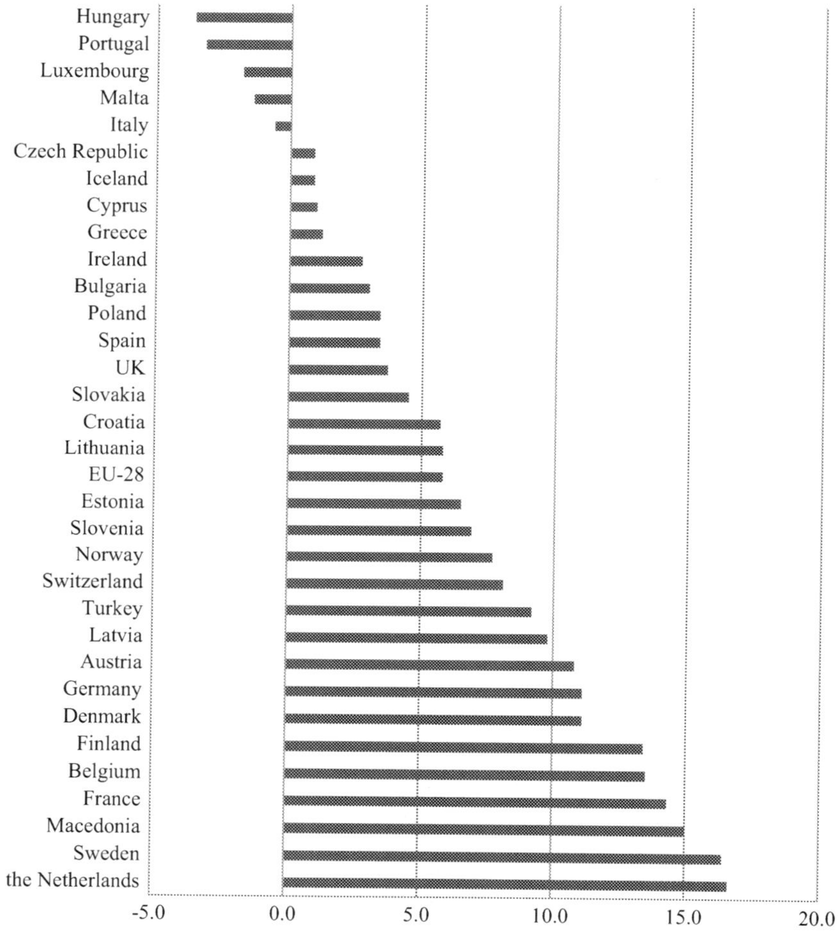

Fig. 7.3 Employment gap between native-born and foreign-born workers in Europe. Source: Eurostat. Differences are stated as percentage points. For example, the employment rate in Sweden is 84.8 percent among native-born workers and 68.4 percent among foreign-born workers, meaning the employment gap is 16.4 percentage points

Labor Market Entry, Human Capital and Redistribution

There is basically consensus among scholars that human capital is the most important factor for individuals to successfully establish themselves at the labor market. Education is the significant factor as to why immigrants so quickly are integrated in the US. In other words, looking at the skills and educational attainment of immigrants provides an indication of the economic outcomes we can expect. The Swedish Entrepreneurship Forum has compared educational attainment in Sweden for native-born individuals and asylum seekers from Syria, Afghanistan, Iraq, Eritrea and Somalia (age group 25–64) during the period of 2011–2015. The comparison shows that the majority of asylum seekers lack higher education and that a high percentage even lacks secondary education, but that the differences across countries are considerable. Among Somali refugees, the share with education equivalent to Swedish compulsory school (nine years) or less is a full 58 percent, while only 12 percent have any form of higher education. There is reason to assume that levels of knowledge are similar for asylum seekers who arrive in the rest of Europe.

In other words, many of these refugees can be presumed to be far from the labor market. There may also be reason to consider the quality of education that refugees received in their home countries, since this is likely to constitute a further barrier to economic integration. Within the OECD countries alone there is considerable variation in levels of knowledge, as reflected in international comparisons (e.g. PISA and PIAAC). It thus seems reasonable to conclude that lower average skills levels are the primary reason for lower employment rates among foreign-born workers. Unemployment is considerably higher for all people with only pre-secondary education, both native-born and foreign-born, but especially so for the latter group.

How large, then, are the welfare transfers? OECD research has estimated that the redistribution between native-born and foreign-born people is in the range of +/- 1 percent of GDP. Studies that include a relatively large number of countries during earlier periods (1980 to the mid-2000s) show positive effects and few or zero displacement effects in the labor market. At the request of the European Commission, researchers d'Artis Kanc and Patrizio Lecca performed a study that shows that the costs for integration of new arrivals to Europe will exceed income for the first seven to ten years (Kancs and Lecca 2017). Thereafter, refugee immigration is estimated to provide a positive contribution to annual GDP growth of 0.2 to 1.4 percent (the level depends on the success of the integration policy). This means that it will take ten to twenty years to fully recover of the costs of integration programs. Economist and migration scholar Joakim Ruist estimates that net transfers to refugees and their relatives from the rest of the population in 2015 amounted to 1.35 percent of GDP in Sweden (Ruist 2018). Added to this are the costs directly related to asylum incurred by the Swedish Migration Agency and other government agencies, which equal 0.65 percent of GDP. The total costs amounts to about 2 percent of GDP.

According to economist Jan Ekberg, income redistribution from the native-born population to the foreign-born population amounts to 1.5–2 percent of GDP annually. In a review of the literature since the 1970s, Ekberg found that the average immigrant to Sweden made a positive contribution to public finances until the mid-1980s, a period dominated by labor force immigration. Somewhere in the transition from the 1970s to the 1980s, immigration shifted towards more refugees and the net contribution to public finances has consequently been negative (Ekberg 2009). That is to say, immigration has constituted a net cost to public finances since the 1980s. This development also coincides with the deterioration of integration in the labor market.

One hypothesis presented in the literature is that public welfare commitments work as "welfare magnets," meaning that immigrants are attracted to countries where welfare transfers are relatively large. Borjas puts it this way:

> The magnet hypothesis has several facets. It is possible, for example, that welfare programs attract immigrants who otherwise would not have migrated to the United States; or that the safety net discourages immigrants who "fail" in the United States from returning to their source countries; or that the huge interstate dispersion in welfare benefits affects the residential location choices of immigrants in the United States and places a heavy fiscal burden on relatively generous states. (Borjas 1999: 608)

Borjas also finds empirical evidence that migrants are attracted to the US states that offer relatively more generous benefits (ibid). The US is an interesting comparison country, especially considering that the social safety net is much less comprehensive than in large parts of Europe. Concerns related to the notion that immigrants would come to the US to benefit from various welfare systems resulted in new legislation that made citizenship a requirement for receiving most welfare transfers. *The Personal Responsibility and Work Opportunity Reconciliation Act* was introduced in 1996 by former US President Bill Clinton who during his election campaign vowed to "end welfare as we know it."

To the best of our knowledge, there has been no study corresponding to Borjas's "welfare magnets" in Europe, but there is be no reason to believe that this effect would be weaker in Europe. On the contrary, it is reasonable to expect a stronger impact in Europe, considering that redistribution policies in the European states is considerably larger than within the US. The tendency of asylum seekers to leave southern Europe for countries in northern Europe, especially Sweden and Germany, is consistent with this interpretation. Economists have presented similar arguments in other contexts and have warned of the risks of what can be considered welfare arbitrage. There is however a need for deeper analysis of the long-term consequences here.

Conclusions: Better Economic Integration and Greater Coordination Within the EU Are Critical Steps in Order to Reap the Benefits from Migration

This chapter has shown that the EU and its Member States are confronting significant challenges in managing the refugee crisis that has been ongoing for several years. In this context, countries like Sweden and Germany are distinguished by their unique combination of comprehensive welfare systems and high rates of asylum reception. The question is, quite simply, how large the economic consequences will turn out to be and whether the costs will become unmanageable over the long term or will be balanced by positive effects in terms of increased labor force participation and more dynamic entrepreneurship. The risk that EU countries will function as welfare magnets can be presumed to be related to the scope and design of the welfare state. In addition, the migration issue is not only dividing public opinion in various European countries, it is sowing discord among EU Member States. Central and eastern European countries are generally more restrictive towards asylum seekers than others, especially Sweden and Germany. In the United Kingdom, the presence of both Polish guest workers and asylum-seekers had strong influence on the outcome of the Brexit referendum. Parts of these differences are based on the view of the effects migration can be expected to have on the welfare state. However, migration in the EU thus far seems not to have undermined the national welfare systems to any appreciable extent. Still, it is obvious that the situation in Europe has created a deep need for fact-based analysis and discussion of the economic consequences for the welfare state.

Obviously certain groups are going to generate a significant net economic cost to welfare states while other groups can be expected to provide positive economic effects. As regards asylum seekers, family reunification immigrants and labor force immigrants, there are also significant differences within and between the various groups. The European countries that have received a high percentage of asylum seekers are going to have to bear substantial costs for the foreseeable future. The net economic effect depends partly on the costs that arise for society and the welfare state when receiving a large number of immigrants, partly on how quickly and effectively asylum seekers are integrated into the economy and the immigrants' levels of productivity and value creation. Similar arguments can be made concerning labor force migrants, of course. In countries with high distribution policy ambitions, the economic contributions made by low-productivity jobs can fall short of the aggregate costs of migration. Still, there is evidence from other countries, the US in particular (although it has much lower welfare policy ambitions), that indicates long-term gains from immigration. Likewise, simulation studies of the economic gains of immigration could also be significant to Europe. Consequently, the success or failure of integration determines whether the economic cost/benefit analysis ends with a plus or a minus.

Providing humanitarian assistance to people in need due to war, conflict or disaster is a worthy mission and a legal reason to be granted asylum. Still, costs should be shared across member States and there should be a coordinated European process for migration and asylum policy to avoid bottlenecks and excessive costs for certain countries. Large-scale immigration requires efficient systems to prepare refugees for entering the labor market. At present, the interval between arrival to Europe and entry to the labor market is far too long, although this differs from country to country. Germany seems to have made the most progress here and large groups of refugee immigrants are ready to enter the labor market after only three months. This is due partly to an improved bureaucratic process, where most matters are managed by one comprehensive agency. Likewise, Germany has devoted considerable efforts to create qualified language courses that are combined with tailor-made and occupation-specific training programs. Germany has also instituted a "3+2" system, in which asylum seekers can train for three years with the right to stay for an additional two years if they find jobs that correspond to their training.

Asylum reception can thus have profound distribution policy consequences in the EU and its Member States, but also contribute to welfare systems becoming more robust over time. Integration policy is key to the long-term outcomes. If nothing else changes, higher welfare transfers to immigrants will mean that more people will have to be in work for the average welfare to be maintained. Rapid integration thus alleviates the public economic costs that unquestionably arise over the short run. At the same time, successful integration can lead to economic opportunities, such as eliminating labor shortages and alleviating skills provision problems. If, on the other hand, it takes a long time before immigrants are established in the labor market, the burden of support will increase for those who are working in the host country, which can have fiscal and distribution policy consequences.

One question that can be asked is whether the economic integration of newly arrived refugees can be accomplished within existing frameworks or whether wider economic and institutional reforms are going to be required? Policy design will determine the impact on the economy and, by extension, the legitimacy of the welfare state as we know it. This issue is consequently essential to the future of the European welfare states that are based on universal, rather than differentiated, welfare systems. In this context, it is important to emphasize that migrants are a heterogeneous group with widely varying backgrounds and possibilities for successful economic integration. It is reasonable to expect entirely different conditions for economic integration and entrepreneurship for immigrants who come to Europe for asylum reasons compared to immigrants driven by labor market reasons.

This means that integration policy in Europe must use several different instruments to succeed: (1) entry barriers to labor markets must be lowered through lower wages, either linked to wage subsidies or a wider wage spread; (2) incentives to enter the labor market must be reinforced, and; (3) training and education programs must be made more effective, especially in the language of the recipient country. These programs should also, to the greatest possible extent, be adapted to refugees of various ethnic and educational backgrounds.

The EU should also establish mechanisms to make it easier for the Member States to learn from each other. At present, integration policy tends to proceed from different points of departure in each country, even though the countries adopted a common policy formulated in the *European Agenda for the Integration of Third-Country Nationals* back in 2011. In the current situation, migration is one of the key policy areas for the European Commission and the aforementioned document has been augmented with *The European Agenda of Migration* from 2015. It presents methods for preventing illegal migration, saving lives and securing external borders, strengthening a common asylum policy and developing a new policy for legal migration. Likewise, the EU has an important role in communicating relevant knowledge of the effects that can be expected from migration, the costs and benefits thereof not least among them. Finally, there is reason to ensure that an effective quota system for the reception of asylum seekers among EU Member States is established, based upon effective sanctions.

References

Aldén, M., & Hammarstedt, L. (2016). Flyktinginvandring: Sysselsättning, förvärvsinkomster och offentliga finanser. *Rapport till Finanspolitiska rådet*. 2016: 1.

Borjas, G. J. (1999). Immigration and Welfare Magnets. *Journal of Labor Economics, 17*(4), 607–637.

Borjas, G. J. (2013). Immigration and the American Worker. *Center for Immigration Studies*.

Brezis, E. S., & Krugman, P. R. (1996). Immigration, Investment, and Real Wages. *Journal of Population Economics, 9*(1), 83–93.

Chatham House. (2017). What Do Europeans Think About Muslim Immigration? Retrieved October 2, 2018, from https://www.chathamhouse.org/expert/comment/what-do-europeans-think-about-muslim-immigration#.

Ekberg, J. (2009). Invandringen och de offentliga finanserna. *Expertgruppen för studier i offentlig ekonomi*. 2009: 3.

Eklund, J. (Ed.). (2016). Immigration, Economic Integration and Entrepreneurship. *Swedish Economic Forum Report 2016*. Swedish Entrepreneurship Forum.

Foged, M., & Peri, G. (2016). Immigrants' Effect on Native Workers: New Analysis on Longitudinal Data. *American Economic Journal: Applied Economics, 8*(2), 1–34.

Hatzigeorgiou, A., & Lodefalk, M. (2015). Trade, Migration and Integration: Evidence and Policy Implications. *The World Economy, 38*(12), 2013–2048.

Kancs, A., & Lecca, P. (2017). Long Term Social, Economic and Fiscal Effects of Immigration into the EU: The Role of Integration Policy. *Joint Research Centre Working Papers in Economics and Finance*. 2017: 4.

Kerr, W. R., & Lincoln, W. L. (2010). The Supply Side of Innovation: H-1B Visa Reforms and US Ethnic Invention. *Journal of Labor Economics, 28*(3), 473–508.

Krugman, P. R. (2010, April 26). The Curious Politics of Immigration. *The New York Times*. Retrieved October 2, 2018, from https://krugman.blogs.nytimes.com/2010/04/26/the-curious-politics-of-immigration/.

Lazear, E. P. (2017). Why Are Some Immigrant Groups More Successful Than Others?. *National Bureau of Economic Research working paper*. 2017: 23548.

NOS. (2016). Timmermans: meer dan helft vluchtelingen heeft economisch motief. Retrieved October 2, 2018, from https://nos.nl/artikel/2082786-timmermans-meer-dan-helft-vluchtelingen-heeft-economisch-motief.html.

OECD. (2010). Open for Business: Migrant Entrepreneurship in OECD Countries. *OECD Publishing*. Retrieved October 2, 2018, from https://doi.org/10.1787/9789264095830-en.

OECD. (2018). National Accounts of OECD Countries: General Government Accounts 2017. *OECD Publishing*. Retrieved October 2, 2018, from https://doi.org/10.1787/na_gga-2018-en.

Peri, G., & Sparber, C. (2009). Task Specialization, Immigration, and Wages. *American Economic Journal: Applied Economics, 1*(3), 135–169.

Ruist, J. (2018). The Prosperity Gap and the Free Movement of Workers. In U. Bernitz, M. Mårtensson, L. Oxelheim, & T. Persson (Eds.), *Bridging the Prosperity Gap in the EU: The Social Challenge Ahead*. Cheltenham, UK: Edward Elgar Publishing.

Sanandaji, T. (2016). *Massutmaningen*. Kuhzad Media.

Wihlborg, C., & Khoury, S. (2018). Trust in the Euro and the EU's Banking Union after the Financial Crisis. In A. Bakardijeva Engelbrekt, N. Bremberg, A. Michalski, & L. Oxelheim (Eds.), *Trust in the European Union in Challenging Times*. Cham, Switzerland: Palgrave.

CHAPTER 8

EU Foreign and Security Policy in a Mediatized Age

Douglas Brommesson and Ann-Marie Ekengren

Introduction

Since the start of the new millennium the EU has been beset by one crisis after another (Rosamond 2017). Constitutional crisis, debt crises and financial crises are just a few of the challenges that have confronted the EU and with it the process of European integration. However, "Brexit" is perhaps the challenge that most clearly has shaken the foundations of the EU. The British people's request to leave the EU and the ensuing exit negotiations is a grave test for the EU, as it goes against the idea of recurring EU expansions and that the EU should encompass all of Europe. Amid this period of recurring crises, the EU is trying to find its place in a changing world order. This is visible in the field of foreign and security policy, which relevance was strengthened by the Treaty of Lisbon and the creation of the European External Action Service (EEAS). Through the treaty revisions, the EU's High Representative for Foreign Affairs and

D. Brommesson (✉)
Lund University, Lund, Sweden
e-mail: douglas.brommesson@svet.lu.se

A.-M. Ekengren
University of Gothenburg, Gothenburg, Sweden
e-mail: ann-marie.ekengren@pol.gu.se

A. Bakardjieva Engelbrekt et al. (eds.), *The European Union in a Changing World Order*,
https://doi.org/10.1007/978-3-030-18001-0_8

Security Policy was granted new capacities and a new institutional role. The first High Representative Javier Solana (1999–2009) held the office of General Secretary of the Council of the European Union. He was succeeded by Catherine Ashton (2009–2014), who, as High Representative, simultaneously held the office of Vice President of the European Commission for External Affairs and permanent Chair of the foreign affairs configuration of Council of Ministers. The High Representative is assisted by the EEAS. As a result of these changes, the person who holds the position of High Representative has become increasingly indispensable at the center of EU foreign and security policy than his/her predecessors (Helwig 2013). This is particularly evident with the appointment of the current High Representative, Federica Mogherini (2014–), who has pursued an active role on the global stage and thus strengthened the High Representative's role as the central EU voice in international politics (Helwig 2017).

Two high representatives have left their mark on the EU through their efforts to develop strategies aimed at carving out a path forward for the EU in international politics. Javier Solana led the work on the European Security Strategy (2003) and Federica Mogherini did the same on the EU's Global Strategy (2016). Although these two strategies have somewhat different areas of focus (the former focuses on security policy; the latter has a more general global perspective), they are often compared because of their central position as comprehensive strategic policy documents covering broad and important components of the EU's external relations (Mälksoo 2016; Tocci 2017). The manner in which the strategies were developed highlights interesting changes regarding how the EU formulates and conducts foreign and security policy at a time when the international order is in transition (Tonra and Christiansen 2010). The process that led to the 2003 Security Strategy centered on the political relations among EU member states and EU institutions. Today, the EU's foreign and security policy is formulated through a process which is markedly more public. The communication efforts regarding the EU's Global Strategy of 2016 have been considered important, both when it was drafted as well as at the time of its launch (Hedling 2018). Mogherini's active use of social media to launch the strategy and her public activities on the diplomatic stage constituted an integral part of this process.

This chapter discusses the mediatization of politics in general and of the EU's foreign and security policy in particular. The questions addressed concern whether the development of the EU's foreign and security policy is influenced by the increase of mediatization and—if so—how. To answer these questions, we compare the EU's strategies from 2003 and 2016 with regard to how the EU's environment is described, how the EU's identity is represented, and how the demand for an EU-level foreign and security policy is perceived by EU citizens and politicians. The overall conclusion is that while there are signs indicating that the mediatization of the EU's foreign and security policy has increased since the beginning of the new millennium, it is mainly a matter of leading representatives of the EU and EEAS civil servants who are trying to make use of the opportunities provided by the media logic to promote EU political goals. This suggests that mediatization needs not be a threat to politics if it is used properly, for example by strengthening the legitimacy for political solutions to societal problems. However, it is extremely important that political leaders in the EU and at the national level use the opportunities that new media offer with combining both style and sensitivity.

Digitalization, "Fake News" and the Mediatization of Politics

A growing body of academic literature argues that politics has been influenced by the growing level of mediatization (Hjarvard 2008; Krotz 2007, 2009; Mazzoleni 2008; Schulz 2014; Strömbäck 2008, 2011). According to media researchers, politics is increasingly described as being mediatized since at least the end of the 1980s. The argument is that, in the past, politics was affected by the media; whereas, today, politics has internalized the media logic (Asp 1986, 1990). Expressed differently, the media logic has colonized the political sphere. Here, media logic can be understood in the spirit of David P. Altheide and Robert P. Snow (1979) as the media's *modus operandi*, even if it is a logic that is not necessarily limited to those actors we associate with the media. Concretely, the media logic is expressed through practices such as personification, intensification, polarization and identification of scapegoats, just to name a few examples.

However, as we have shown in our recent book *The Mediatization of Foreign Policy: Political Decision-making and Humanitarian Intervention*, there are strong reasons to assume that foreign policy is particularly resistant to mediatization (Brommesson and Ekengren 2017: 3–18). Foreign policy is traditionally seen as a conservative policy area characterized by caution and prudence. Because foreign policy decisions are frequently made in small, closed groups, it is not publicly debated as frequently as other policy areas. Foreign policy issues are therefore less public and debate in the media is more limited. These characteristics stand in sharp contrast to the media logic, with its shortsightedness and focus on individual cases along with its sensationalism rather than long-term perspective. Foreign policy can thus be described as a critical case of mediatization. That is, if we can identify examples of mediatization in the area of foreign policy we can assume that mediatization occurs in many other political areas as well.

At the same time, the traditional view of foreign policy as a policy area particularly resistant to mediatization has been put in question by the emergence of digital diplomacy. Cornelia Bjola and Marcus Holmes (2015) acknowledge that it is still too early to say whether we have reached a shared definition of digital diplomacy. Nonetheless it requires the use of modern information technology to achieve diplomatic goals or solve foreign policy problems. As these forms of diplomacy become more common, we may conclude that diplomacy has transformed from a political practice conducted away from the public view to one that is present in everyone's social media feeds. Digitalization allows the public to witness diplomatic moves on social media platforms like Twitter and Facebook, as foreign ministries or individual foreign ministers seek to market their own state and its international activities (often referred to as "national branding" or "place branding") or even, sometimes, themselves as forceful leaders. Digital diplomacy can be understood as the consummation of a mediatized foreign policy. Such a development implies that policy is adapted to the requirements of the media. This implies that a farsighted, strategic perspective has been replaced by shortsighted, vivid, polarizing gambits in which particular individuals are from time to time granted a central role. The rapid spread of information, little opportunity for explanation and development (Twitter's limit of 140 characters is a particularly conspicuous example) and intensified polarization are some of the risks of the digital diplomacy.

When Donald Trump was elected president of the United States we witnessed an extreme example of politics adapting to the format of digital media. Trump's constant attacks on political opponents and the "dishonest media" as well as his sweeping promises of a grand future for America, enabled him to win support outside traditional political channels. According to Hunt Allcott and Matthew Gentzkow (2017), key to his election victory was the running of his campaign as a unifying rally with an apparently successful digital strategy. In the wake of the 2016 US presidential election, the related question of "fake news" (intentionally falsified news) has emerged (Bakir and McStay 2018). Donald Trump claims that he gave birth to the concept. Regardless whether this is true or not, Trump succeeded in painting the mainstream media's (e.g. New York Times and CNN) coverage of him as biased. According to him, these biases led to a distorted reporting characterized by political correctness to the extent that the news became essentially false. The speed with which information spreads and the difficulty to correct erroneous information clearly reveal the potential power of social media during an election campaign.

Since the US presidential election, the big question has been whether Trump was aided by actors with connections to Russia, and whether it actually was these actors who planted and spread fake news in social media in order to harm Trump's opponent and create a momentum in favour of him. It is not the task of this chapter to sort out this contentious issue. However, taken together, the debate about digital diplomacy, digital political campaigns and phenomena such as "fake news" suggest that we are witnessing the development of an increasingly intense and polarized political reality—one that can be seen as an expression of media adaptation—a clear example of a mediatized political practice.

In keeping with our argument, the adaption to media norms and rhythms acts as a strong indicator of the standard arguments in mediatization research, i.e. that the media logic (or the media's *modus operandi*) has successfully colonized politics. This narrative suggests that power is located within the framework characteristic of media structures, regardless of whether we are considering new social media or traditional media. However, it is also possible to see things from the opposite perspective. From the point of view of politics, it is reasonable to keep the question of who influences whom open to empirical investigation. This makes it possible to ask whether political actors are actually using the media's short-sighted perspective to strengthen farsighted political goals (Brommesson and Ekengren 2017: 188–190; Hedling 2018). If so, this implies that the media logic has not colonized politics, but, rather, that politics has snapped up the media logic as an increasingly integrated tool in the service of politics.

Returning to the issue of "fake news" and undue influence over popular opinion, many observers argue that various Russian actors with more or less strong connections to the Kremlin use fake news and other activities in social media, "alternative media" and even traditional media to strengthen Russia's standing in the West (or to discredit opponents in the West). The purpose is to promote Russia's long-term strategic interests. Again, it is not our task here to determine the degree to which Russian actors have engaged in such behavior. However, such action creates awareness of the fact that state actors can use mediatization as an instrument in the service of politics, and that this can be done strategically. As Elsa Hedling shows in her doctoral thesis (Hedling 2018), this gives us reason to ponder about the power relations between politics and the media. The "role of the victim", often ascribed by research to politics actually seems drastically overstated. Rather, it may be that mediatization has become a new means to gain legitimacy for more or less traditional political goals.

Following from this argument, we have reason to view the EU as a political actor which most probably also uses the opportunities offered by mediatization. This is because the EU is an actor which, in many respects, lacks, or has limited recourse to, opportunities to gain legitimacy through traditional ways due to the absence of a shared public European sphere, the weak role played by European parties remain compared to national counterparts, and feeble citizen mobilization at the grassroots level. According to Asimina Michailidou and Hanz-Jörg Trenz, mediatization and the media logic do offer opportunities the EU can use to deal with the Union's legitimacy deficit (Michailidou and Trenz 2018).

Regardless of whether one believes that politics has difficulties fending off mediatization or whether politics and politicians regularly use the opportunities offered by mediatization, our argument is rather that we should expect significant variation in mediatization from case to case and over time. That is, there is no reason to assume that mediatization will steadily increase over time. In the next section we develop our argument in support of this view. Following that, the remaining part of the chapter is devoted to providing evidence of variation in mediatization. This is achieved by analyzing the strategies of the EU in the area of external relations mentioned above. In our view, the analysis illustrates ways in which degree of mediatization varies which this can be connected to specific prerequisites which in turn create a favorable context for increased mediatization.

Mediatization of the EU's Foreign and Security Policy

A not insignificant part of the mediatization literature leaves the impression that the political sphere will increasingly be "invaded" by the media. This is communicated by the fact that politics is expected to be forced to adapt to the media's agenda, speed and story-telling techniques. Jesper Strömbäck (2008, 2010, 2011) notes that, in this context, media logic means simplification, polarization, intensification, personification, visualization, stereotyping and framing politics as a game or competition. The media logic is portrayed as the more powerful force, one that subordinates the logic of politics. In a story about the EU's external relations, this could mean painting simple stories about one-dimensional threats to the EU, communicating lively descriptions of other actors who stand for something radically different from the EU and—by doing so—portraying the struggle over political influence and economic benefits as a competition among the strong actors of the world.

Political logic can be described as collective processes that contribute to the redistribution of power in society. Political actors behave in various ways in order to gain influence, and the ideological basis for various decisions is part of political logic. Another important aspect of political logic is when collective political actors operate within the framework of political institutions to win support for their ideologies. This includes getting citizens to vote for them in elections and striving to implement the policies articulated in the election process. In this narrative, political logic is closely connected to an idealized view of representative democracy. In a narrative about the EU's external relations, it might involve describing the importance of the institutions for creating political meaning, the value system that is the foundation of the EU's existence, and the multilateral processes that contribute to changing the conditions for exercising influence and engaging in trade.

Our argument is that certain conditions determine the degree to which political logic or media logic becomes dominant. It simply cannot be assumed that mediatization will continually increase. Rather, it should be expected to vary across different contexts, time periods and types of questions. Based on theoretical arguments and previous research by media scholars (Strömbäck and Esser 2009; Djerf-Pierre et al. 2014; Isotalus and Almonkari 2014), we argue that mediatization of foreign policy is more likely under certain circumstances. Among others, Rachel Folz (2011) points to factors such as uncertainty, identity and resonance as contributing to explaining variation in terms of outcomes. Our own previous research also shows that degree of mediatization tends to vary across different types of questions (and over time) if there is variation in these factors. It is thus not reasonable to simply assume that the EU's external relations will be characterized by more and more mediatization over time. Rather, mediatization depends on the conditions discussed below.

Uncertainty plays an overarching role and is thus one of the most important factors that can contribute to an increased use of media logic (Folz 2011). By uncertainty we mean whether decision-makers are faced with an entirely new strategic landscape, e.g. a new issue that they have not dealt with before or the weakening or renegotiation of previously stable institutions. In such situations, it is reasonable to assume that mediatization—consciously or unconsciously—creates frames of reference for how a question should be described and understood. Media logic creates an intuitive framework outside the existing political lines of division. The media's ability to create shared stores contributes to impact of the media logic. Given this, we can assume that the probability that media logic will be used is greater today, because the EU's role has become more contested in recent years. In addition, the world order is in greater flux today, which also suggests that we are facing greater uncertainty. This also suggests that media logic is more likely to play a role in foreign policy.

A second factor that contributes to the increased use of media logic is *identity* (Folz 2011). By this we mean whether decision-makers identify themselves in a meaningful manner with characterizations associated with mediatization. For example, the likelihood that a decision-maker will see media logic as a natural way to communicate about political issues increases if he/she self-identifies as a champion of the rights of individuals or tends to use polemic descriptions.

Our third factor is *resonance* (Folz 2011). Resonance means that decision-makers experience some form of pressure from an external audience regarding an issue at hand or policy under consideration. Such pressure—from member states, the public, political parties or other organizations—increases the likelihood that media logic offers a way to interpret the question or policy.

As noted previously, we use two EU strategies to illustrate how mediatization tendencies vary depending on the prevalence of these three conditions. For each strategy, we will discuss how the conditions for mediatization vary in terms of:

1. Uncertainty about the global situation or Europe's role,
2. Identity in line with media logic's focus on individuals, polemic, simplification, etc.
3. A sense of strong pressure from an external audience about foreign policy.

Given variation in these conditions, we discuss the degree to which there are indications that EU foreign policy is more or less mediatized.

While our primary ambition is to illustrate an overarching line of reasoning about the mediatization of politics in relation to the EU's foreign policy, it is useful to briefly discuss what mediatized and non-mediatized politics can be expected to look like. Reasoning largely aimed at gaining support for policy within the framework set by existing institutions is seen as an expression of political logic primarily focused on processes (form). Reasoning aimed at formulating strategies based on ideological values in order to solve particular problems is an expression of political logic primarily focused on policy (content). Political logic as strategy in contrast to media logic has been discussed by Strömbäck (2008) and Meyer (2012). If the EU acts to meet demands that the media claims to represent the majority opinion and if it formulates its media strategy in a vivid and personalized way, then it is an expression of media logic focused on process (form). However, it is also possible that the EU's global strategies are formulated based on the view that dominates a polarized debate at a given point in time. For example, foreign policy is characterized by a global focus on security and the rights of individuals (content). It should be noted that both logics can manifest themselves simultaneously, albeit in relation to different policy questions.

From European Security Strategy to Global Strategy for the EU

When Javier Solana presented the European Security Strategy (ESS) 2003, the EU's position was strong. The Euro had been recently launched and the EU's large eastward expansion was imminent. Researchers and practitioners who had predicted that European integration would deepen seemed prescient. The Euro and enlargement both testified to an integration process that was reaching heights never seen before in Europe. At the same time, internal divisions about the Iraq War demonstrated the need to develop a shared understanding about security along with a strategy to promote it. The British Prime Minister Tony Blair clearly stood on the side of the US giving his support to the 2003 invasion of Iraq, while France and Germany were critical. The latter countries did not accept the view that a preventive war was necessary in order to keep Iraq from developing weapons of mass destruction. They argued that the UN weapons inspectors under the leadership of Hans Blix should be given more time to complete their work. Different views about the UN's role in the conflict were also evident in the debate among European leaders.

Thirteen years later, in 2016, Federica Mogherini presented the EU's global strategy (EUGS). It was intended to be an overarching, comprehensive approach to foreign and security policy, at the center of which was the EU's role in a changing world. According to Nathalie Tocci (2016), who not only conducts research on the EU's foreign and security policy, but also participated in preparing a draft of the EUGS, the strategic considerations that led the EU's heads of state and government to task Mogherini with formulating a new strategy for the EU were largely based on an understanding that the global scene had deteriorated greatly since 2003. This was also stated in the introduction of the EUGS: "We need a stronger Europe. This is what our citizens deserve; this is what the wider world expects. We live in times of existential crisis, within and beyond the European Union."

According to Mogherini, both the world outside the EU and the EU itself was experiencing an existential crisis. Externally, the EU was depicted as being surrounded by conflicts, particularly in the east (Ukraine, the Crimea), southeast (Syria, Iraq, Yemen) and south (Libya, Egypt). There were also threats and conflicts inside the EU: a seemingly constant stream of terrorist attacks (Brussels, Paris, Nice, Manchester, Stockholm, Barcelona—to name only the most recent incidents), financial crises, waves of migrants that the EU was ill-equipped to deal with, and the EU institutions put under pressure by the growth of new EU-skeptical movements (see also Fägersten and Blombäck in this volume).

At the launch of the EUGS, the EU saw itself as located in a world characterized by crisis at a time when it is having difficulty dealing with its own internal crises. Developing a strategy aimed at carving out the organization's own place in the world at such a momentous time opened the door to existential reflections. This should be compared to the situation which reigned at the launch of the ESS, which took place at a time when the process of integration was seen as having acquired almost eternal and unstoppable characteristics. When the zeitgeist is such, existential questions are not at the forefront, but the narrative focuses instead on how the success story can be protected and put to work. Another way to summarize the fundamental contextual differences is to note that the ESS is a document to guide the EU's security policy on the global scene, while the EUGS is a document to create legitimacy for the very presence of the EU on the global scene.

At the same time, it is important to keep in mind that all strategies of this kind are written with communicative ambitions. Maria Mälksoo (2016) argues that both strategies are aimed at bringing clarity about the EU's role in the world, as well as efforts to try to bring clarity about who the EU is and what it wants to be. Thus, despite contextual differences, both documents can be understood from a communicative perspective. This makes the form that the documents are taking an interesting object of study and which brings us close to the question of legitimacy, in the sense that political actors can be expected to communicate their policies in an effort to gain legitimacy, either internally or externally.

Nonetheless, the forms of communication change, and new forms can lead to changes in the logic guiding communication. Expressed differently, the paths to legitimacy can change direction. In the following sections we will look more closely at the EU's strategies by studying the way in which, and to what degree, media logic and political logic coexist side-by-side in official documents. This will give us a sense of the reach and depth of mediatization in EU foreign policy.

Solana Strategy: Europe Has Never Been So Secure and the EU Can Do More to Contribute to Peace and Security in the World

When the European Security Strategy (EES) was formulated in 2003, the end of the Cold War was fading into the distant past. Moreover, due to the crisis in Yugoslavia, NATO's role had changed from a strict military alliance to an organization with peace-keeping ambitions. Because many EU members were also members of NATO, the latter had long been an important component of Europe's security. From the beginning of the new millennium, discussions about the creation of an independent European security identity had intensified within NATO. The US was less inclined to contribute as much as it had historically to the defense of Europe.

Therefore, discussions about how the European countries themselves could be persuaded to contribute more to their own defense became part of the NATO agenda.

It is partially in the light of these discussions that the development of the ESS should be understood. Sten Rynning (2003) argues that, at the time, Europe was faced with the problem that within the EU, member states' strategic evaluations of their own countries' security situation differed from what was regarded as the best policy for Europe. For some countries, the trans-Atlantic connection was fundamental; for others it was problematic. Some members were attracted to an independent Europe. However, despite these differences in national strategic evaluations, discussions on strategy at the European level were based on a shared understanding of the EU's capabilities and limitations. The contents of the strategy can be seen as an illustration of the degree to which and in what ways EU foreign policy shows signs of, on the one hand, a media logic and, on the other, a political logic.

The very first sentence of the ESS declares: "Europe has never been so prosperous, so secure and so free." The high level of security that has been achieved is explicitly compared to previous periods in Europe's history, including the two world wars that took place on European soil. The creation of the EU is seen as a factor that has greatly contributed to freedom and stability. The EU's institutions, rule of law and consolidated democracies are depicted in the ESS as a successful mix that promotes peace and prosperity. Even global developments are understood in terms of more stable institutions, and the ESS expresses a desire for further development of international institutions. International agreements to control the export of weapons of mass destruction are said to be effective, and the role of the UN and the Security Council in managing conflict is deemed to be very important and in need of greater support. The ESS also notes that more countries are now members of multilateral trade organizations. Overall, the international order is described as resting on international institutions and norms designed to promote peace, prosperity and conflict resolution.

However, the ESS identifies challenges that hint at the possibility that more uncertain times are in the offing. The conflict in the Balkans is mentioned as a reminder that war can break out in Europe also. Nonetheless, the issue that gets most attention is the problem of weak states, which can be taken over by terrorists, lawlessness and organized crime—for example Somalia, Liberia and Afghanistan. Already at the time, Christopher Hill

(2004) warned of more uncertain times ahead for the EU, not least due to terrorism and the risk of rising fragmentation within the organization. Nonetheless, the most central parts of the ESS are dominated by an absence of uncertainty about global developments as well as the EU's security policy role in the world and Europe. Although the Iraq War created a clear dividing line among the central members of the EU, there is nothing in the document that suggests uncertainty about the overall security policy situation or the EU's role. Thus, uncertainty, which is an important theoretical prerequisite for the likelihood that media logic will be used as a framework for the narrative about the EU's security policy strategy in the beginning of the 2000s, is missing.

The EU is described as a global actor, with implies that the EU is expected to step up its attention to global matters. The ESS expresses this in terms of: "The increasing convergence of European interests and the strengthening of mutual solidarity of the EU makes us a more credible and effective actor." European identity is formulated in relation to common values and the common interests and embedded in institutions that have been set up. Identity in these sections has no connection to the characteristics of media logic. European identity is partly formulated in contrast to non-democracies and weak states with ineffective political institutions. It is rather clear that terrorists and criminal networks do not share the EU's normative foundations. Thus, in the description of the EU's international role there is a degree of polarization in relation to these groups, which is in keeping with media logic's tendency to paint extreme differences and polarize different points of view.

On the other hand, there are no signs of personification, simplification or visualization to any significant degree. Rather, the ESS repeatedly refers to complex and unpredictable situations that can arise due to the absence of institutions or poorly managed institutions. The "new threats are dynamic" and the EU is expected to act in "multi-faceted situations". Few identity markers in the ESS follow the media logic, even if there is some tendency to polarize when the EU's identity is contrasted with terrorists, professional criminals and failed states.

In the strategy itself, references to an external audience, the media and other forms of organized expressions of opinion, are almost completely absent. If those involved in formulating the ESS felt a strong sense of pressure from elite or public opinion on issues of security policy, it is not given a central role in the reasoning put forth in the document. One formulation in the ESS could be interpreted as recognition that there might be external pressure—a section that states that "global communication increases awareness in Europe of regional conflicts or humanitarian tragedies anywhere in the world." Despite this, given the rather undeveloped connection between global communication and opinion, there are no grounds to argue that there is resonance in the matter of a European security policy. As discussed above, resonance is one of the prerequisites that increases the likelihood of media logic. Its absence suggests that we should not expect media logic to have had any significant role in the formulation of the EU's foreign and security policy in the early years of the twenty first century.

Mogherini Strategy: The World Is Increasingly Uncertain and the EU's Common Values Are More Strongly Emphasized

The EUGS was drawn up under the leadership of High Representative Federica Mogherini and published 13 years after the ESS was approved by the EU's heads of state and government in December 2003. It is a new strategy in a new era and, as noted above, it was produced against a background of apprehension and uncertainty. While the ESS under Solana's leadership in 2003 painted a positive picture of the EU as being at the height of its prosperity, under the leadership of Mogherini in 2016, the EUGS adopts a completely different tone. The depiction of the EU changed from being a union that had never been so prosperous and peaceful (2003), to an organization characterized by an existential crisis (2016). The Global Strategy states that, "We live in times of existential crisis," and that the crisis exists both "within and beyond the European Union." The crisis is so deep that the very existence of the union is threated. In addition, the EUGS proclaims that, "Our European project, which has brought unprecedented peace, prosperity and democracy, is being questioned." Internally, the EU is portrayed as lacking cohesion. Externally, it is not least developments in "the east, [where] the European security order has been violated."

Another indication that the EUGS is intended to respond to an uncertain world is its focus on "resilience" (endurance and the ability to recover). The threats that are appearing inside and around the EU are multi-faceted and the challenges are great. Everything, from terrorism to a more offensive Russia, is challenging the EU. The need for a robust EU that can withstand pressures is thus significant. The Global Strategy's recipe to reaching this goal is to tie many political areas together –foreign policy, crisis management, refugee policy and the fight against terrorism.

Mogherini's background as Italy's foreign minister is interesting in this context. During her years as Italian foreign minister, Mogherini was required to devote considerable attention to the refugee question due to repeated catastrophes that resulted in the deaths of many refugees in the Mediterranean. She brought this experience with her to the office of the High Representative for Foreign and Security Policy, and she communicated a clear picture of the need for the EU to be able to manage migration with the help of stricter border control, transfer of competence to border states, and greater naval presence in the Mediterranean.

The EUGS thus bears clear marks of a dramaturgy with vivid and drastic formulations. Without exaggeration we can say that uncertainty, which we identified as the primary condition enabling media logic to gain a foothold, is obviously present. The very fact that uncertainty has grown so strong in such a short period of time points to the emergence of a dramatic and revolutionary period promoting the rise of dramatic, and quite literally, existential references. We can thus conclude that uncertainty is, in fact, accompanied by media logic forms of expression that are used to argue that the EU must play a clearer role on the global stage. At the same time, mediatized rhetoric is used to argue for a clearer European presence in global politics that builds on established structures of cooperation. The Global Strategy states that, "The EU will promote a rules-based global order with multilateralism as its key principle and the United Nations at its core."

Taken together, what emerges is a picture of an uncertain context that motivates dramatic and drastic forms of expression to describe the situation in which the EU finds itself. These forms of expression are easy to relate to the media logic. However, while media-logic forms of expression are used to describe the present situation, the media logic is not used to motivate dramatic shifts in policy—in any case, not shifts in the direction we might expect of a mediatized policy. Rather than greater focus on the rights of individuals and human security, what emerge are relatively traditional political solutions as the way to resolve the EU's crisis. Expressed differently, media logic is used as a means to gain legitimacy for a political logic in a context characterized by uncertainty.

The period during which the ESS was formulated was characterized by the eastern enlargement and a rather open EU. Thirteen years later, the pendulum has swung. The dimension of identity, our second precondition favorable to mediatization, is more focused on what the EU member states share. Even identity is communicated against a backdrop of uncertainty, a situation in which, according to the EUGS, the EU is to be guided by "our shared interests, principles and priorities." The EU's values, which the Union must live up to and which are the foundation for its shared global tasks, include, "respect for and promotion of human rights, fundamental freedoms and the rule of law. They encompass justice, solidarity, equality, non-discrimination, pluralism and respect for diversity." These identity markers had a strong position in 2003 as well; in large part the EU's foreign policy identity remains the same. Unity on these values is, according to the Global Strategy, not only a matter of law, but also "[one] of ethics and identity." "Unity" is unambiguously the central foundation for EU's action in the world, and when cohesiveness, and thus shared identity, comes under pressure, the response of the EUGS is to further emphasize the common values in which a shared identity is rooted (see also Wennerström in this volume).

While a shared identity justifies an EU that acts in the world on the basis of traditional political considerations—rooted in political logic and trust in international law and multilateral institutions—the values that are connected to identity reflect a more mediatized perspective. The emphasis on values such as diversity and non-discrimination are highlighted at a time when countries close to the EU are accused of having violated these very same values. This element of the EUGS differs from the ESS, because the latter does not focus on these values to the same degree. The strongly value-based approach of the more recent document can thus also be seen as an initial expression of polarization with a clear signal directed at an implied counterpart. In sum, identity justifies political utterances that can be connected to political logic as well as utterances that can be connected to media logic.

We have also identified resonance—essentially a bottom-up phenomenon—as a condition that can be expected to promote mediatization. If resonance occurs, politics is linked to a bottom-up pressure that motivates mediatized policy. As regards the EU's Global Strategy, however, the relationship is almost the reverse. Citizens and their interests are clearly present in the strategy, but almost always from a top-down perspective. The interests of the citizens are to be promoted, but exactly what these interests are has to be determined through a political process. It is also difficult to find any particularly footprint from citizens in the development of the

Global Strategy. Rather, Mogherini and bureaucrats at the EEAS act as if to rouse opinion, not least among Europe's politically interested elite, through active presence in both social and traditional media.

In the Global Strategy, the top-down perspective appears in formulations like the "European Union will promote peace and guarantee the security of its citizens and territory," and, "[T]he EU will advance the prosperity of its people." According to the document, the EU will also, "foster the resilience of its democracies and live up to the values that have inspired its creation and development." Objectively, it is of course difficult to argue against the ambition to strengthen peace, security and democracy, but it is worth nothing that these efforts are not motivated by the experiences or demands of the citizens. The ambitions are instead the result of political considerations. In other words, political logic is the basis of the references to the citizens of the EU. It should perhaps be pointed out that this is not necessarily wrong. It is reminiscent of the honorable intentions of politicians who want to understand the needs of the citizens and provide them with workable solutions. However, whether to base policy on the challenges identified by political institutions or on those that people experience in their daily lives nevertheless reflects a choice in favor of one of our two logics—political logic and media logic. In relation to security policy, the decision can also be seen as a choice between traditional security perspectives, with the security of the state at the center, or a more critical security perspective that puts the individual at the center—a perspective often referred to as "human security".

In sum, resonance is weak even in the EUGS. Additionally, where it does appear, it is a top-down perspective rather than something clearly connected to the views of the European people. Here, the Global Strategy reflects a political logic. At the same time, Mogherini's communicative activity can be seen as a way to adapt the framing of the Global Strategy to media logic in order—if possible—*to create* resonance at a time when the very existence of the EU is being questioned in parts of Europe. However, again, the type of bottom-up resonance that promotes a mediatization process cannot be said to exist in 2016.

Media Logic and Political Logic in the Solana and Mogherini Strategies

Our analysis of the ESS shows that the political logic is clearly dominant. There is an institutional framework for policy and given norms that political actors must respect. At the same time, more developed institutional arrangements are the solution to the problems identified in the ESS. An examination of EU foreign policy more generally also confirms the significance of general political frameworks and institutions as the central focus. A vision of European security policy is formulated in terms of unity, democracy, peace and expansion. To the extent that these values are mentioned in the strategy, they serve as a normative foundation for thinking about the global problems facing Europe. This corresponds well with what the political logic characterizes as the foundations of policy content. On the whole, media logic must be seen as entirely absent from the ESS. There are very few elements that indicate a desire to follow opinions expressed in the media, and there is nothing that indicates that policy is considered to be a game or competition. There is also not much in the strategy that suggests that the debate is polarized or that the EU as a phenomenon is subject to pressure or is being called into question. The focus lies rather on institutions than individuals and their rights. Nonetheless, at the time, researchers and practitioners expressed concerns about the disunity in the EU—for example as it manifested itself during the war in Iraq– and about a lack of legitimacy, either of which would weaken the EU's ability to act in foreign policy matters.

By 2016, the way the EU communicated its foreign and security policy had changed and adapted to media logic. The EUGS is motivated using vivid and rather dramatic descriptions of an existential character. The EU's existence is at stake. The period during which the EUGS is being developed under Mogherini's leadership is characterized by the fundamental condition that fosters mediatization, i.e. uncertainty. In relation to the theoretical assumptions of mediatization literature (and even from theoretical perspectives in security studies), such mediatized rhetoric might be used to promote dramatic political decisions rooted in a clear polarization. However, while there are elements in the policy that seem to be rooted in a shared European identity, the strategy articulated in the EUGS ultimately builds on traditional institutionalized measures. Taken together, the EUGS is a strategy that, in a time of uncertainty, uses rhetoric that is in tune with media logic's form, but it does so to promote a message that reflects political logic.

The EU Must Strike a Balance Between the Opportunities and Challenges of Mediatization in a Changing World Order: Build Legitimacy and Resist Polarization

From multiple perspectives, 13 years is a short period of time, offering only limited possibilities to trace larger structural changes. However, this is not true for the history of EU foreign policy. A comparison of the Solana and Mogherini strategies and the situation of the EU during the periods during which they were drawn up shows that the surrounding context changed considerably and, therefore, so did efforts to formulate a common foreign policy. Over the same period, elements of media logic in the EU's central foreign policy document increased, even if the media logic's dramaturgy was used primarily to win support for traditional political solutions. We argue that this state of affairs illustrates that the media logic, in certain circumstances, becomes more palpable. One could argue that what the EU offers its member states and their citizens has not fundamentally changed, but how it is framed is different.

Compared to the role it plays in the EU's process of foreign policy formulation, the media logic has made greater inroads in the surrounding world. As discussed in the introduction, American President Donald Trump has taken Twitter diplomacy to new levels. Trump's actions have raised questions about the use of that channel of communication and sparked discussion about the problems it can create if the content communicated comes as a surprise even to those in relevant political and diplomatic circles. The EU's High Representatives have struggled with problems linked to the fact that they are not always understood to be spokespeople for the foreign policy of the whole EU. In the same way, the EU itself has to live with being called into question and with (occasionally) weak public support for its common policy. It is thus noteworthy that elements of the media logic are not actually stronger than they are. Nevertheless, the sense of uncertainty and the presence of existential threats against the states of Europe are stated in much more forceful terms in 2016. In 2003, the world was understood to be rather predictable and certain. The political and institutional solutions provided by the EU were understood as the key to that sense of security. In 2016, the situation was completely different: military conflicts just beyond the EU's borders and differences of opinion inside the EU. Thus, there was greater uncertainty in 2016, a situation that, theoretically speaking, creates conditions for greater use of media logic.

At the same time, the shared identity that is advocated in the formulations of EU foreign policy in 2003 and 2016 is largely the same. It rests on shared values like democracy, freedom, respect for human rights and the rule of law. In other words, there is a strong belief in the fundamental political institutions of the liberal state. The characteristics of the media logic are in large part completely absent in the construction of European identity. Nonetheless, in both of the policy formulations, there are certain identity markers in line with the media logic. In 2003, there is a polarized description of European identity that is set in contrast to terrorism, organized crime and failed states. In 2016, there is a polarized description in which European identity, among other things, is based on diversity and non-discrimination, in contrast to those who do not support these values. Thus, in both cases there are elements of a polarized identity, which creates conditions for the use of the media logic. There is nothing in the texts that communicates the existence of strong opinions on EU foreign policy among the population, various organizations in society or other European actors which policy-makers normally feel obliged to take into consideration in formulating policy. Rather, the views of political elites are expected to serve as a guide. In other worlds, policy development is connected to institutions that are associated with the political logic.

We believe that the discussion presented in this chapter shows that it is false to state that politics is largely mediatized and that media logic guides the form and content of policy. This applies also to the EU. Foreign policy is one of the policy areas that is traditionally seen as resistant to the media logic, but even here we find variations, probably because particular prerequisites are required for the media logic to have an impact. For example, we can see that a sense of uncertainty and changed expectations for an actor like the EU can, in some situations, create a fertile soil for the media logic. That was true for EU's foreign policy in recent years, when the EUGS was launched under Mogherini's leadership. We even see elements of polarized descriptions of identity in the ESS under Solana, but elements of media logic are quite limited. Compared to understandings of identity, uncertain situations and existential crises are probably more important prerequisites for the emergence of the media logic. This means that self-reinforcing processes occur in crisis situations—i.e. uncertainty creates a fertile soil for media logic which, in turn, exacerbates uncertainty, thus leading to additional polarization and the visualization and depiction of politics as a game of winners and losers.

This brings us to a couple of recommendations aimed at both political and media actors on the European and national levels. To begin with, it is extremely important to try to remain cool-headed and focus on policy and institutions. This probably requires ability to stay focused on policy rather than on one's self and one's political opponents. Farsightedness and clear rules of the game are desirable alternatives to the narrative techniques of the media logic. Also, channels of rapid communication (like Twitter) can be problematic insofar as they leave little room for nuance and reflection.

It is also possible that the problems need not be very large or require significant sacrifices. It is thus worth reiterating that even if we have seen more media logic in the EU's foreign policy in recent years, it is not primarily intended to motivate a new policy, but rather to motivate previously charted courses. This puts the spotlight on the question of who is serving whom. While some research has described mediatization as a process by which the logic associated with the media colonizes other social spheres, including the political one, the EU's Global Strategy shows that politics can instead use media logic to promote political solutions it wants to prioritize.

Thus, our final recommendation is this: by all means, use media logic, but use it correctly. Media logic can offer a tool that promotes legitimacy, makes it possible to engage with people and reveals fundamental lines of difference in society. In other words, used correctly, media logic can be an instrument for gaining legitimacy for solutions to societal problems that fundamentally rest on a political logic. At the same time, we understand that there is a fine line between building legitimacy in a new way and falling into media logic's exaggerated tempo and polarization. Wisdom as a political virtue is as relevant today as it has ever been.

References

Allcott, H., & Gentzkow, M. (2017). Social Media and Fake News in the 2016 Election. *Journal of Economic Perspectives, 31*(2), 211–236.

Altheide, D. L., & Snow, R. P. (1979). *Media Logic*. Beverly Hills, CA: SAGE.

Bakir, V., & McStay, A. (2018). Fake News and the Economy of Emotions: Problems, Causes, Solutions. *Digital Journalism, 6*(2), 154–175.

Bjola, C., & Holmes, M. (Eds.). (2015). *Digital Diplomacy: Theory and Practice*. London: Routledge.

Brommesson, D., & Ekengren, A.-M. (2017). *The Mediatization of Foreign Policy, Decision-making and Humanitarian Intervention*. New York: Palgrave Macmillan.

Djerf-Pierre, M., Ekström, M., Håkansson, N., & Johansson, B. (2014). The Mediatization of Political Accountability: Politics, the News Media Logic and Industrial Crises in the 1980s and 2000. *Journalism Studies, 15*(3), 321–338.

European Council. (2003). *The European Security Strategy*. Retrieved October 3, 2018, from http://eur-lex.europa.eu/legal-content/EN/TXT/HTML/?uri=LEGISSUM:r00004&from=EN.

European External Action Service. (2016). *The EU's Global Strategy*. Retrieved October 3, 2018, from http://eeas.europa.eu/archives/docs/top_stories/pdf/eugs_review_web.pdf.

Folz, R. (2011). Does Membership Matters? Convergence of Sweden's and Norway's Role Conceptions by Interaction with the European Union. In S. Harnisch, C. Frank, & H. W. Maull (Eds.), *Role Theory in International Relations: Approaches and Analyses*. Oxon: Routledge.

Hedling, E. (2018). *Blending Politics and New Media Mediatized Practices of EU Digital Diplomacy*. Lund: Department of Political Science.

Helwig, N. (2013). EU Foreign Policy and the High Representative's Capability-expectations Gap: A Question of Political Will. *European Foreign Affairs Review, 18*, 235.

Helwig, N. (2017). Agent Interaction as a Source of Discretion for the EU High Representative. In T. Delreux & J. Adriaensen (Eds.), *The Principal Agent Model and the European Union*. Basingstoke: Palgrave Macmillan.

Hill, C. (2004). Renationalizing or Regrouping? EU Foreign Policy Since 11 September 2001. *JCMS: Journal of Common Market Studies, 42*(1), 143–163.

Hjarvard, S. (2008). The Mediatization of Society. *Nordicom Review, 29*(2), 102–131.

Isotalus, P., & Almonkari, M. (2014). Mediatization and Political Leadership: Perspectives of the Finnish Newspapers and Party Leaders. *Journalism Studies, 15*(3), 289–303.

Krotz, F. (2007). The Meta-Process of Mediatization as a Conceptual Frame. *Global Media and Communication, 3*(3), 256–260.

Krotz, F. (2009). Mediatization: A Concept with Which to Grasp Media and Societal Change. In K. Lundby (Ed.), *Mediatization Concept, Charges, Consequences* (pp. 21–40). New York: Peter Lang.

Mälksoo, M. (2016). From the ESS to the EU Global Strategy: External Policy, Internal Purpose. *Contemporary Security Policy, 37*(3), 374–388.

Mazzoleni, G. (2008). Mediatization of Society. *The International Encyclopedia of Communication*.

Michailidou, A., & Trenz, H.-J. (2018). The Media as Public Intermediaries in Europe: From Deliberation to Democratic Legitimacy. In C. Holst, M. Warat, & M. Góra (Eds.), *Expertisation and Democracy in Europe*. London: Routledge.

Rosamond, B. (2017). The Political Economy Context of EU Crises. In D. Dinan, N. Nugent, & W. E. Paterson (Eds.), *The European Union in Crisis*. London: Palgrave Macmillan.

Rynning, S. (2003). The European Union: Towards a Strategic Culture? *Security Dialogue, 34*(4), 479–496.

Schulz, W. (2014). Reconstructing Mediatization as an Analytical Concept. *European Journal of Communication, 19*(1), 87–101.

Strömbäck, J. (2008). Four Phases of Mediatization: An Analysis of the Mediatization of Politics. *The International Journal of Press/Politics, 13*(3), 228–246.

Strömbäck, J. (2010). Mediatization and Perceptions of the Media's Political Influence. *Journalism Studies, 12*(4), 423–439.

Strömbäck, J. (2011). Mediatization of Politics. Towards a Conceptual Framework for Comparative Research. In E. Bucy & R. L. Holbert (Eds.), *Sourcebook of Political Communication Research*. London: Taylor and Francis.

Strömbäck, J., & Esser, F. (2009). Shaping Politics: Mediatization and Media Interventionism. In K. Lundby (Ed.), *Mediatization. Concept, Changes, Consequences*. New York: Peter Lang.

Tocci, N. (2016). The Making of the EU Global Strategy. *Contemporary Security Policy, 37*(3), 461–473.

Tocci, N. (2017). From the European Security Strategy to the EU Global Strategy: Explaining the Journey. *International Politics, 54*(4), 487–502.

Tonra, B., & Christiansen, T. (2010). *Rethinking European Union Foreign Policy*. Manchester: Manchester University Press.

CHAPTER 9

Populism as a Challenge to Liberal Democracy in Europe

Sofie Blombäck

Introduction

The Brexit referendum and the election of Donald Trump to the US presidency, both in 2016, have become the starting point for a renewed interest in populism and its consequences for how modern democracies function. The many national elections in the EU countries in 2017 were largely analysed through a populist lens. Would the populist Freedom Party become the largest party in the Netherlands? Would Marine Le Pen become France's first right-wing populist president? In both cases, the "populist wave" that many commentators feared failed to materialize. At the same time, progress for populist parties in several European countries, raises the issue of how populists will affect democratic governance in these countries.

A possible "populist wave" in the EU can also be expected to have an impact on the role of the EU in a changing world order in two different ways. Increased influence for populist parties and politicians in the EU can change the content of the Union's common foreign policy, and perhaps

S. Blombäck (✉)
Mid Sweden University, Sundsvall, Sweden
e-mail: Sofie.Blomback@miun.se

A. Bakardjieva Engelbrekt et al. (eds.), *The European Union in a Changing World Order*,
https://doi.org/10.1007/978-3-030-18001-0_9

also the will to pursue such a policy at all. An EU characterized by populist thinking would likely change its stance versus other countries, on issues ranging from migration policy to free trade. Opposition to elites is a fundamental component of populism. Since the EU is often perceived as an "elite project" it is difficult to see populist politicians condoning the EU attempts to influence other parts of the world. The second way populism can affect the EU's global role is more indirect, but perhaps also more fundamental. Large support for populist parties could challenge the EU project itself and thus also the capacity of the Union to be a united actor in the global arena. Additionally, the current international instability can also be thought of as an opportunity for populists. Crises can be beneficial for populists, as they often promise to resolve situations which the established elite has failed to address.

This chapter first takes a step back from the current political situation and discusses what populism is and how it relates to liberal democracy. Since the assumption is that the existence of populist parties in itself constitutes a challenge to the prevailing political order, the aim of the chapter is not to assess if populism is "good" or "bad". The question is, instead, what is the current state of populism in Europe, given the many parallel crises we experience? Moreover, in what ways could populist parties influence the future development of European integration? To answer these questions, a theoretical discussion of populism's relationship to the EU and to liberal democracy is followed by an overview of the populist parties in the EU institutions and Member States, and their electoral successes over the past decade is analysed. The chapter concludes with a discussion of populist parties as both a threat and a wake-up call for the EU and its member states, arguing that if they are unable to deliver political solutions to problems such as "Brexit" and the migration crisis, they will remain vulnerable to populist challenges.

What Is Populism?

The first step is to discuss what populism actually is. The use of the term is widespread, both in political debate, in media and in academia, to describe widely different phenomena, often without specifying what is meant by the term. Populism is notoriously difficult to define—political scientists do not even agree if populism is a political style, a political strategy or a political ideology (see e.g. Jagers and Walgrave 2007; Moffitt 2016; Mudde 2004; Weyland 2001). The conceptual confusion is increased by the frequent combination of populism with other labels, such as "left-wing", "radical right-wing" and so on.

This chapter adheres to the view that the core of populism, whether we regard it as a political style or as an ideology, is the idea of an opposition between "the people" and "the elite". Cas Mudde and Cristóbal Rovira Kaltwasser (2016) have written extensively on this foundational component in the populist worldview, and its consequences. "The people" are homogeneous and have one common interest and one common will.[1] "The people" can be a certain ethnic or national group, or simply defined as "the common people" (Canovan 1984: 315ff). "The elite", for its part, can consist of for example an economic or political elite, but politicians and established parties are usually included in the definition of the elite. The elite is in an almost moral opposition to the people, usually rules at the expense of the people, and often co-operates with groups, ranging from large corporations to ethnic minority groups, that are not counted as "the real people" in a way that adversely affects the people (see also Kriesi 2014). Jan-Werner Müller (2016: 26ff) argues that populism thus becomes anti-pluralist. If there is only *one* people and *one* true popular will, and the people are morally always right, there is no need for different views or a discussion about different political options. Therefore, in the populist world image, there is no room for a legitimate opposition when the populists have come to power. Those who oppose the populist politicians or parties are by definition not included in the people. Müller (2016: 20) summarizes this core message of populists with their claim that "…they, *and only they*, represent the people".

This rather minimal definition of populism is precisely the reason that we find populists on both sides of the political left-right spectrum. Researchers sometimes call populism a 'thin (centred) ideology' (Kriesi 2014; Mudde 2004; Mudde and Rovira Kaltwasser 2016) because it is well suited to combining with other ideological positions. Thus, there is a link between movements on the left side that accuse the elite of being in the pocket of large corporations, such as some of the anti-capitalist movements in the United States after the financial crisis of 2008, and nationalist movements accusing the elite of allowing unchecked immigration and siding with ethnic minority groups. In both cases, the "common people" are losing out, although the two types of populist movements define "common people" in very different ways.

[1] See also Taggart (2000) on the concept of the "populist heartland".

The idea that there is a unified people with a common interest means that there logically must be a single correct way to act in any given political situation. Similarly, there are only two types of actors, those who are with the people and those who oppose the people. Therefore, populist movements are often opposed to negotiations and compromises in politics, instead advocating simple solutions based on common sense and the will or interest of the people. Actors who disagree with this approach, ranging from rival parties to international bodies such as the European Court of Justice, can by definition not be acting in the interests of the people (Mudde and Rovira Kaltwasser 2016: 80ff; Liang 2016: 11).

Many of today's European populist movements are strongly associated with their leaders, from Geert Wilders, the leader and sole party member of the Dutch Freedom Party to comedian Beppe Grillo, the leading figure of the Italian Five Star Movement. Benjamin Moffitt (2016) is one of several scholars who has focused on this phenomenon. His book on populism as a political style focuses on the leaders, and the important role they play. At first glance, a type of political movement that advocates popular government and dislikes elites, but at the same time emphases leadership and often has low levels of internal democracy does not seem to add up. There are some examples of populist movements that do not have a single strong leader. The Populist Party that had a brief period of success in the United States in the nineteenth century is one such example, the Occupy Wall Street movement is another. These are, however, exceptions; the movements with a strong leader are considerably more common.

Aside from the fact that becoming a successful party usually requires a certain measure of organization, which in turn requires some form of leadership, there is an inherent logic in the populist movements' preference for strong leaders. Since there is only one popular will, no internal decision-making structure is needed except for a leader who can formulate and preferably implement this will. The rest of the movement's role is to support the leader. Because the leader is the interpreter of the true popular will, all criticism, both internal and external, is illegitimate. The leader's role is thus rather peculiar in populist movements. The leader must of course be a part of the people, not of the elite, but must at the same time appear to be strong enough and effective not to be challenged in their role as interpreters of the will of the people (Mudde and Rovira Kaltwasser 2016: 62ff; Müller 2016: 32ff). One way populist leaders mark their distance from the elites is by refusing to follow conventions for how political leaders are expected to look or behave within a certain given context

(Moffitt 2016). Donald Trump is an excellent example of this. Despite his fortune and his close ties to various elite groupings in the United States, he successfully depicted himself an “outsider” in relation to the political class and during the presidential campaign of 2016 he continually broke the expectations of how a presidential candidate should act.

Populism and Democracy

Populism as an ideology is a challenge for representative democracy, as the representative democracy requires a chosen political elite. Therefore, populist movements often advocate direct contact between the people and the leader, for example through referendums and other direct-democratic elements, with several scholars noting that these referendums are primarily intended to ratify the leaders’ interpretation of the popular will (Müller 2016: 29). At the same time, the populist parties in this chapter are all acting within the framework of representative liberal democracies in Europe. There are few or none of those who expressly advocate transition to a different type of government other than representative democracy. On the other hand, the majority of the populist parties are obviously critical of the functioning of representative democracy today. One common criticism is that if the representative democracy really worked properly and fairly, then the populists should be in government, since only they represent the real popular will (Müller 2016: 31f). Demands for increased direct-democratic elements and less power to the political parties are common, as are demands for the removal of other barriers that impede the implementation of the popular will, such as constitutional courts.

The strongest populist challenges of liberal democracy have occurred in South America, where populist movements with strong leaders has led to the dismantling of the rule of law and increasingly authoritarian rule in for example Venezuela (Mudde and Rovira Kaltwasser 2012b). Similar developments, however, can also be seen in Europe. In both Poland and Hungary, populist parties have won elections and subsequently implemented reforms of the legal and media systems. These reforms were strongly opposed and have led other EU countries to express concern about the rule of law and the continued democratic rule. Another example is the argument put forward during the Brexit referendum campaign that leaving the jurisdiction of the European Court of Justice would mean improved popular governance in the United Kingdom (Ringeisen-Biardeaud 2017). In this instance, the representatives of the British

Parliament were portrayed as better interpreters of the popular will than a supranational court.

Does populism thus endanger democracy in the long run? There is no academic consensus on whether populism and democracy are inherently contradictory or if a combination of the two could be possible. Some researchers emphasize populism as a threat to democracy, citing either the empirical examples that exist or the inherent difficulty of combining the populist ideal of a single popular will with the pluralism that democratic governance presupposes (e.g. Müller 2016). Others are somewhat more positive and instead see populism as a kind of safety valve or alarm (e.g. Mudde and Rovira Kaltwasser 2012a). According the this view, populist movements occur when the political parties and leaders become too distant from the people, but can be neutralized relatively easily if the established parties respond to the dissatisfaction in an adequate manner. Finally, there are those who believe that populism can strengthen democracy, for example by linking formerly politically apathetic citizens to the political process or by challenging an elite that has actually become corrupt. Which of these positions is taken depends largely on our attitude towards liberal and representative democracy. An advocate of radical democracy, such as Chantal Mouffe (2005) and Ernesto Laclau (2005), will argue that all politics almost inevitably have an element of populism. A defender of strictly representative democracy is likely to be significantly more negative to populism.

Nor do all populists share the same views on democracy (see e.g. Kriesi 2014). As mentioned earlier, some populist movements advocate restrictions in the prevailing democratic institutions because they prefer a strong leader who, with a minimum amount of barriers, can implement policies that are in the true interests of the people. At the same time other populist movements are strong advocates of introducing further direct-democratic elements. Both of these demands may be seen as a challenge of how the current representative democracies are organized, but are hardly a threat to basic democratic ideals.

However, the different ways of looking at populism usually meet in the view that populism can be used as an indication of (ill) health in the political life of democratic countries. No smoke without fire, we tend to believe. If there are populists, there must be popular dissatisfaction with the current regime. However, there are researchers who do not fully agree with this assessment. Research shows, for example, that the very existence of credible populist parties creates a demand for populism. Stijn van Kessel's

(2015) book on populist parties is a good example of this. Other research suggests that populist parties can also influence their own destinies, for example by trying to raise issues that they can politicise. Populism is often associated with crisis and many researchers argue that populists often do better in times of crisis. Moffitt (2016) argues that a crisis creates an opportunity for the populists; there is an urgent problem that requires a radical and effective solution. In addition, the populist narrative of the corrupt or incompetent elite is reinforced—they have been responsible for governing the country and now it is in crisis. However, it is not simply that populist parties arise as a result of crises in a society. Populists can "create" crises, for their own benefit. This does not mean that populist leaders consciously create problems. Rather, they identify possible problems, which exist in every society, and formulate a narrative portraying this particular problem as a crisis. The crisis is affecting the people, and is caused or aggravated by the elite. The only way to solve the crisis is to replace the elite with a popular regime; naturally in the form of the populist party or populist leader. If this is a successful strategy is of course dependent on how many people can be persuaded to agree that this particular problem exists and constitutes a crisis.

Whether we think the crises are created narratively or "naturally occurring", the social debate in Europe since the mid-2010s has been characterized by a series of crises—the global financial crisis (Kriesi and Pappas 2015), the refugee crisis and, not least, "Brexit" as a crisis for the EU. In addition, many, including many politicians, warn of a more "low-intensity" crisis in the form of declining trust in established parties, governments or the EU itself (Armingeon and Ceka 2014; Dalton and Weldon 2005; Foster and Frieden 2017). All of these fit very well into the rhetoric of different populist parties, although the case of "Brexit" is usually portrayed as the withdrawal from the EU as a solution to a crisis for Britain. If crises are opportunities for populist parties, then the period since the mid-2010s should have been favourable. Has this really been the case, and if so, what are the possible consequences for the political systems in the EU and its Member States?

Populist Parties and European Integration

However, before we can answer these questions, we need to say a few words about how populist parties can influence the EU in theory. The starting point is still the discussion of how populism and (liberal, representative) democracy go together. In one sense, the EU a collaboration between liberal democracies, but the organization itself has also developed state-like traits. Even though the Union is not a fully functioning state, the EU does often operate as a liberal democratic state. In cases where the EU does not act as a liberal democratic state, it is usually since the Member States have retain the decision making power at the national level. In other words, decisions in the EU are either made through a set of institutions that mimic those in a democratic state or by a set of 28 (more or less) liberal democracies negotiating amongst themselves.

In both these cases, populist parties can be a challenge. Partly in the form of EU sceptical parties, which are often populist and question the EU's prevailing political order (Krouwel and Abts 2007). Partly in the form of populist parties at national level challenging liberal, representative democracy within the Member States themselves. As mentioned earlier, there is a great deal of research on the relationship between populism and democracy. In Mudde and Rowira Kaltwasser's (2012b) research on populism and democracy, it appears that established democracies are relatively resilient to populist challenges. In these countries populists cause policy changes, for example by raising previously sensitive or un-politicized issues onto the agenda, but do not fundamentally change how the political system works. Established institutions such as independent judiciaries, free and fair elections and a free media are just a few examples of actors and institutions who oppose the pressure for institutional reform from populist leaders and parties. Non-consolidated democracies, on the other hand, are more sensitive to the challenge of populist parties. In these cases, there is a risk that the system will develop in an authoritarian direction if a populist leader comes to power.

The EU is a special case here, since although most of the Member States are established democracies, the EU itself is not. While it has state like features, such as a directly elected parliament that participates in legislating, it is ultimately the Member States who control the direction of the union. Additionally, the EU's political institutions are not consolidated. There are groups in all the Member States opposing the very idea of a European union, and even more widespread demands for changes in how the EU is governed. "Brexit" is an example of the former; the many reforms of the EU institutions, such as the European Parliament's increased influence over EU legislation (Hix and Høyland 2013), are examples of the latter. We can therefore posit that the functioning of the EU itself can be affected by populist actors. For example, several populist parties demand referendums for their respective countries withdrawal from the EU (Lyons and Darroch 2016). An EU without France, which populist Front National wishes to see, would be a different organization than today's EU. Populist parties on the left side are often also highly Eurosceptic (Halikiopoulou et al. 2012; Hobolt 2015; Hooghe et al. 2002).

We can also imagine that the EU is one of the sensitive topics that the political establishment in a Member States avoids discussing, creating the conditions for populist parties to raise the issue (Krouwel and Abts 2007). This has been seen in several of the early EU Member States, where it was long assumed that there was a permissive consensus (Hooghe and Marks 2009) that allowed political leaders to manage European integration. No great interest or enthusiasm for the integration project was expected from the general population, but as long as the integration delivered results in terms of economic growth, no major objections were foreseen. In addition, the consensus among the established parties was that integration was desirable, which led to the absence of public debate. In several of these countries, such as the Netherlands, France and Germany, the issue of EU membership has since been politicized by populist parties. The most obvious example is, of course, "Brexit". Although the referendum was initiated by the Conservative Party, the continuing success of the UKIP certainly influenced that decision (Hobolt 2016). In addition to more drastic changes such as withdrawing from the Union altogether, politization of the EU-membership may also force a more restrictive approach to enhanced integration within the EU in countries with strong populist parties. We therefore see two ways in which populist parties could fundamentally challenge the EU. In this case challenging does not entail undermining the liberal democratic system, for example by weakening the rule of law or the freedom of the press, but rather challenging the very idea of having a European Union that functions as it does today.

As pointed out earlier, the climate of crisis that largely characterized the period before and after the European Parliament elections in 2014 should have provided an opportunity for populist parties to attract more voters.[2] Having the support of a large number of voters is of course a prerequisite for exercising influence for any political party. Actually investigating the influence of populist parties throughout the EU and its Member States is

[2] See Kriesi and Pappas (2015) for an overview of the effect of the recession on populist parties in Europe. See also Hobolt and De Vries (2016) on support for Eurosceptic parties.

beyond the scope of this chapter. As a first step we will investigate the extent of the populist presence in the EU decision-making institutions, and in the Member States. In the Member States, we can also see if support for populist parties has increased over time, given the Brexit vote, the current refugee crisis and other crises being discussed. With regard to the presence of the populist parties in the European Parliament, we will not see any impact of the recent crises until the elections in the summer of 2019.

Which Parties Are Populist?

Before we can say something about how prominent populists are in the EU and its Member States, we need to clarify which parties we actually mean. As with the meaning of the word "populism", there is a debate both inside and outside academia about which parties are actually populist. We get very little guidance from the parties themselves, there are many who do not want to describe themselves as populists because the word has negative connotations. In some cases, however, we can get some information from the names of the parties, such as the Slovak Party "Ordinary People and Independent" or Czech "Action of Dissatisfied Citizens", which both suggests that the party represents 'common people'. In other cases, the names are much less helpful. Many European countries have a People's Party, where the name is often meant to signal that the party wants to represent the entire people, regardless of class. This does not always entail that the "people" are in opposition to an "elite", however. The Swedish Liberals, until 2015 called the People's Party, are not populists by any definition. Other parties with similar names, like the Danish People's Party and the People's Party of Our Slovakia, on the other hand, are generally considered to be populist. Moreover, as has previously been pointed out, purely populist movements are very rare. Instead, we see populism combined with other issues or ideologies. This means that there are left-wing populists, although most left-wing parties are not populists. On the other side of the political spectrum, there are the right-wing populists that we most often think about when discussing populism, but not all parties on the far right are populists. For example, purely fascist or Nazi movements are usually not included among the populists, because they lack the dominant idea of an opposition between the common people and a corrupt elite.

It might not be useful to consider populism as a trait that parties either have or not. Most parties have some populist elements or sometimes use populist messages or strategies. In order to identify the group "populist parties", we must specify a criterion for a party to be considered sufficiently populist to be included in the group. This chapter uses a minimalist definition that focuses on the dichotomy of people and elite that unites all populists, whether they combine populism with right- or left-wing ideology or with any other issue. Populist parties are those who often and consistently raise the idea that there is a homogeneous people who are in opposition to an equally homogeneous and in addition corrupt elite, and that political decisions should be based on the will of the people without being filtered through elite institutions, such as the established political parties.

To make a review of all parties in Europe and to determine if they are populists or not would be a very extensive work, and therefore are not possible within the scope of a single book chapter. Instead, we rely on other researchers' assessments, primarily on van Kessel's (2015) list of populist parties, which is based, inter alia, on expert surveys. Van Kessel's study uses a definition similar to the one used here and covers populists on both the right and the left. As the survey only covers the period up to 2013, it has been updated with parties that were founded or received their first electoral successes in the period 2014–2017. In order to determine if a party is to be considered populist we have relied on scholarly descriptions of the party.[3] In borderline cases, the rule has been to be as inclusive as possible, so as not to underestimate the number of populist parties and their electoral support.

Table 9.1 shows that populist parties have been elected to the national parliament and/or to the European Parliament in 24 of the 28 EU Member States. In most of the countries, there are one or two populist parties, but in Bulgaria as many as five populist parties have been represented on at least one occasion during the period in question. However, the number of parties is less interesting than the influence they have, both in the form of electoral support and in government participation and holding other positions of power. The next section discusses populist parties in the EU itself, the following section discusses the parties at Member State level.

[3] The coding of new parties is primarily based on descriptions of the parties in election reports in *Electoral Studies* and in *European Journal of Political Research Political Data Yearbook* (http://www.politicaldatayearbook.com), supplemented with the *Chapel Hill Expert Survey*'s question on how important anti-elite rhetoric is for the parties (www.ches-data.eu). In cases where the party is not mentioned in either of these sources, descriptions from media accounts and the parties' websites have been used.

Table 9.1 Populist parties in EU Member States 2010–2018

Austria	Freedom Party of Austria (FPÖ)
	Team Stronach (TS)
Belgium	Flemish interest (VB)
	List Dedecker (LD)
Bulgaria	Attack (Ataka)
	Citizens for European development of Bulgaria (GERB)
	National Front for the salvation of Bulgaria (NFSB)
	Bulgaria without censorship (BBZ)
	Will (Volya)
Croatia	Croatian Labourists—labour party (CL-LP)
	Croatian Party of Rights (HSP-AS)
	Human shield (Zizi)
Czech Republic	Action of dissatisfied citizens (ANO)
	Dawn of direct democracy (UPD)
	Freedom and direct democracy (SPD)
	Czech pirate party (pi)
Denmark	Danish Peoples Party (DF)
Estonia	Free party (EV)
Finland	True Finns (PS)
France	National front (FN)
Germany	The left (Linke)
	Alternative for Germany (AfD)
	German pirate party (pi)
Greece	Popular orthodox rally (LAOS)
	Coalition of the Radical Left (SYRIZA)
	Independent Greeks (AE)
Hungary	Hungarian civic union (Fidesz)
	Movement for a better Hungary (Jobbik)
Ireland	Sinn Féin (SF)
Italy	North league / Lega (LN)
	Go Italy (FI)
	Five star movement (M5S)
Latvia	For Latvia from the heart (NsL)
Luxembourg	Alternative democratic reform party (ADR)
Netherlands	Party for freedom (PVV)
	Forum for democracy (FvD)
Poland	Law and justice (PiS)
	Kukiz'15
	Congress of the new right (KNP)
Romania	Greater Romania party (PRM)
	People's party—Dan Diaconescu (PP-DD)
	Save Romania union (USR)

(*continued*)

Table 9.1 (continued)

Slovakia	Slovak National Party (SNS)
	Ordinary people and independent (OLaNO)
	People's party our Slovakia (KLsNS)
	We are family (SR)
Slovenia	Slovenian National Party (SNS)
Spain	We can (Podemos)
Sweden	Sweden democrats (SD)
United Kingdom	British National Party (BNP)
	UK Independence party (UKIP)

Source: van Kessel (2015), author's coding

The Direct Challenge: Populists in the EU Institutions

With the exception of the European Parliament, populist parties and politicians have been largely absent from most of the EU's central institutions. There are usually few or no populist politicians in the European Commission, the European Court of Justice or the European Central Bank. One reason, is that positions in these bodies are indirectly elected and it is therefore the governments of the Member States who appoint them. Some particularly important posts, such as the President of the European Commission, the High Representative for Foreign Affairs and Security Policy, and the President of the European Council, are jointly appointed by all the Member States. Populist politicians tend not to do well in such conditions—it is literally the established party elites that the populists oppose that are in charge of appointments. Given that many populist parties oppose the EU membership, it is also not self-evident that their representatives would be interested in holding such offices, but there have been some attempts. One example is the leader of the Greek party Syriza, Alexis Tsipras, who ran for the post as President of the Commission in 2014. The campaign was not successful, in the sense that Tsipras was not elected to the Commission, but it was a rare example of several parties and movements on the left in several European countries rallying behind a joint candidate from a populist party.

In the Council of Ministers, the situation is somewhat different. Since populist parties have long been excluded from the government in most Member States, they have also been absent from bodies composed of government members. However, as populists have come to power in a number of Member States, this has obviously changed. Examples include Viktor Orbán from Hungarian Fidesz, Silvio Berlusconi from Italy and the previously mentioned Tsipras who since 2015 is Prime Minister of Greece. To date, there is little systematic research on the level influence populist politicians actually wield in the European Council or the Council of Ministers. Naturally, it depends on which Member State they represent and how successful they are in building alliances with other countries. We do know that populists in either council can create tensions (Batory and Puetter 2013). We saw examples of this when former Polish Prime Minister Donald Tusk was to be re-elected to the post of the European Council President in the spring of 2017. Poland's new prime minister Beata Szydlo from the populist party Law and Justice strongly opposed this election (BBC 2017), even though there is a tradition of respecting the appointments made by previous governments. For a populist party, however, this type of tacit agreement is offensive, as an example of elites colluding for their mutual benefit.

Populist parties are more frequently found in the European Parliament. Ever since the first direct elections to the European Parliament in 1979, researchers have noted that non-government parties, small parties and non-established parties have often done better in the European Elections than in national elections (e.g. Hix and Marsh 2011). The phenomenon is often explained by the fact that the European elections are second-order national elections. Voters, parties and the media care less about the European elections than national elections and the results are interpreted in relation to the national political situation. Therefore, voters dare to take a chance on unknown party, or protest vote to express frustration with the established parties. The idea of applying the second-order election theory to the European Parliament elections was put forward by Karlheniz Reif and Hermann Schmitt (1980), and has been discussed in countless scientific publications ever since. Many of the hypotheses put forward have been challenged. It is for example unusual for entirely new parties to reach their first electoral successes at the European level (Blombäck 2015). Of the populist parties in Table 9.1, only seven were elected to the European Parliament before they were elected to their national parliament.

However, even if there is a debate about whether EP elections are actually the second order national elections, research consistently shows that non-established parties do well and government parties lose on average. Thus, we can also expect populist parties to perform well, as they, with some exceptions, are neither in government nor part of the established parties. In the European Parliament elections in 2014, populist parties received approximately 16 percent of the votes on average in EU member states, but the between-country variation is large. Figure 9.1 shows the percentage of votes the populist parties received in each of the Member States. In five countries, no populist party received votes, while in five other countries more than one third of the votes went to populists. Among the latter we find Italy, Poland, Greece and Hungary, all of which had

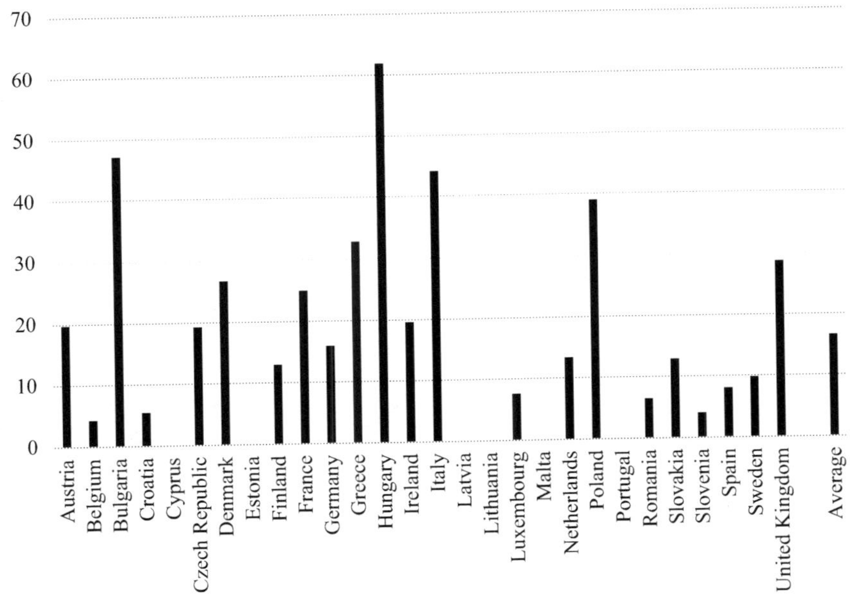

Fig. 9.1 Share of votes for populist parties in the 2014 European Parliament elections. Source: ParlGov database (Döring and Manow 2018), author's calculations. Comment: The collective share of votes for all populist parties that have been represented in the European Parliament or their national parliament in 2010–2018 (see Table 9.1), in the European Parliament election in 2014

populist governments. Other countries with high numbers of populist parties are Denmark, reflecting a good result for the Danish People's Party, and Britain where Eurosceptic and populist UKIP became the largest party.

Is it the case that populist parties do extraordinary well in European elections? Figure 9.2 shows the difference between the latest national elections in each country before 2014 and the European Parliament elections. Here too, there are large differences between countries. The biggest gap is found in the UK, where UKIP, as noted earlier, became the largest party in the EP elections, but only received a few percent of the votes in the national elections in 2010. There are also several countries where the populist parties received a lower vote share in the European elections, such as Romania, the Czech Republic, Austria, Finland and Italy. Germany is an interesting case. Although the difference in overall votes for populist

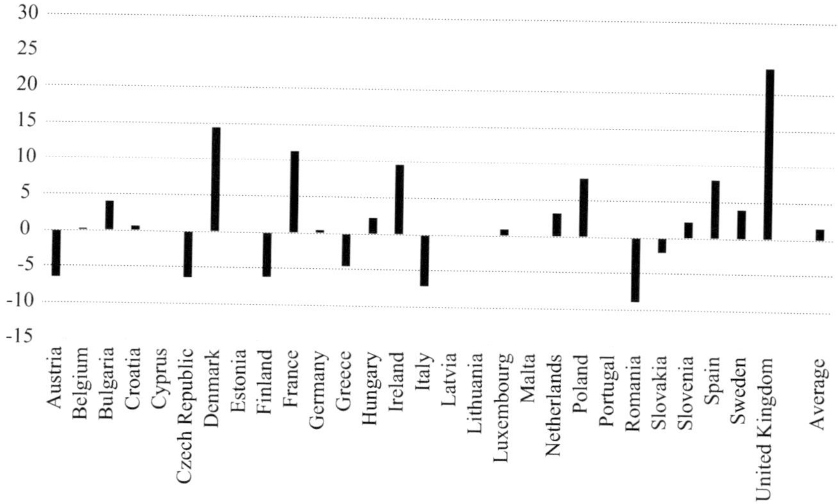

Fig. 9.2 Difference in vote share for populist parties between national and European Parliament elections 2010–2014. Source: ParlGov database (Döring and Manow 2018), author's calculations. Comment: The collective share of votes on all populist parties that have been represented in the European Parliament or their national parliament in 2010–2018 (see Table 9.1) in the European Parliament elections in 2014 minus the share of votes for the same parties in the national parliament elections immediately preceding 2014

parties was small between the two elections, two new populist parties were elected to the European Parliament. For one of them, however, the explanation is that the previous 5 percent electoral threshold for elections to the European Parliament was abolished in Germany. Alternative for Germany (AfD) received over seven percent of the votes and thus would have had representation even without this rule change, but the same is not true for the Pirate Party, which with only 1.4 percent got one of Germany's 96 mandates. All in all, the theory that populist parties do better in the European Parliament is confirmed, but the difference is small. At the aggregated level, the difference between the two groups of election results is only 1.6 percentage points.

To sum up, there is a certain presence of populist actors in the EU institutions themselves, and populists are found in the two bodies responsible for legislating—the European Parliament and the Council of Ministers—although to a limited extent. Through their presence in these institutions, the populist parties have the opportunity to influence EU policies by taking part in legislating and budgeting. There is also a theoretical possibility that the EU project itself could be altered, for example by populist demands for measures to reduce the democratic deficit. The European Parliament in particular has a history of demanding changes to the way the institutions operate (Hix and Høyland 2013), although the parliament does not have formal decision-making power on these issues. So far, populist parties have not been able to effect such changes, partly because they are far from having the majority in any one of the institutions, partly because the populist parties are not united in a single political group with a common agenda (Jungar 2018). They do not share left-right ideology or a single attitude towards the EU. Moreover, since only Member States can fundamentally change the nature of European integration, if populists are going to seriously challenge the liberal democratic regime in the EU, it must be done at Member State level.

The Indirect Challenge: Populists in the Member States

Studying populists at the national level is necessary in order to say something about their ability to challenge EU political governance. It is of course also important in terms of developments in individual Member States. Even though we expect established democracies to be resistant to the populist challenge, the potential consequences if democracy is curtailed are much more serious at the national level compared with the European level.

Figure 9.3 shows the percentage of votes that populist parties received in the latest national elections in EU member states, up until early September 2018. The average is just over 20 percent, thus higher than in the 2014 European parliamentary elections, which contradicts the thesis that populist parties should do better in European elections than in national elections. There are two possible explanations for this. These results include a number of new parties formed after the 2014 European Parliament elections. Since the principle was to include rather than excluding borderline cases, we may have included parties that would not have been deemed populist by the expert surveys carried out for the parties formed before 2013. The second possible explanation is that there is actually a so-called "populist wave", perhaps in the wake of the crises that characterized the EU in 2014–2018.

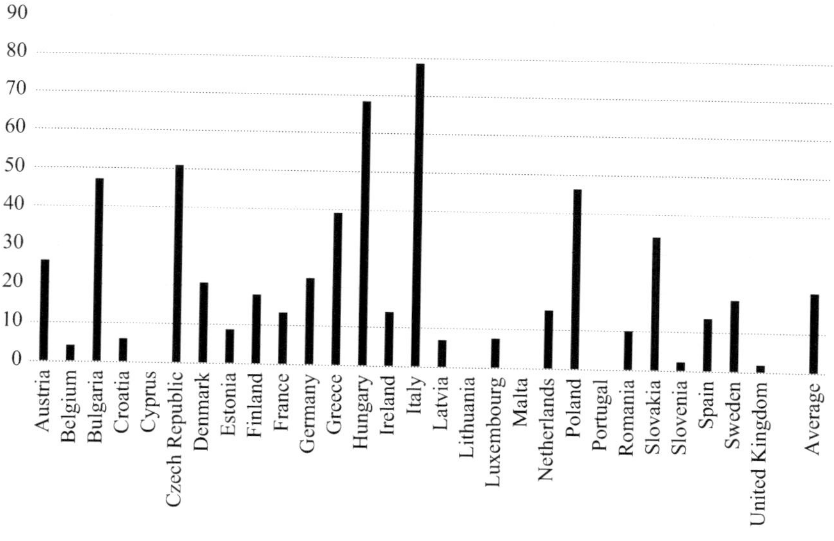

Fig. 9.3 Share of votes for populist parties in national parliaments in 2018. Source: ParlGov database (Döring and Manow 2018), author's calculations. Comment: The collective share of votes for all populist parties that have been represented in the European Parliament or their national parliament in 2010–2018 (see Table 9.1), in the latest national parliament elections before September 2018

If we look at the countries where there has been an increase in electoral support for populists, the picture is mixed. There are cases with several populist parties as well as increases that depend entirely on a single new party. The countries with the biggest increases are Italy, Slovakia and the Czech Republic. In Italy the two populist parties Lega and the Five Star Movement formed a government. In the Czech Republic, two new populist parties received representation and ANO became the largest party with almost 30 percent of the vote, its leader Andrej Babiš becoming the new Prime Minister. Overall, the populist parties received more than half the votes. In Slovakia, the results for the populists in the parliamentary elections in 2016 were more than 20 percentage points higher than that in the European Parliament elections in 2014. This includes a new party, We are Family (Sme Rodina), but the three already existent populist parties all improved on their 2014 European Parliament results in the 2016 national elections. In Slovakia we can thus speak of a very successful election for populist movements. The entire Estonian increase, on the other hand, is due to a single new party, Estonian Freedom Party, which is harder to classify because it formed very shortly before the election and has not been the subject of much research. Here we cannot as unambiguously conclude that there is an increased level of populism. The situation in Latvia is similar, with the whole increase due to the new party For Latvia from the Heart, which campaigned on a message of greater transparency in politics. In Spain, left-wing Podemos increased its share of the votes, while in Poland, both the Law and Justice and the new anti-establishment movement Kukiz'15, led by musician Pawel Kukiz, increased their support. In the Austrian elections in October 2017, the Freedom Party did slightly better than in previous elections, and entered into a coalition government. In Germany, finally, Alternative for Germany, which originally was a Eurosceptic party, received more than 12 percent of the votes, thus clearing the 5 percent threshold with a wide margin.

Finally, it should of course be noted that there are several countries where the presence of populist parties is lower than it is in the European Parliament, as can be seen in Fig. 9.4. Both Britain and France exhibit the classic pattern with much lower support for populist parties in national parliamentary elections. Here it is important to remember that both countries use different electoral systems in the two types of elections. In most EU countries, the rules differ very little between national and European elections, with proportional voting systems at both levels. France and the United Kingdom, on the other hand, have different variants of majoritarian

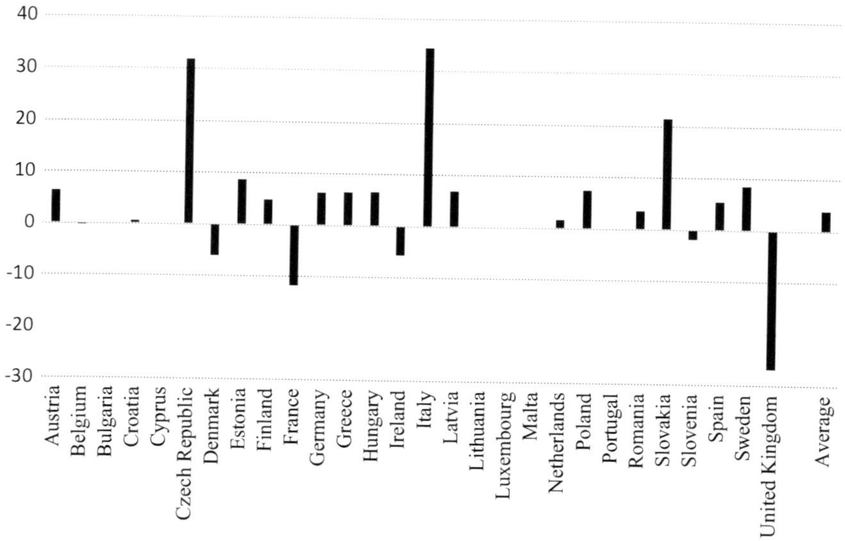

Fig. 9.4 Difference in vote share for populist parties between European Parliament elections 2014 and the latest national elections. Source: ParlGov database (Döring and Manow 2018), author's calculations. Comment: The collective share of votes on all populist parties that have been represented in the European Parliament or their national parliament in 2010–2018 (see Table 9.1) in the latest national parliament elections minus the share of votes for the same parties in the European Parliament elections in 2014

systems in the national elections. Simply put, majoritarian systems tend to favour large parties and disadvantage non-established parties (Blombäck 2015: 37–38). Here too, the Brexit vote plays an important role. The parliamentary elections in Britain in 2017 took place after the decision to leave the EU was made, and thus UKIP had lost its main issue.

Parliamentary presence alone is not enough to seriously challenge or change the political system. In order to be able to effect that kind of change, either within a country or in a country's EU policy, government portfolios and preferably a parliamentary majority for the populist parties are required. As previously noted, populist parties and politicians have achieved this in some of the EU member states. One of the early cases was Italy, where a major political corruption scandal in the mid-1990s caused a collapse of the established party system and paved the way for populist parties such as Lega Nord and Forza Italia. Forza Italy's party leader Silvio

Berlusconi, who on several occasions was the Italian Prime Minister, has been accused of corruption as well as using his private media empire to strengthen his position. At the same time, the period when these populist parties held power was characterized by institutional reforms, among other things of the electoral system (see e.g. Renwick et al. 2009).

Another relatively early case was Austria, where the Austrian Freedom Party under Jörg Haider's leadership was part of a coalition government with the Austrian People's Party in the early 2000s. The other EU countries reacted strongly by imposing sanctions (Merlingen et al. 2001), as this was the first case of a right-wing populist party in a government. However, the party's time in office did not lead to any changes to the political system itself in Austria at an institutional level. While undermining the controversial "proporz system", where the two major established parties distributed many important posts within the public sector between themselves, was one of the stated goals of the party, there is some debate about how much this was realised as well (Müller and Fallend 2004). At the EU-level, the consequence of the FPÖ's government participation was partially the cause of the so called Article 7 procedure for when states are in violation of the Charter of Fundamental Rights of the European Union (Menéndez 2002). It is therefore a case of deepening cooperation, which may not be what we imagine when we think of the influence populist parties have on the EU's development.

The EUs ability to respond to threats to democracy within Member States has been tested by developments in two other countries with populist parties in government.[4] In Hungary, Fidesz has a large majority in parliament, which the party has used in order to implement a number of reforms of, inter alia, laws governing the media and the civil society. Since the Law and Justice came into government in Poland, Poland has implemented several controversial legislative changes that, among other things, reduce the independence of the judiciary. These are thus two examples of countries where populist parties with strong parliamentary and government positions seriously challenge the political system and its institutions. Many of the other Member States, as well as the European Commission (2017a, b), are highly critical of developments in both countries. To date, however, the criticism has not caused either country to abandon its reforms, and there is no consensus among the Member States on using the sanctions that have been put in place in the treaties.

[4] See the special issue of *Journal of European Public Policy* vol. 24, no. 3, introduced in Keleman and Blauberger (2017) for an in-depth discussion.

Potentially more challenging for the project of European integration itself was the major electoral success of Syriza in Greece, as the party opposed the austerity measures required for the country to be granted emergency loans, thus endangering the entire Euro system. However, since the party won the election, it has enforced most of the measures demanded by the EU and the IMF, without ceasing its criticism of these institutions. At the time of writing, the crisis seems to have abated.

Is Populism in the EU a Growing Challenge?

This chapter has mapped the presence and electoral strength of the populist parties in the EU, and discussed how populist parties can pose a challenge to the current political order in both the EU and its Member States. It is important to emphasize that populism is not a marginal phenomenon within the EU. The vast majority of member states have at least one populist party represented in their national parliaments and just over 16 percent of the votes went to populist parties in the latest European Parliament elections. It is however also important to emphasize that the variation between EU countries is high. Cyprus, Malta, Lithuania and Portugal completely lack populist parties while in Hungary, Fidesz holds governmental power and a sufficiently large majority in parliament to amend the Constitution on its own. The trend is also one of a slightly increasing vote share for populist parties. In the European Parliament elections in 2014, they received somewhat higher support than they had in the last previous national elections, and in 2018, the average populist representation in national parliaments had increased yet again.

In terms of populism as a threat to prevailing liberal representative democracy, the results are also mixed. Although there are parties in several countries that wish to change the political system to a greater or lesser degree, they have in the majority of cases been unsuccessful, either because their vote share is low and / or because the established parties have ruled out cooperation with them. In addition, changes in the political system are not always the main goal of the populist parties. If they have a chance to influence policy, they might choose to change migration policy, economic policy or something else. At EU level, despite a much talked of 'wave of success' for populist parties, we have also not seem any great impact on the political system.

However, there are exceptions to this general trend of limited influence and it is important to highlight the real threats populist reforms post for the rule of law and freedom of the press in some EU Member States. Another example that has been mentioned several times throughout the chapter is "Brexit", which is, at least indirectly, a result of the electoral success of the populist party UKIP. What these examples show is that although populist parties in general have little influence over the political systems in the EU, there is reason to take their challenge seriously. If and when populist parties get influence, the consequences can be serious.

Responding to the Challenge of Populist Parties Requires the Right Kind of Policy: Do Not Copy Them, Provide Political Solutions to Social Problems

Despite a rigorous academic and societal debate on how liberal democracies should respond to the challenge from populist actors (Mudde and Rovira Kaltwasser 2016: 97ff; Müller 2016: 75ff; Rovira Kaltwasser and Taggart 2016) there is no consensus in sight. We do know that populist parties rarely disappear if ignored. Demonising them tends to play into their narrative about themselves as underdog challengers to an elite that unfairly does not want to share the power. Trying to tame them by bringing them to coalition government or by adopting their issues has shown very varied results. This is due, in part, to the fact that populism rarely occurs in a "pure" form. It is usually combined with other ideological content. Although there is no universally accepted correct way to respond to populist parties, it is worth highlighting some points that are important to remember in the ongoing debate on populist parties, their role in democratic governance and their impact on developments in the EU.

The first is that we should avoid using the word populist as a general insult against all political opponents. The populist challenge is precisely in its ability to politicise a real or perceived conflict between "political elites" and "common people", and is thus something completely different from parties who completely want to abolish democratic governance or, for that matter, from a politician who is being opportunistic in order to win voices.

Since the group of populist parties to some extent overlaps other groups, such as extreme right or left parties, it is easy to clump them into a single group when discussing parties on the fringes of the party systems. Populism, however, as the chapter has shown, has a special kind of dynamic that is the result of the tension between "people" and "elite", and by its insistence that the people are a homogeneous group with a single common interest. By not overusing the word populism, we can preserve it as a useful concept. Only in this way can it help us understand how a populist parties, movement or politicians function and argue.

A related recommendation is to distinguish populism and other forms of protest movements. Müller (2016: 98) stresses that there is a difference between the populists' "we, and only we, are the people" and the "we are also the people" of marginalized groups. The latter form of anti-elite policy does not require the construction of a homogeneous people, can serve to lift important issues that have previously been overlooked and do not in itself constitute a threat to either pluralism or the liberal democratic system. To dismiss these groups as "mere populists" instead risks driving these movements into actually becoming populists, as it signals that the elite really does not take their demands and needs seriously.

Populism can be dealt with politically by the established parties, but this does not mean that established parties must adopt populist policy proposals. As noted earlier in this chapter, an important part of the populists' strategy is to exploit the crises that currently dominate the public debate. An effective, but unfortunately difficult-to-implement, strategy should therefore be to solve social crises and problems. Corruption scandals should be tackled with effective investigations and sanctions, economic crises should be reversed or at least relieved, and in the case of the EU, stable and constructive solutions to the Brexit issue and the migration crisis are needed, to name but a few examples. Unless the EU and its member states are able to deliver such solutions, they will continue to be vulnerable to populist challenges. Obviously, there is nothing preventing the populists from politicising new crises, but every solution to a crisis makes the populists' arguments about an incompetent and corrupt elite all the weaker.

In the end, there are two ways that other parties and politicians can respond to the populist challenge. One is to see populism as a threat, something that is to be combated with everything from good counter arguments to legislation. The second is to see populism primarily as a warning, something that causes self-reflection about how the political system works and if there is an opportunity to "undermine" the populists by strengthening democracy. Whichever route is chosen, it is also important not to be overly preoccupied with to the current policy positions of the populist parties. They also represent, through their way of looking at society and politics, a challenge to the prevailing political order in Europe and western societies in general. As we have seen, the consequences of these challenges can be far-reaching and likely far more difficult to reverse than changes in current policy. A change in migration or economic policy can be reversed, a dismantling of the independent judiciary or a withdrawal from the EU is significantly harder to change back when the populist parties no longer control the political agenda, sit in parliament or form part of the government.

References

Armingeon, K., & Ceka, B. (2014). The Loss of Trust in the European Union During the Great Recession Since 2007: The Role of Heuristics from the National Political System. *European Union Politics, 15*(1), 82–107.

Batory, A., & Puetter, U. (2013). Consistency and Diversity? The EU's Rotating Trio Council Presidency After the Lisbon Treaty. *Journal of European Public Policy, 20*(1), 95–112.

BBC. (2017, March 17). Poland fails to stop Donald Tusk EU Re-election. *BBC.*

Blombäck, S. (2015). *Making Their Way Home from Brussels. New Parties in European and National Elections*. Gothenburg: University of Gothenburg.

Canovan, M. (1984). "People", Politicians and Populism. *Government and Opposition, 19*(3), 312–327.

Dalton, R. J., & Weldon, S. A. (2005). Public Images of Political Parties: A Necessary Evil? *West European Politics, 28*(5), 931–951.

Döring, H., & Manow, P. (2018). *Parliaments and Governments Database (ParlGov): Information on Parties, Elections and Cabinets in Modern Democracies. Development Version.*

European Commission. (2017a, December 7). *Infringements –European Commission Refers Hungary to the Court of Justice for its NGO Law (Press release).*

European Commission. (2017b, December 20). *Rule of Law: European Commission Acts to Defend Judicial Independence in Poland (Press release).*

Foster, C., & Frieden, J. (2017). Crisis of Trust: Socio-economic Determinants of Europeans' Confidence in Government. *European Union Politics, 18*(4), 511–535.

Halikiopoulou, D., Nanou, K., & Vasilopoulou, S. (2012). The Paradox of Nationalism: The Common Denominator of Radical Right and Radical Left Euroscepticism. *European Journal of Political Research, 51*(4), 504–539.

Hix, S., & Høyland, B. (2013). Empowerment of the European Parliament. *Annual Review of Political Science, 16*, 171–189.

Hix, S., & Marsh, M. (2011). Second-order Effects Plus Pan-European Political Swings: An Analysis of European Parliament Elections Across Time. *Electoral Studies, 30*(1), 4–15.

Hobolt, S. B. (2015). The 2014 European Parliament Elections: Divided in Unity? *JCMS: Journal of Common Market Studies, 53*, 6–21.
Hobolt, S. B. (2016). The Brexit Vote: A Divided Nation, a Divided Continent. *Journal of European Public Policy, 23*(9), 1259–1277.
Hobolt, S. B., & De Vries, C. (2016). Turning Against the Union? The Impact of the Crisis on the Eurosceptic Vote in the 2014 European Parliament Elections. *Electoral Studies, 44*, 504–514.
Hooghe, L., & Marks, G. (2009). A Postfunctionalist Theory of European Integration: From Permissive Consensus to Constraining Dissensus. *British Journal of Political Science, 39*(1), 1–23.
Hooghe, L., Marks, G., & Wilson, C. J. (2002). Does Left/right Structure Party Positions on European Integration? *Comparative Political Studies, 35*(8), 965–989.
Jagers, J., & Walgrave, S. (2007). Populism as Political Communication Style: An Empirical Study of Political Parties' Discourse in Belgium. *European Journal of Political Research, 46*, 319–345.
Jungar, A.-C. (2018). Repercussions of Right-Wing Populism for European Integration. In U. Bernitz, M. Mårtensson, L. Oxelheim, & T. Persson (Eds.), *Bridging the Prosperity Gap in the EU: The Social Challenge Ahead*. Cheltenham: Edward Elgar Publishing.
Kelemen, R. D., & Blauberger, M. (2017). Introducing the Debate: European Union Safeguards Against Member States' Democratic Backsliding. *Journal of European Public Policy, 24*(3), 317–320.
Kriesi, H. (2014). The Populist Challenge. *West European Politics, 37*(2), 361–378.
Kriesi, H., & Pappas, T. S. (Eds.). (2015). *European Populism in the Shadow of the Great Recession*. Colchester: ECPR Press.
Krouwel, A., & Abts, K. (2007). Varieties of Euroscepticism and Populist Mobilization: Transforming Attitudes from Mild Euroscepticism to Harsh Eurocynicism. *Acta Politica, 42*(2–3), 252–270.
Laclau, E. (2005). Populism: What's in a Name? In F. Panizza (Ed.), *Populism and the Mirror of Democracy*. London: Verso.
Liang, C. S. (2016). *Europe for the Europeans*. Abingdon: Routledge.
Lyons, K., & Darroch, G. (2016, June 27). Frexit, Nexit or Oexit? Who Will Be Next to Leave the EU. *The Guardian*.
Menéndez, A. J. (2002). Chartering Europe: Legal Status and Policy Implications of the Charter of Fundamental Rights of the European Union. *JCMS: Journal of Common Market Studies, 40*(3), 471–490.
Merlingen, M., Mudde, C., & Sedelmeier, U. (2001). The Right and the Righteous? European Norms, Domestic Politics and the Sanctions Against Austria. *JCMS: Journal of Common Market Studies, 39*(1), 59–77.
Moffitt, B. (2016). *The Global Rise of Populism: Performance, Political Style and Representation*. Stanford: Stanford University Press.

Mouffe, C. (2005). *On the Political.* London: Routledge.
Mudde, C. (2004). The Populist Zeitgeist. *Government and Opposition, 39,* 542–563.
Mudde, C., & Rovira Kaltwasser, C. (2012a). Populism and (Liberal) Democracy. In C. Mudde & C. Rovira Kaltwasser (Eds.), *Populism in Europe and the Americas: Threat or Corrective for Democracy?* Cambridge: Cambridge University Press.
Mudde, C., & Rovira Kaltwasser, C. (2012b). Populism. In C. Mudde & C. Rovira Kaltwasser (Eds.), *Populism in Europe and the Americas: Threat or Corrective for Democracy?* Cambridge: Cambridge University Press.
Mudde, C., & Rovira Kaltwasser, C. (2016). *Populism: A Very Short Introduction.* Oxford: Oxford University Press.
Müller, J.-W. (2016). *What Is Populism?* Philadelphia: University of Pennsylvania Press.
Müller, W., & Fallend, F. (2004). Changing Patterns of Party Competition in Austria: From Multipolar to Bipolar System. *West European Politics, 27*(5), 801–835.
Reif, K., & Schmitt, H. (1980). Nine Second-order National Elections–A Conceptual Framework for the Analysis of European Election Results. *European Journal of Political Research, 8*(1), 3–44.
Renwick, A., Hanretty, C., & Hine, D. (2009). Partisan Self-interest and Electoral Reform: The New Italian Electoral Law of 2005. *Electoral Studies, 28*(3), 437–447.
Ringeisen-Biardeaud, J. (2017). "Let's Take Back Control": Brexit and the Debate on Sovereignty. *Revue Française de Civilisation Britannique. French Journal of British Studies, 22,* XXII–XXI2.
Rovira Kaltwasser, C., & Taggart, P. (2016). Dealing with Populists in Government: A Framework for Analysis. *Democratization, 23*(2), 201–220.
Taggart, P. (2000). *Populism.* Buckingham: Open University Press.
van Kessel, S. (2015). *Populist Parties in Europe: Agents of Discontent?* Basingstoke: Palgrave Macmillan.
Weyland, K. (2001). Clarifying a Contested Concept: Populism in the Study of Latin American Politics. *Comparative Politics, 34*(1), 1.

CHAPTER 10

Can the EU Protect Its Fundamental Values?

Erik O. Wennerström

Introduction

It seemed in 2003 that the European Union and the United States were both confirming Robert Kagan's description of the world in his book published that year, *Of Paradise and Power.* Under the leadership of former French President Giscard d'Estaing, the European Convention presented its draft Treaty Establishing a Constitution for Europe, aimed at taking the building of a normative European state closer to the realization of the Kantian paradise based on laws and rules. That same year, it seemed that the position of the United States as sole global superpower in an unsettled world was confirmed when the US, without a United Nations mandate, invaded Iraq and toppled the ruling regime. According to Kagan, this seemed rather to reflect the world once described by Hobbes, where the strong seek security in their own strength, while the weak look for it in norms. From the vantage point of 14 years later, the world is no less unsettled and the structure and "EUphoria" that informed the European Convention has been supplanted by deep pessimism. The European integration project is no longer state building on the offensive; it is a defensive

E. O. Wennerström (✉)
The Swedish National Council for Crime Prevention, Stockholm, Sweden
e-mail: erik.wennerstrom@bra.se

A. Bakardjieva Engelbrekt et al. (eds.), *The European Union in a Changing World Order*,
https://doi.org/10.1007/978-3-030-18001-0_10

EU being battered from the inside by Brexit, separatism and the illiberal agendas of certain Member States, exacerbated by the challenges of migration, xenophobia, populism and EU scepticism. For the moment, the actions of neither Russia nor the US are helping to ease these woes (Kagan 2003: 3–12).

But Kagan was right in that it is the robust regulations that hold the structure together and the political and economic advantages they give to participating states were and remain the strength of the EU. In these regulations, EU Member States and EU institutions have repeatedly pointed to the central, shared values that are the foundation of the structure. At first, to hold up as a yardstick that states seeking entry must be measured against, lest they be allowed in only to damage the common structure with their faults; later, to hold the same yardstick against next to all Member States and watch out for serious breaches of the common values contract (Tuori 2016: 225ff).

When Polish President Duda used his veto in July 2017 against two of the three controversial bills from the governing Law and Justice Party (the president's own party, *Prawo i Sprawiedliwość*, PiS), many thought this to be the result of both foreign and domestic reactions. If we disregard the domestic reactions, we see that both the EU Commission and the president of the European Council issued statements prior to debate and voting on the bills—statements that signalled that, in the eyes of the EU, Poland was about to cross the Rubicon of the rule of law. These events, if not a victory, seem at least to mark a temporary stalemate in a process that has been ongoing since the Law and Justice Party came to power in 2015. If this stalemate can in some sense still be regarded as a success, partly attributable to EU actions, this begs the questions: which EU mechanism made this successful foray possible, and what values were defended?

This chapter sheds light on aspects of EU efforts to ensure that the established common values are respected by the Member States. The most germane question addressed is whether the mechanisms created to protect the values are effective. To answer the main question, we must first discuss the established values and whether the mechanisms created are intended to protect those values. The chapter begins, first, with an account of how the values now called the EU's common fundamental values (laid out in Article 2 TEU) emerged and how they are used and, secondly, an outline of the various mechanisms created to verify compliance with these values. The EU's use of these compliance mechanisms, especially the preventive and sanction mechanisms (Article 7 TEU) and the enlargement mechanism (Article 49 TEU), is then described. This is followed by an analysis of whether a convergence of values can be observed based on developments in the EU. Finally, there is a discussion of the significance of these developments to the EU's capacity to assert its values in a world order in transformation. The chapter concludes with a couple of recommendations for action that indicate the EU should develop its Rule of Law Framework and strengthen collaboration with the Council of Europe.

The Emergence of the EU's Fundamental Values

All exercise of power, whether through action, legislation or positions taken in negotiations, is based on values in the sense of a balancing of interests in furtherance of a particular orientation. If this balancing fails, the exercise of power will be impaired in strength, quality or legitimacy. It has seemed important to achieve consensus on the values, or more accurately principles, in the EU ever since the idea of a political union was put into action. The need has been further emphasized in connection with major enlargements of the EC/EU. Such arguments were made as far back as the incorporation of the former military dictatorships of Greece, Portugal and Spain into the EC in the 1980s, but particularly ahead of the major eastward enlargement after the end of the Cold War. This is reflected in the Maastricht Treaty, the first incarnation of the Treaty on European Union (TEU). It is there established that "The Union shall respect the national identities of its Member States, whose systems of government are founded on the principles of democracy." The Treaty also confirms the Union's respect for fundamental rights as guaranteed by the European Convention for the Protection of Human Rights and Fundamental Freedoms (ECHR). With the entry into force of the Lisbon Treaty, the fundamental values of the EU and the ECHR are regulated in separate articles. But it is important to point out that the "Maastricht values" are defensively structured. The EU must *respect* the national identities of the Member States, which already *are* founded on principles of democracy, regardless of what they are (and regardless of whether that is actually the case) (Sadurski 2010).

The pithily stated Maastricht values were not terribly helpful in the 1990s ahead of the imminent enlargement talks with all countries in Eastern and Central Europe. The EU's accession criteria (the "Copenhagen criteria") were therefore established during the 1993 meeting of the European Council in Copenhagen:

1. Stability of institutions guaranteeing democracy, the rule of law, human rights and respect for and protection of minorities.
2. A functioning market economy and the ability to cope with competitive pressure and market forces within the EU.
3. Ability to take on the obligations of membership, including the capacity to effectively implement the rules, standards and policies that make up the body of EU law (the "acquis"), and adherence to the aims of political, economic and monetary union.

When the TEU was amended in Amsterdam, the reference to "principles" was retained, but then not only the principles of democracy. It was also established that the EU is founded on the principles of liberty, democracy, respect for human rights and fundamental freedoms, and the rule of law, principles which are common to the Member States. It was with the Treaty Establishing a Constitution for Europe (TCE) of 2004 that the principles were first called "values" and their number further expanded:

> The Union is founded on the values of respect for human dignity, freedom, democracy, equality, the rule of law and respect for human rights, including the rights of persons belonging to minorities. These values are common to the Member States in a society in which pluralism, non-discrimination, tolerance, justice, solidarity and equality between women and men prevail (Article I-2, TCE).

Now, the TCE never entered into force, as it was voted down in referenda in France and the Netherlands in 2005. But the description of the values (Article I-2) was transferred virtually unabridged to the TEU when it was amended in Lisbon in 2007. The same six values upon which the EU is founded are listed (Article 2(1) TEU) (i.e. respect for human dignity, freedom, democracy, equality, the rule of law and respect for human rights, including the rights of persons belonging to minorities), along with six characteristics of the kind of society considered desirable by the parties to the Treaty (i.e. pluralism, non-discrimination, tolerance, justice, solidarity and equality between women and men).

There is no obvious causality between the values and the characteristics. Why should these not have been accorded the same legal gravitas? Which one or more of the six values can give rise to the characteristic of "solidarity", what is distinctive of the prevalence of the value of "dignity" and so on? The question is whether the characteristics have any legal value at all.

Table 10.1 EU values as defined by the Treaty on European Union

Human dignity
Freedom
Democracy
Equality between women and men
The rule of law
Respect for human rights, including the rights of persons belonging to minorities

Source: Treaty on European Union

It is only the six values that are subject to operationalization in the treaty, through references to them in the preventive and sanction mechanisms (Article 7 TEU) and the enlargement mechanism (Article 49 TEU) (see Table 10.1).

How Have EU Values Been Used in Practice Vis-à-vis Candidate Countries?

Although scholars have argued that the EU has failed to transmit the values the Union claims to be defending to the newer EU Member States (see e.g. Kochenov 2008; Pech and Schappele 2017), the EU's major enlargement process in 1997–2004 must be regarded as the prime example of application of the EU's values. (European Commission 2000) The dozen or so candidate countries willingly subjected themselves to the initially rather cursory mechanisms established by the EU to examine the countries' ability to fulfil the obligations of EU membership, as well as their capacity to respect the values of the Union as then defined. The 1997 opinions from the European Commission on the readiness of the candidate countries for EU membership set the tone for the subsequent screening process. Although certain adjustments were made in each subsequent year regarding the parameters considered important to fulfil the rule of law, the requirements remained relatively constant. The EU determined that respect for the rule of law was one of the prerequisites of membership (Articles 49 and 2, TEU). For a long time, the only definition of the rule of law in the EU was, for all practical purposes, derived from enlargement praxis, i.e., the various sub-criteria to the rule of law according to the Copenhagen criteria. The empirical information derived from the European Commission's documentation of its assessments and the decisions of the Council contains four main areas of assessment: respecting the supremacy of law, the separation of powers, judicial independence, procedural fundamental rights, and a fifth value (or, more accurately, activity) that is unique in this context, active measures to prevent corruption (Sadurski 2010: 385ff; Wennerström 2007: 197ff).

Slovakia is a clear example of a candidate country sanctioned during the membership negotiations. In its 1997 conclusions on Slovakia, the European Commission states that Slovakia's situation "presents a number of problems" in respect of the Copenhagen criteria. The most significant of these is that the government does not sufficiently respect the powers devolved by the constitution to other bodies, demonstrated, for example, by how the government had disregarded the rulings of the Constitutional Court. The Slovakian government also failed by disregarding the rights of the opposition. The Commission thus recognized a need for "substantial efforts" to ensure fuller independence of the judicial system and pursue the fight against corruption with greater effectiveness. The Commission's language on protection of minorities is no harsher than that used about other countries with similar problems, which nevertheless received a positive opinion. The Commission ended its opinion thus:

> In the light of these elements, although the institutional framework defined by the Slovak constitution responds to the needs of a parliamentary democracy where elections are free and fair, nevertheless the situation is unsatisfactory both in terms of the stability of the institutions and of the extent to which they are rooted in political life. Despite recommendations made by the European Union in a number of demarches and declarations, there has been no noticeable improvement (European Commission 1997).

The observation that the situation was "unsatisfactory" was a clear rejection of Slovakia's efforts to fulfil the Copenhagen Criteria and membership talks were indeed suspended until a new election had brought a new Slovak government to power in 1998 that was willing to accept the challenges the Commission had identified (ibid, see also Wennerström 2007).

Despite the political overtones of the enlargement process, there was early doubt about the willingness of the EU (and its Member States) to fully use the mechanism established to project the values set out in the treaties. The vigour of the enlargement sanction mechanism (non-accession or delayed accession) is both credible and significant. Time seems to be an additional factor at play here: the values project is allowed to take time, with the proviso that if it takes too long the threshold can be lowered in certain cases (most of the candidate countries that joined in 2004 did not meet all conditions) and in other cases, the deadline is extended (as with Bulgaria and Romania, which became Member States in 2007). It seems as if the mechanisms for cooperation and verification established for Bulgaria and Romania prior to their accession to the EU were a way to manage the shortcomings in both countries. These, unlike the treaty procedures, were used to deal with faults in respect of supremacy of the rule of law and should be regarded as mechanisms for upholding the Copenhagen criteria after accession (Kochenov 2004: 30ff).

The EU's enlargement mechanisms thus contain a more detailed and refined monitoring system than the treaty system. The annual structured observations show progress or lack of progress over time and allow for comparison with other states that are or have been monitored by the same mechanism. There are two main shortcomings to this form of assessment. First and foremost, there are no gradations of how well states have met the criteria. Put simply, they either have or they have not. Secondly, the sanctioning function of the enlargement mechanism is entirely political, as an agreement on membership can often be achieved *without* full alignment. Thus, only Slovenia was in full alignment with the criteria when the political reward of membership was handed out to all candidate countries in Central and Eastern Europe (Kochenov 2004).

It is important to note that when it comes to the practical application of respect for the EU's fundamental values, the EU Commission still, in 2018, uses the Copenhagen criteria in relation to imposing demands on the candidate countries, and thus *not* the Treaty's catalogue of values. There are probably several reasons for this, but two seem especially relevant. Firstly, the Commission has established a considerable enlargement acquis over the years. This now covers 35 different negotiating chapters with firmly established practices from the major eastward enlargement from which the Commission, on solid grounds, does not wish to depart. Second, there is a critical difference between the Treaty's description of the Union's values and the corresponding description in the Copenhagen criteria that makes the Commission prefer the latter. While the Treaty refers to "human rights, including the rights of persons belonging to minorities", the Copenhagen criteria refer to "human rights and respect for and protection of minorities". The difference is not insignificant. While the Treaty establishes that certain *individual* rights must exist and be respected, the Copenhagen criteria refer to minorities as a *collective*. Although individuals can enjoy the same individual rights as other individuals in the society in question, it is not unusual for minorities as a group to be discriminated against in various ways in the countries that have applied for membership since the 1990s. The Commission has a more far-reaching mandate to combat discrimination against minorities under the Copenhagen criteria than under the Treaty (Kochenov 2008: 311ff; Sasse 2008: 842ff).

Mechanisms for Protecting EU Values

Leading European scholars of law and political science such as Carlos Closa, Dimitry Kochenov and Laurent Pech have tracked the development of various mechanisms and processes at the EU level to promote and protect the fundamental values of the EU (Closa 2016; Kochenov 2016; Pech and Schappele 2017; Kochenov and Pech (2015a); Kochenov and Pech (2015b). Among the central mechanisms, we find the preventive mechanism (Article 7.1 TEU) that allows EU institutions to act in situations where there is clear risk of a serious breach by a Member State of one of the fundamental values, as well as the sanction mechanism (Article 7.2 TEU) for situations where there is a serious and persistent breach of such a value. The values that have equivalents in the Charter of the Fundamental Rights of the European Union (the EU Charter) are also continuously monitored through judicial review in individual cases, which may set legal precedent. Among the central mechanisms we also find the enlargement mechanism (Article 49 TEU) for the accession of new states to the Union, which refers to the fundamental values, as well as the traditional infringement procedures (Articles 258-260 TFEU). It can be argued that the infringement proceedings before the Court of Justice of the European Union (CJEU) are the Union's most important legal mechanism for implementing common norms and values. The judicial review is, however, limited mainly to areas where the EU has exclusive and shared competence (Articles 3-4 TEU) and will not affect the systems of Member States and rarely the general quality of their domestic exercise of power (Pech et al. 2016).

There is also non-binding or "soft law" tools, including annual reports drafted by EU institutions that address issues related to the fundamental values. In 2014, both the EU Commission and the Council introduced two new mechanisms. The Commission adopted a Rule of Law Framework and the Council undertook to organize an annual Rule of Law Dialogue among the Member States. Information about the Member States' respect for democracy, the rule of law and fundamental rights in the Member

States is also gathered by other international organizations including the Council of Europe and the UN (to which all EU Member States are member states). This information is also used as input for monitoring by the EU of Member States' respect for the fundamental values (Pech et al. 2016).

In connection with the launch of the European Commission's Rule of Law Framework, Commissioner Viviane Reding emphasized that the mechanism is based on three fundamental principles:

1. It can only be activated when there is a "systemic threat" to the rule of law. The framework is not designed to deal with isolated cases of breaches of fundamental rights or miscarriages of justice.
2. The criteria for activating the mechanism will be apply in the same way to all Member States.
3. The EU Commission has a crucial role in the new mechanism in its role as the Guardian of the Treaties.

The mechanism, or Framework, complements existing mechanisms, particularly the preventive and sanction procedures and the EU Commission's infringement procedures. The mechanism is directed exclusively at the rule of law, which was positively defined by the Commission for the first time when the Framework was introduced. The Commission's express intention is to activate the mechanism in situations where there is a systemic breach of the rule of law in a Member State, but not in isolated situations or isolated breaches of fundamental rights. While the Commission plays a central role in the Framework as the Guardian of the Treaties and the independent Guardian of the Union's Values, the Commission also acknowledges a need to draw on the expertise of other EU institutions and international organizations (notably the European Parliament, the Council, the Fundamental Rights Agency, the Council of Europe and the Organization for Security and Co-operation in Europe) (European Commission 2003: 6–8, 2014: 6–9, 2013).

The Framework can be described as a three-stage mechanism whose purpose is to prevent the emerging of a threat to the rule of law in a Member State, which could develop to the level that would potentially trigger the use of treaty procedures. It exists as an attempt to prevent the application of EU preventive and sanction mechanisms. The first stage consists of an assessment by the Commission of whether there are clear indications of a systemic threat to the rule of law. If the Commission is of the opinion that there is a systemic threat to the rule of law, it will initiate a dialogue with the Member State concerned by sending a "Rule of Law Opinion," which should be considered a warning to the Member State. At this point, the Commission gives the Member State concerned the possibility to respond (Pech et al. 2016; European Commission 2014: 6–9; Wennerström 2014: 618ff).

If the first stage does not lead to satisfactory resolution of the problem, the second stage is a formal "Rule of Law Recommendation" issued by the Commission and addressed to the Member State (the recommendation is similar to the reasoned opinions that the Commission uses in infringement proceedings). The recommendation, which will be made public, will request the Member State to solve the problems identified within a fixed time limit and inform the Commission of steps taken to that effect.

In the third stage, the Commission will monitor the follow-up to the recommendation. If there is no satisfactory follow-up within the time limit set, the Commission can resort to one of the mechanisms set out in TEU (Article 7 TEU). The entire process is based on a continuous dialogue between the Commission and the Member State concerned. The Commission also keeps the Parliament and the Council informed (ibid).

The Commission Framework was launched in 2014, but was not applied in earnest until 2016, in response to developments in Poland. (European Commission 2016a; European Commission 2016b; European Parliament (2016)) In the press release in which the Commission introduces the Framework, it explains that what the Framework describes is the intended approach when a situation in a Member State threatens one of the fundamental values: the rule of law. The method is a structured way to apply pressure and scrutiny to the country concerned along the path towards the formal triggering of the sanction mechanisms. In addition, the EU has a duty to promote the Union's values in all international relations (Article 21 TEU, with reference to Articles 2 and 3 TEU); that is, not only internally and not only in connection with enlargement. Doubtless, the intention is for the same values to be promoted in the EU's international relations, but the mechanisms are different and are not addressed in this chapter (ibid).

How Have the Values and Tools Been Used Vis-à-vis EU Member States?

The possibility of sanctioning Member States that do not respect EU values was introduced with the Amsterdam Treaty, which entered into force on 1 May 1999. The quality of the sanction mechanism introduced (in

Articles 2 and 7 (ex 6 and 7) TEU) was put to the test by the end of the same year. After the parliamentary election in Austria on 3 October 1999, the sitting Federal Chancellor began talks on forming a coalition government with the populist far-right Freedom Party of Austria (*Freiheitliche Partei Österreichs*, FPÖ). Following informal consultations, the other fourteen EU Member States agreed that they considered the developments in Austria to constitute a clear risk that an Austrian government in which FPÖ was involved would disregard the values then laid out in the Treaty. The Fourteen also agreed, however, that they could not take any action via EU institutions because the sanction procedure could not be triggered based on merely the *risk* that EU values would be disregarded. The disregard must be manifest in action by the "suspect" Member State before the treaty procedure could be engaged (Wennerström 2007: 141ff).

A similar situation arose in 2001 when a coalition government was formed in Italy under the leadership of the Forward Italy party (*Forza Italia*), under Silvio Berlusconi, together with the controversial National Alliance (*Alleanza Nationale*) and North League (*Lega Nord*) parties. The EU Fourteen quickly agreed that since there was no "smoking gun" in the form of concrete actions, they should strictly apply the treaty provisions, that is, pursue a cautious wait-and-see policy. It was because the other Member States were unable to use the only existing mechanism to defend the Union's values on two occasions within a short period of time that all Member States in Nice accepted the proposed amendments to the sanction provisions that are still found in the TEU.

The Austrian and Italian cases underscore the importance of creating effective mechanisms for sanctioning serious breaches. The existence of the mechanisms (assuredly not only the values as such) can be a deterrent, albeit obviously an inadequate one. The cases also show the importance of continuous vigilance regarding developments in the Member States in relation to the common values. Responsibility for monitoring the values and any threats against them is the purview of the Member States and the Commission.

When the Nice Treaty entered into force on 1 February 2003, the Union's capacity to take action against a Member State that disrespects the values increased. While the Amsterdam Treaty only sanctioned breaches that had occurred, the Nice Treaty also gave the EU a mandate to take preventive action when there is a threat that the common values might be breached, albeit not to act as vigorously as when an actual breach has occurred. Beyond the Austrian and Italian experiences, what underlies this reform is the fact that when a situation that justifies sanctions arises, it is unlikely to be a clear and isolated event, as the Amsterdam Treaty suggests. It is more likely to be a process, a chain of events that take place over a period of time and combined take the country closer to a breach of the values, which requires different steps and thresholds to be managed. Since Nice, the Treaty offers a sanction mechanism that can be used once a serious and persistent breach exists (Article 7.2 TEU), while a preventive mechanism can be triggered earlier, when a risk and threat of a serious breach arises (Article 7.1 TEU). The mechanisms were carried over to the Lisbon Treaty unchanged and can be used independently of each other (Pech et al. 2016).

The breach, or the risk of a breach, is not required to encompass policy areas within EU jurisdiction, but can extend far beyond the treaty framework, unlike the EU Charter, for example. This reflects the fact that a Member State is examined and monitored upon accession to the EU with regard to more than only application of that found in the Treaty. The political nature of the mechanism is underlined by the Council's latitude in judgment when a proposal is issued by the European Parliament, the Commission or one-third of the Member States. The Council can decide to accept the proposal but is not obligated to do so. Even if the Council were to decide to accept a proposal, the Treaty does not require the Council to proceed and actually apply the sanctions.

With the introduction of the preventive mechanism, the watchdog mandate of the Union's bodies also increased. The risk for breach that could be identified but not acted upon in the Austrian case can be described as follows. Based on proclamations from the FPÖ leadership, there seemed to be a clear risk that a government influenced by that party would be highly xenophobic and take measures that conflict with EU common values. If such a government had acted in accordance with its proclamations, the situation would no longer constitute a risk, but qualify as a direct breach that could be deemed serious and persistent. Whether or not a risk or breach is serious must be assessed based on the purpose and the results of the breach. If the purpose and the results of the breach are causal, the gravity of the breach is more apparent. If, for example, a government's objective is to deter people from seeking asylum in the country by abolishing the right to appeal against decisions in asylum cases, there is complete causality between the purpose and the results, which in turn violates the rule of law, which usually entails a right to appeal against official decisions directed at individuals. If, on the other hand, a government intends to lighten the caseload in all administrative proceedings—for economic reasons perhaps—and therefore reduces opportunities to appeal, the case is less clear-cut.

One indicator of the gravity of a breach might be a concurrent breach of more than one of the EU's common values. For a breach to be considered persistent, which is only relevant to the sanction mechanism, the duration of the breach must be measurable. Enactment of a law is a durable act in and of itself that would qualify more or less immediately, as soon as no further implementation measures are required. Repeated cases of isolated breaches may also be an indicator of such a persistent breach. If a Member State's actions have also been criticized by other normative bodies, such as the CJEU or the Council of Europe Venice Commission, and the Member State persists in its actions, this may also be an indicator to consider (Pech et al. 2016; European Commission 2003: 6–8; 2014: 6–9).

Lost Opportunities for Application or Justified Haphephobia?

There were two mechanisms available to the Council after the Nice Treaty entered into force. The latest addition (the preventive mechanism) was created in response to the difficulties of applying the first (the sanction mechanism). Application of both procedures is entirely political as regards decision-making by the Council. The CJEU has jurisdiction only to assess the legality of the decisions made by the Council, not the substantive basis of the decisions. The procedures are difficult to apply precisely because they are so political and especially the sanction mechanism, which has been called the "atomic bomb." There has been (especially after the Nice amendment of the Treaty) no lack of opportunities that should at any rate have led to deliberations on the procedures. It could be argued, for example, that the coalition government in Denmark following the 2001 election should have led to a discussion like that after the Austrian election in 1999, considering that the Danish coalition included the Danish People's Party (*Dansk Folkeparti*), whose platform was not entirely unlike that of FPÖ. The party was later a member of new coalition governments in Denmark after the elections in both 2005 and 2009, without triggering such deliberations. After the 2010 election in the Netherlands and until 2012, the Dutch Party for Freedom and Progress (*Partij voor Vrijheid en Vooruitgang, PVV*) was also part of a supportive alliance with the conservative minority government. Much of PVV's political platform had to do with xenophobia and criticism of Islam, but the formation of the coalition did not lead to discussions of the possibility of using the procedures.

In 2010, France expelled almost a thousand ethnic Romani back to Romania and Bulgaria, where they were citizens. The action was controversial in the EU and Commissioner Reding threatened to launch infringement procedures against the French government for what she considered forced expulsion. Although Bulgarians and Romanians, as EU citizens, had the right to enter France without a visa, they must still according to French immigration rules have a work permit or residence permit to stay longer than three months. The EU Commission regarded the French actions as collective measures based on ethnicity and consequently in breach of the European Convention on Human Rights. The actions were also thought to violate corresponding principles of EU law and the 2004 Citizens' Rights Directive on free movement, which is a fundamental principle for the EU although not a fundamental value in the sense meant by the Treaty. The French government obstructed the rights of the Bulgarian and Romanian citizens in France to exercise that right, in violation of EU law and the EU Charter (Article 21 TEU). The Commission issued a formal notice to France, in which it demanded full implementation of the Directive. Where traditional legal mechanisms under EU law are available, it is understandable that the Commission opted to go that route (Pech et al. 2016).

The newly elected *Fidesz-KDN* government in Hungary initiated a process in 2011 to amend the Hungarian Constitution, as well as several other legislative measures that were thought to violate the rule of law. The passage of "cardinal laws" (laws of quasi-constitutional value that require a supermajority to be amended by future Hungarian parliaments) accelerated. A law that strengthened the government's control of the media was passed. The retirement age of judges was drastically reduced. The data protection ombudsman was dismissed before his contract had expired. Institutional changes were made that reduced the independence of the central bank. Several of these measures violated EU law and, together, they led in a direction that breaches the EU fundamental values, especially the rule of law. The measures taken and constitutional amendments made in Hungary have led to serious international criticism and the adoption of soft law measures by the European Parliament but did not trigger the treaty procedures (although the constitutional experts at the Venice Commission have commented on and criticized the Hungarian legislative measures) (European Parliament 2015a; European Parliament 2015b; European Parliament 2015c; European Parliament 2017; Pech et al. 2016).

Under the leadership of Victor Ponta, the Romanian government issued an "emergency decree" in 2012 after the parliament voted to remove the country's president from office. Under the constitution, a removal must be confirmed by a referendum, regarding which the Romanian Constitutional Court ruled that participation by a majority of citizens enrolled on the permanent electoral lists was required for the referendum to be valid. The emergency decree defied the Court's judgment and claimed that the mere holding of the referendum, regardless of its outcome, sufficed to confirm the president's removal. The Commission and the EU President harshly criticized Prime Minister Ponta's government and referred to the possibility of acting through treaty procedures ahead of the European Council meeting in July 2012. At that meeting, Prime Minister Ponta provided assurances that his government would not undermine the Romanian justice system by implementing the emergency decree, which the EU accepted (Pech et al. 2016; Tuori 2016: 237ff). The Venice Commission has also expressed an opinion on these matters (Wennerström 2014: 617).

This takes us to the as-yet undecided tug of war between the EU and individual Member States that are for various reasons challenging the obligations of EU membership in the matter of respect for Treaty values. The prime example in this respect is Poland. The relationship to the EU has become increasingly strained since the conservative Law and Justice Party won a majority in the Polish parliament in October 2015, primarily due to several legislative measures taken and proposed on constitutional matters. As in Hungary, the reforms began with a reform of public service broadcasting laws, which gave the government direct influence over the media. The process of nominations to the Polish Constitutional Court was changed thereafter so that the sitting government could appoint most judges to the court. Reform of the Polish judicial system has since continued, despite the scathing objections of the EU Commission and the Venice Commission. The Polish Supreme Court is the target of the legislative amendment that was the focus of EU criticism in the summer of 2017 and aims at changing the appointment procedure (and, retroactively, the age of retirement for judges) for the Supreme Court as well, so that the parliamentary majority is given primary control (European Commission 2017a).

In the spring of 2016, the EU Commission, entirely in accordance with the method explained in its Rule of Law Framework, initiated a dialogue with the Polish government concerning the threat to EU fundamental values it observed in the Polish reform efforts. In the absence of progress in the dialogue, the Commission issued a formal recommendation to Poland on 27 July 2016 and a further recommendation on 21 December 2016. On 26 July 2017, the Commission issued a new recommendation to Poland concerning four new Polish legislative acts: The Law on the Supreme Court, the Law on the National Council for the Judiciary, the Law on the Ordinary Courts Organization and the Law on the National School of Judiciary. The first two proposed acts had been vetoed by President Duda, whereupon the bills went back to the parliament for redrafting. They were thus not withdrawn, and the President's veto was probably purely cosmetic. In its final recommendation, the Commission asked the Polish government to address the identified problems in the proposed legislation within one month (European Commission 2017a).

Regarding one of the problems, retirement age for judges based on gender, which is contrary to Directive 2006/54 on gender equality in employment, the Commission simultaneously prepared formal infringement proceedings against Poland. The package of measures implied that the Commission drew a line in the sand: if the Polish government initiates procedures to dismiss or force retirement of sitting judges on the Supreme Court, the Commission is prepared to trigger the preventive procedure (naturally, the Venice Commission has also commented on the Polish reforms) (European Commission 2017a, b, c). In September 2018, the Commission decided to refer Poland to the CJEU due to the violations of the principle of judicial independence created by the new Polish Law on the Supreme Court. The Commission also asked the Court to order interim measures until it has issued a judgment on the case (European Commission 2018).

Do the Mechanisms Strengthen EU Values?

A protective mechanism that does not work or is impossible to use can harm the value it was created to protect. When the sanction of fining people who crossed the street against a red light was abolished in Sweden in 1987, it was not because there was doubt about the value (traffic safety for pedestrians), but because the protective mechanism did not serve its purpose. An unsuitable protective mechanism may harm the value it is meant to protect in that it makes the legislature and the government seem unwilling or unable to protect the value. Both the EU Commission's Rule of Law Framework and the Council's Rule of Law Dialogue are intended to cure the paralysis that the design of the preventive and sanction mechanisms seems to have caused in the EU. But, irrespective of how lawful these measures are, there is reason to ask how the entirety of the values has evolved since they were redrafted. Is there really the same "pressure" in all six values?

There is reason to linger at the EU Commission's understanding and action in this connection, not only as the Guardian of the Values, but also as impartial actor in relation to the motives and domestic policy of individual Member States. From the point it ratified the Nice amendment of the Treaty, the Commission demonstrated its belief in a hierarchy among the Union's values, regardless of how this is expressed in different treaty versions. There are, so to speak, fundamental values for the existence of the Union that apply whether or not they are listed in the Treaty catalogue. In the 2003 communication from the Commission on "Respect for and promotion of the values on which the Union is based," the Commission explains that it will focus its efforts on democracy, human rights and the rule of law (that is, the first Copenhagen criterion), as a subset of the common values then laid out in the Treaty catalogue. When the Commission discussed its Rule of Law Framework eleven years later, it did not find it necessary to explain why it had chosen to create a more distinct mechanism in defence of the rule of law in particular, out of all the various EU values (European Commission 2003: 6–8, 2014: 6–9).

When the Council initiated a Rule of Law Dialogue in the Conclusions of the Council of December 2014, it can be said that the EU Member States accommodated the Commission's perspective on the internal relationships between the common values. Over the years, the Council, the Commission and the Parliament have also acted through various soft law measures regarding compliance with the values in a manner that reinforces the impression that certain values simply cannot be managed institutionally, while the three Copenhagen values seem to be those that can be put into practical action. The following list of such instruments demonstrates this state of affairs (see Table 10.2).

Table 10.2 Lists of mechanisms to protect EU values

Preventive mechanism (Article 7)	Can formally be applied with regard to all six fundamental values in Article 2, but has only been invoked in connection with protection of the rule of law value
Sanction mechanism (article 7)	As above.
Enlargement mechanism (article 49)	Even though article 49 refers to article 2, the application is narrowed to the three values also found in the Copenhagen criteria: Democracy, the rule of law and human rights.
Infringement procedures (articles 258–260, TFEU)	Usually refers to isolated legal acts and the relationship to the treaties but is applied by the CJEU in the light of the charter of fundamental rights of the European Union.
Peer review procedure (article 70)	This could refer to any of the six values, but so far has not occurred.
Commission's rule of law framework	Exclusive protection for the rule of law value.
Council's annual rule of law dialogue	Exclusive protection for the rule of law value.
Strategy for effective implementation by the EU of the charter of fundamental rights in the European Union	Refers to implementation of the EU charter, i.e., the human rights value.
Guidelines on methodical steps to be taken to verify compatibility with fundamental rights by the Council's preparatory bodies	Refers to implementation of the EU charter, i.e., the human rights value.
European Commission annual report on the application of the charter of fundamental rights in the European Union	Refers to implementation of the EU charter, i.e., the human rights value.
European council conclusions on fundamental rights and the rule of law	Regular conclusions regarding two of the values: Human rights and the rule of law.
European Parliament's annual report on the situation of fundamental rights in the EU	Refers to implementation of the EU charter, i.e., the human rights value.
Annual report on fundamental rights	Refers to implementation of the EU charter, i.e., the human rights value.
Justice scoreboard	Refers to functions in EU member states that protect the values of human rights and the rule of law.
Anti-corruption report	Refers to functions in EU member states that protect the rule of law value.

Sources: EU treaties, the European Commission and the Council.

Are All Values Equal?

There are six different values in the EU Treaty catalogue that, judging by the Treaty articles, are of the same or at least similar gravitas and worth. Now, that does not necessarily have to be so. Through its actions, the EU can demonstrate that it is more important to protect certain values than others at any given time. If the illiberal developments in Central and Eastern Europe are a particular challenge to two of the six values (the rule of law and fundamental rights), the EU's focus on those two makes sense. Over time, it may also prove that certain values have been left fallow for a long time, either because they have never been challenged or because although they have been challenged they are nevertheless not equipped with appropriate protective tools. In 2016, the European Parliament instructed its research service to prepare a proposal on an EU mechanism for democracy, the rule of law and fundamental rights, a proposal that had existed since October of that same year. With this step, the three central EU institutions have all explicitly supported the focus on three of the Union's values that the Commission had been promoting and acting in accordance with since 1993. The Treaties may change, but these three values seem to endure while the other three are becoming increasingly obsolete (see Table 10.1).

The only fundamental values defined with legal predictability to date are those in the human rights subset found in the Charter of Fundamental Rights of the European Union. Certain values have direct equivalents among the fundamental rights. The value of respect for "human dignity" corresponds verbatim to Article 1 of the Charter, just as the value of "liberty" corresponds to Article 6. The value of "equality" corresponds to Title III, Articles 20–26. Things get trickier from there. The value of "democracy" has no perfect equivalent among the rights, although Article 39, "Right to vote and to stand as a candidate at elections to the European Parliament" and Article 40 "Right to vote and to stand as a candidate at municipal elections" are key components of democracy. However, the EU Charter says nothing about the relationship of the political majority to power or to the minority, for example. Nor can the value of the "rule of law" be broken down into various individual rights but is rather a fundamental rule among the various branches of government. Respect for the country's constitution, for the hierarchy of norms and jurisdictional rules among public bodies falls outside a description of a country under the rule of law that is focused on the individual. To the extent that government ultimately impacts individuals, there are partial equivalents among the rights, primarily Articles 41–44 regarding the relationship between the individual and public administration, and Articles 47–49 regarding justice and the rights of individuals to effective remedy and a fair trial. Almost half of all rulings in the CJEU in 2016 that cite a specific article in the EU Charter referred to the articles in the Charter that correlate to the rule of law (European Commission 2014: 6–9; European Commission 2017d; Toggenburg and Grimheden 2016: 147ff).

Finally, as regards the sixth value, "respect for human rights, including the rights of persons belonging to minorities," seeking its equivalent in the particulars of the Charter becomes something of a tautological exercise. But it should be underlined here that when EU legal documents, including the Treaties, to which the Charter belongs, refer to *human* rights, they are not referred to in the Charter as such. When rights are cited in the Charter, the term used is *fundamental rights.* Respect for human rights thus entails at least respect for the rights set out in the European Convention on Human Rights (ECHR) and their equivalents in the Charter. However, the Charter contains further rights and principles that are not covered by the reference to human rights.

When the EU Commission issued its Rule of Law Framework, the Commission also presented its definition of the rule of law. The communication indicates that this is the definition the Commission will be applying as the standard from which non-compliance will be monitored. The Commission's definition relies heavily on the definition presented by the Venice Commission in 2011. This is understandable, since the Venice Commission is the only other institution in Europe with a clear mandate to monitor the constitutional level of the rule of law in Europe. The EU Commission's definition of the rule of law encompasses six sub-principles: (1) legality; (2) legal certainty; (3) prohibition of arbitrariness of the executive powers; (4) independent and impartial courts; (5) effective judicial review including respect for fundamental rights; and (6) equality before the law (European Commission 2014: 6–9; Venice Commission 2011).

Despite the establishment of new instruments and processes to uphold the EU's fundamental values, serious problems remain regarding their effectiveness. The Commission's Rule of Law Framework was triggered for the first time in response to the constitutional crisis in Poland. Although it is too early to evaluate its effectiveness, it seems thus far not to have successfully ensured the respect of the Member States for the values. Nor does it seem to have deterred the parties concerned from implementing their "illiberal" agendas. The first round of the Council's Rule of Law Dialogue on 17 November 2015 did not lead to any concrete measures to deal with any of the challenges identified above, instead leaving the initiative largely up to the Member States to identify their own shortcomings and promote solutions through a confidential, and thus not particularly deterrent, process of self-reflection (Baratta 2016).

But, bit by bit, the Commission has carved out an area where it has proven itself ready, willing and able to act to protect certain values. It has been methodically marshalling its forces for a long time in relation to the rule of law and human rights. Here, the Commission benefits from relatively clear definitions of the values that must be respected. And the Commission is not alone. The Council of Europe works in parallel in these specific areas through the European Court of Human Rights and the Venice Commission. This normative interaction makes it possible for the Commission to refer to something outside of itself and outside the EU, that is, to other contexts in which the Member States are voluntarily included and submit to examination. The three values of the Council of Europe are democracy, human rights and the rule of law, which also seem to be what the EU Commission is willing to work for (Venice Commission 2011).

Yet, like the EU, the Council of Europe does not have much to offer as regards judicial norms in respect of democracy, even though the organization regards it as one of three cornerstones. Is democracy, perhaps, the value that human rights and the rule of law are meant to represent? In such case, the argument is familiar from the UN system, which has since the days of Kofi Annan (and his special adviser in these matters, Lakhdar Brahimi) from the mid-1990s and later driven the line that the trio of values—democracy, human rights and the rule of law—constitute a trinity. The UN talks about the "triangle of freedom" with mutually reinforcing parts. Considering all established mechanisms (see the tables above), it is striking that the values that are upheld are relatively constant and that this rarely involves all six fundamental values. The convergence that emerges is found not so much in that various institutions' definitions of one value or another are beginning to resemble one another, but rather that convergence occurs over time in the number of values that are considered crucial (Brahimi 2002; European Parliament 2013; United Nations 2004, 2006, 2008, 2009).

The EU Should Develop the Rule of Law Framework and Deepen Cooperation with the Council of Europe

In the light of the developments outlined above, it is fair to direct a few recommendations for action to both the Member States and EU institutions, as well as all actors that in various ways advise them. It is, naturally, not easy for any part of the EU to take political action against measures taken by individual Member States that threaten the values when those states enjoy domestic political support for the measures. The political forces that advocate *Alleingang* in terms of values are often populist *and* Eurosceptic, which is why all measures originating in the EU system are at risk of fulfilling populist prophecies (see also Blombäck in this volume). It is therefore hardly surprising that the EU Commission under Jean-Claude Juncker has signalled a higher level of ambition than its predecessors (for instance, by putting Commission Vice President Frans Timmermans in charge of compliance with the rule of law in the EU) and has taken more vigorous action than before following both the 2016 British referendum and Dutch parliamentary election. The protection of values must be managed so that it does not impair the respect of values (or the values themselves). We perhaps see here one of the advantages to that the Commission is not legally obligated to respond to *every* breach of the values.

But, on the other hand, the Commission cannot remain passive only to avoid the potential awakening of Eurosceptic forces in the Member States. If the Commission allows flagrant challenges of fundamental values to pass, this undermines both the values and the mechanisms for protecting them. Against this backdrop, officials, academics and civil society groups have suggested several measures to strengthen the EU's capacity to act. Some of these proposed measures would require amendment of the Treaty and should perhaps therefore be regarded more as general reflections. These include a proposed obligatory exit, that is, amendment of the Treaties to include a new provision that makes it possible to "expel" a Member State that systematically and repeatedly breaches the EU values. In light of the fact that the treaty procedures as they are have already generated profound haphephobia, one might ask how much actual political appetite there is for automating them. More modest changes to the procedures have also been proposed, however, such as an adjustment to lower the thresholds for the decisions foreseen in the Treaty (Pech et al. 2016).

Another suggestion would be to make an amendment to the EU Charter (Article 51.1), so that all fundamental rights become directly applicable in the Member States, instead of only when EU law is concerned. Albeit this might be an interesting proposal, it carries the weakness of strengthening the opportunity to act upon breaches in isolated cases. Systematic breaches of the fundamental values could possibly be picked out from the crowd of Charter matters, but would not, for example, identify breaches related to the division of power or norm-hierarchical challenges as in the Slovakian enlargement case. Another proposal would be to implement a "reverse Solange doctrine" (Von Bogdandy et al. 2012). Under this proposal, in a situation where human rights are being systematically abused in a Member State, that country's national courts could invite EU bodies (and especially the CJEU) to review and deliberate on the compatibility of national measures and the fundamental values of the treaty. At present, the CJEU has no standing to do this. The idea of a new watchdog body, a kind of "Copenhagen Commission" tasked with monitoring respect for the Article 2 values, has also been raised, as has the possibility of delegating this task to the Venice Commission of the Council of Europe. None of the proposals, however, are characterized by any great measure of political realism (Pech et al. 2016; Tuori 2016: 228ff).

There have also been proposals to reinforce the Commission's Rule of Law Framework. The interesting thing here is that the mechanism could be modified, with no legislative amendments, to add clarity to the criteria and guidelines that govern triggering of the framework. Greater transparency concerning the dialogue to be held between the Member State concerned and the Commission is also desirable. EU-funded capacity building programs, like those opened to candidate countries in the enlargement processes, could be directed at national courts, civil society organizations and other institutions in the Member States to strengthen the protection of democracy, the rule of law and the fundamental rights. Legislative amendments would probably be required to implement these proposals, however.

Considering how long it has taken to develop national constitutional violation mechanisms and the external pressure usually required for international mechanisms for normative compliance to work, it is not particularly surprising that the EU has not progressed further. The values as laid out in the Treaty were hardly created with the precision required for them to be applicable in practice. The development described above points to two key factors. The first is the normative quality of the individual values. It is difficult to see how values like human dignity, liberty and equality could develop into parts of something resembling a legal rule of the type "if x [human dignity] is threatened, then *y* [the treaty mechanism]". These three values are not characterized by equal precision and maturity in the context of application. The second, and perhaps more important, factor takes us back to the theme of this volume. This can be said to be the greater political context in which the EU takes action to protect the values. If the EU had forged ahead with regard to values utterly devoid of resonance in the practical and legal reality in which EU Member States otherwise work, the EU would have stood alone with no allies or supportive actors outside the Union's own institutions. There is no Venice Commission for human dignity, nor a court in Strasbourg or anywhere else for matters of liberty alone. If the efforts of the EU to protect the Union's values are to have any hope of success, the Union must act in step with external forces that are working to promote the same values. These forces are and have been a vital element of the liberal world order that has emerged over several decades and which is now being challenged in several ways (see, for example, Fägersten and Cramér in this volume).

So, what should be done? As regards the values, the EU should clearly indicate its position that it should continue to assert three out of the six fundamental values vis-à-vis the Member States: democracy, the rule of law and human rights. Unless greater clarity has been created surrounding the meaning of the other three (human dignity, liberty and equality), along with an idea of how they should be applied, it would be better to move them from the first to the second sentence of Article 2 TEU or perhaps eliminate them entirely. The risk is that they will over the long-term damage the credibility of the EU fundamental values that can actually be applied. This would also align EU values and the values of the Council of Europe and the UN. The European Commission is hardly likely to be allowed to create its own Venice Commission for EU purposes and will likely remain dependent upon these types of external actors. Full alignment of values between the EU and the Council of Europe and their respective courts will also increase opportunities to act to protect the common values. Conversely, greater differences between the descriptions of values increase relativism and scope for breaching the values for various reasons.

Regarding mechanisms, it seems, as far as can be judged, wiser to continue working with the existing mechanisms than to broach new solutions to problems that there is limited political appetite to solve. The Commission should continue unremittingly to apply the Rule of Law Framework against Member States that challenge the rule of law. The possibility, within existing structures and treaties, of coordinating several infringement matters against a single Member State that is also the subject of interest under the Commission's Rule of Law Framework should be further considered in the light of the proceedings brought against Poland in 2017. If this turns out to be a practicable route, it can be combined with more assiduous references to the common values in Article 2 once the Commission has, so to speak, already entered the CJEU via infringement cases.

Finally, it is essential that the Member States support the Commission in its efforts. It would be good if the Council's Rule of Law Dialogue could act in support, but Member States that want to safeguard the EU's fundamental values must be perspicacious enough to see the limitations to what the Council can contribute. After all, it is the institution designed to work politically down to the lowest common denominator. That notwithstanding, the rule of law in the EU should not be further watered down, as long as there is no desire to entirely abandon the Kantian vision of cooperation among the states and citizens of Europe that Robert Kagan described in 2003.

References

Baratta, R. (2016). Rule of Law "Dialogues" Within the EU: A Legal Assessment. *Hague Journal on the Rule of Law, 8*(2), 373–419.

Brahimi, L. (2002). *The Rule of Law at Home and Abroad. The 2002 Dag Hammarskjöld Lecture*. Uppsala: Dag Hammarskjöld Foundation.

Closa, C. (2016). Reinforcing EU Monitoring of the Rule of Law: Normative Arguments, Institutional Proposals and the Procedural Limitations. In C. Closa & D. Kochenov (Eds.), *Reinforcing Rule of Law Oversight in the European Union*. Cambridge: Cambridge University Press.

European Commission. (1997). Commission Speech (1997) Commissioner Hans van den Broek's address to the EU meeting in Noordwijk 1997 "The Rule of Law in the Context of Enlargement", SPEECH/97/144.

European Commission. (2000). Commission Communication COM (2000) 97. EU Bulletin Supplement, 5/97.

European Commission. (2003). Commission Communication COM (2003) 606. Article 7 of the Treaty on EU – Respect for and promotion of the values on which the Union is based

European Commission. (2013). Commission Speech (2013) Vice President Reding's Speech "Safeguarding the Rule of Law and Solving the "Copenhagen Dilemma": Towards a New EU-mechanism", European Commission – SPEECH/13/348.

European Commission. (2014). Commission Communication COM (2014) 158. A New EU Framework to Strengthen the Rule of Law.

European Commission. (2016a). Commission Recommendation (EU) 2016/1374 of 27 July 2016 Regarding the Rule of Law in Poland.

European Commission. (2016b). Commission Recommendation COM (2016) 8950 of 21.12.2016 Regarding the Rule of Law in Poland Complementary to Commission Recommendation (EU) 2016/1374.

European Commission. (2017a). Commission Proposal COM (2017) 835 final 2017/0360 of 20.12.2017. Reasoned Proposal in Accordance with Article 7(1) of the Treaty on European Union Regarding the Rule of Law in Poland.

European Commission. (2017b). Commission Recommendation COM (2017) 5320 of 26.7.2017 Regarding the Rule of Law in Poland Complementary to Commission Recommendations (EU) 2016/1374 and (EU) 2017/146.

European Commission. (2017c). Commission Recommendation COM (2017) 9050 of 20.12.2017 regarding the rule of law in Poland complementary to Commission Recommendations (EU) 2016/1374, (EU) 2017/146 and (EU) 2017/1520.

European Commission. (2017d). Commission Report (2017) Annual Report on the Application of the EU Charter of Fundamental Rights, COM (2018) 396.

European Commission. (2018). Rule of Law: European Commission Refers Poland to the European Court of Justice to Protect the Independence of the Polish Supreme Court. Press release, 24 September 2018.

European Parliament. (2013). European Parliament Study on The Triangular relationship between Fundamental Rights, Democracy and the Rule of Law in the EU – Towards an EU Copenhagen Mechanism (PE 493.031).

European Parliament. (2015a). European Parliament Resolution of 10 June 2015 on the Situation in Hungary (2015/2700(RSP)).

European Parliament. (2015b). European Parliament Resolution of 8 September 2015 on the Situation of Fundamental Rights in the European Union (2013–2014) (2014/2254(INI)).

European Parliament. (2015c). European Parliament Resolution of 16 December 2015 on the Situation in Hungary (2015/2935(RSP)).

European Parliament. (2016). European Parliament Resolution of 13 April 2016 on the Situation in Poland (2015/3031(RSP)).

European Parliament. (2017). European Parliament Report (2017) on a Proposal Calling on the Council to Determine, Pursuant to Article 7(1) of the Treaty on European Union, the Existence of a Clear Risk of a Serious Breach by Hungary of the Values on Which the Union Is Founded (2017/2131(INL)).

Kagan, R. (2003). *Of Paradise and Power: America and Europe in the New World Order*. New York: Alfred A. Knopf.

Kochenov, D. (2004). Behind the Copenhagen Façade: The Meaning and Structure of the Copenhagen Political Criterion of Democracy and the Rule of Law. *European Integration Online Papers, 8*(10), 1–24.

Kochenov, D. (2008). *EU Enlargement and the Failure of Conditionality: Pre-accession Conditionality in the Fields of Democracy and the Rule of Law*. The Hague: Kluwer Law International.

Kochenov, D. (2016). The Missing EU Rule of Law? In C. Closa & D. Kochenov (Eds.), *Reinforcing Rule of Law Oversight in the European Union*. Cambridge: Cambridge University Press.

Kochenov, D., & Pech, L. (2015a). Monitoring and Enforcement of the Rule of Law in the EU: Rhetoric and Reality. *European Constitutional Law Review, 11*(3), 512–540.

Kochenov, D., & Pech, L. (2015b). Upholding the Rule of Law in the EU: On the Commission's 'Pre-Article 7 Procedure' as a Timid Step in the Right Direction. *European University Institute Working Papers*. 24(2015). Florence: European University Institute.

Pech, L., & Schappele, K. (2017). Illiberalism Within: Rule of Law Backsliding in the EU. *Cambridge Yearbook of European Legal Studies, 19*, 3–47.

Pech, L., Wennerström, E., Leigh, V., Markowska, A., De Keyser, L., Gómez Rojo, A., & Spanikova, H. (2016, April). An EU Mechanism on Democracy, the Rule of Law and Fundamental Rights. *European Parliamentary Research Service*. Available at SSRN: https://ssrn.com/abstract=2768938.

Sadurski, W. (2010). Adding a Bite to a Bark? A Story of Article 7, the EU Enlargement, and Jörg Haider, *Sydney Law School Research Paper*. 10(1). Available at SSRN: https://ssrn.com/abstract=1531393.

Sasse, G. (2008). The Politics of EU Conditionality: The Norm of Minority Protection During and Beyond EU Accession. *Journal of European Public Policy, 15*(6), 842–860.

Toggenburg, G., & Grimheden, J. (2016). The Rule of Law and the Role of Fundamental Rights: Seven Practical Pointers. In C. Closa & D. Kochenov (Eds.), *Reinforcing Rule of Law Oversight in the European Union*. Cambridge: Cambridge University Press

Tuori, K. (2016). From Copenhagen to Venice. In C. Closa & D. Kochenov (Eds.), *Reinforcing Rule of Law Oversight in the European Union*. Cambridge: Cambridge University Press

United Nations. (2004). *The Rule of Law and Transitional Justice in Conflict and Post-conflict Societies*. Report S/2004/616.

United Nations. (2006). *Uniting Our Strengths: Enhancing United Nations Support for the Rule of Law*. Report A/61/636–S/2006/980.

United Nations. (2008). *Strengthening and Coordinating United Nations Rule of Law Activities*. Report A/63/226.

United Nations. (2009). *Strengthening and Coordinating United Nations Rule of Law Activities*. Report A/64/298.

Venice Commission. (2011). Document CDL-AD (2011) 003 rev.

Von Bogdandy, A., Kottmann, M., Antpohler, C., & Dickschen, J. (2012). Reverse Solange-protecting the Essence of Fundamental Rights Against EU Member States. *Common Market Law Review, 49*(2), 489.
Wennerström, E. (2007). *The Rule of Law and the European Union*. Uppsala: Iustus.
Wennerström, E. (2014). The EU Commission Defines the Rule of Law and a Mechanism for Applying It Inside the EU. *Europarättslig tidskrift* 3.

Index[1]

[1] Note: Page numbers followed by 'n' refer to notes.

A. Bakardjieva Engelbrekt et al. (eds.), *The European Union in a Changing World Order*,
https://doi.org/10.1007/978-3-030-18001-0

Printed in the United States
By Bookmasters